UNDERSTANDING CHILDREN'S WORRY

This accessible guide offers a concise introduction to the science behind worry in children, summarising research from across psychology to explore the role of worry in a range of circumstances, from everyday worries to those that can seriously impact children's lives.

Wilson draws on theories from clinical, developmental and cognitive psychology to explain how children's worry is influenced by both developmental and systemic factors, examining the processes involved in pathological worry in a range of childhood anxiety disorders. Covering topics including different definitions of worry, the influence of children's development on worry, Generalised Anxiety Disorder (GAD) in children, and the role parents play in children's worry, this book offers a new model of worry in children with important implications for prevention and intervention strategies.

Understanding Children's Worry is valuable reading for students in clinical, educational and developmental psychology, and professionals in child mental health.

CHARLOTTE WILSON is a clinical psychologist and assistant professor in clinical psychology at the University of Dublin, Trinity College.

Essays in Developmental Psychology

North American Editors:
Henry Wellman
University of Michigan at Ann Arbor

UK Editors:
Claire Hughes
University of Cambridge
Michelle Ellefson
University of Cambridge

Essays in Developmental Psychology is designed to meet the need for rapid publication of brief volumes in developmental psychology. The series defines developmental psychology in its broadest terms and covers such topics as social development, cognitive development, developmental neuropsychology and neuroscience, language development, learning difficulties, developmental psychopathology and applied issues. Each volume in the series will make a conceptual contribution to the topic by reviewing and synthesizing the existing research literature, by advancing theory in the area, or by some combination of these missions. The principal aim is that authors will provide an overview of their own highly successful research program in an area. It is also expected that volumes will, to some extent, include an assessment of current knowledge and identification of possible future trends in research. Each book will be a self-contained unit supplying the advanced reader with a well-structured review of the work described and evaluated.

Published

White & Hughes: *Why Siblings Matter: The Role of Brother and Sister Relationships in Development and Well-Being*

Crone: *The Adolescent Brain*

Needham: *Learning About Objects in Infancy*

Hughes: *Social Understanding and Social Lives*

For updated information about published and forthcoming titles in the *Essays in Developmental Psychology* series, please visit: https://www.routledge.com/Essays-in-Developmental-Psychology/book-series/SE0532

UNDERSTANDING CHILDREN'S WORRY

CLINICAL, DEVELOPMENTAL AND COGNITIVE PSYCHOLOGICAL PERSPECTIVES

Charlotte Wilson

LONDON AND NEW YORK

First published 2021
by Routledge
2 Park Square, Milton Park, Abingdon, Oxon OX14 4RN

and by Routledge
52 Vanderbilt Avenue, New York, NY 10017

Routledge is an imprint of the Taylor & Francis Group, an informa business

© 2021 Charlotte Wilson

The right of Charlotte Wilson to be identified as author of this work has been asserted by her in accordance with sections 77 and 78 of the Copyright, Designs and Patents Act 1988.

All rights reserved. No part of this book may be reprinted or reproduced or utilised in any form or by any electronic, mechanical, or other means, now known or hereafter invented, including photocopying and recording, or in any information storage or retrieval system, without permission in writing from the publishers.

Trademark notice: Product or corporate names may be trademarks or registered trademarks, and are used only for identification and explanation without intent to infringe.

British Library Cataloguing-in-Publication Data
A catalogue record for this book is available from the British Library

Library of Congress Cataloging-in-Publication Data
A catalog record has been requested for this book

ISBN: 978-0-8153-7887-7 (hbk)
ISBN: 978-0-8153-7888-4 (pbk)
ISBN: 978-1-351-22766-7 (ebk)

Typeset in Minion Pro
by codeMantra

CONTENTS

Acknowledgements ix

CHAPTER 1	**WHAT IS WORRY?**	**1**
	Definitions of worry	2
	Problem solving and worry	4
	Negative affect and worry	7
	Verbal-linguistic nature of worry	9
	The function of worry	13
	Measurement of worry in children	15
	Assessment of children's worry	15
	Assessing the processes involved in children's worry	21
	Conclusions about the measurement of children's worry	25
CHAPTER 2	**CHILDREN'S WORRY AND DEVELOPMENT**	**26**
	Worry in a developmental context	27
	Development of worry across childhood	27
	Components of worry	30
	Future thinking	31
	Problem solving	39
	Executive functions	43
	Catastrophisation	47
	Conclusions	50
CHAPTER 3	**CHILDREN'S WORRY AND THE FAMILY**	**52**
	Concordance between child and parent anxiety and worry	53
	Parenting behaviours and worry	56

Attachment and worry	65
Worry processes in parents and children	67
Meta-cognitions in parents and children	68
Intolerance of uncertainty in parents and children	69
Parents' involvement in the treatment of worried children	70
Conclusion	75

CHAPTER 4   WHEN CHILDREN'S WORRY BECOMES A PROBLEM   **76**

Processes involved in problematic worry	77
Beliefs about worry	78
Cognitive/experiential avoidance	87
Problems with strategies for managing difficulties or emotions	89
Problematic relationships with internal experiences	92
Heightened internal experiences	94
Intolerance of uncertainty	98
Attachment and previous trauma	100
Models of GAD: similarities and differences for children and adults	101

CHAPTER 5   CHILDREN'S WORRY AND PSYCHOLOGICAL DISORDERS   **103**

Generalised anxiety disorder in children	104
Worry in anxiety disorders in childhood	107
Worry in depression and mood disorders in children and adolescents	110
Worry in psychosis	111
Worry in eating disorders	112
Worry in insomnia	114
Worry in pain	116
Worry in autistic spectrum conditions	119
Worry in attention deficit hyperactivity disorder	121
Treatment of worry	123
Treatment of children with GAD	123
Treatment of worry	126
Conclusions about worry across different psychological disorders	127

CHAPTER 6	A NEW DEVELOPMENTAL UNDERSTANDING OF WORRY	**130**
	Key issues	131
	The developmental progression of worry from infancy to adolescence	133
	The development of problematic features of worry	138
	Summary of a new developmental understanding of worry	139
	Implications of this new understanding of worry	141
	Developmental implications	141
	Clinical implications	142
	Systemic and wider system implications	146
	Where next? Setting a research agenda for children's worry	147
	Conclusions	149

Bibliography 151
Index 203

ACKNOWLEDGEMENTS

My interest in the development of worry in children started while I was working as a full-time clinical psychologist and I found myself trying to help and support a number of young women whose worries were significantly impacting their lives. Without their trust, and their willingness to share with me their experiences, I would have never started this journey. Along the way I have met lots of worriers, young and old, who have challenged me to think deeply about worry and to try and make sense of it. I have had countless conversations with colleagues who have shaped my thinking, and I have had the pleasure of working with brilliant students and trainees who have found answers to some of my questions and who have made me ask other, more important, questions. I want to acknowledge all these people.

Most of all I want to acknowledge the most important worriers and non-worriers in my life, Paul, Katherine, Lizzy, George, Hazel, Margriet, and Derek. Thank you for all your love and support.

This book has been a long time in the making. From my original ideas about worry, through numerous studies carried out with the help of lots of different students, to actually putting all my thoughts down on paper, it has been a long process. It is therefore somewhat strange to be finalising this book and writing this foreword in the middle of a global pandemic. At the very start of 2020 the COVID-19 virus started spreading throughout the world. It hit Ireland in February and schools and college shut on 12th March. For the past one hundred days or so I have been at home with my two daughters, noticing my own worries and responding to theirs. There has perhaps never been quite such an apt time to be writing about children's worry. The CoSpace study (https://emergingminds.org.uk/co-space-study-news/) has been tracking children and families' mental health through the earlier stages of the pandemic, when many countries were in lockdown, through to current stages where we have more freedoms, but perhaps also more uncertainty about the future. Unsurprisingly, their children's wellbeing was one of UK parents' most prominent stressors. They reported that their children and adolescents were worried about catching COVID-19 themselves, and worried about someone they love catching it, as well as reporting that they were worried about missing school. Younger pre-school children were reported to be worried about missing social events with friends and were worrying about seeing their friends. Although these are somewhat reasonable worries, nearly 15% of parents reported that their children and adolescents were worried about leaving the house at all, suggesting that these worries could be having a significant impact for some. The most prominent worries for children and adolescents were similar, with uncertainty being the most prominent worry for both age groups. Adolescents had more worries about returning to school in terms of the possibility of catching COVID-19, being put under pressure academically due to lost time, and managing their new workloads. These worries were even more prevalent in children with additional needs, whether these were special educational needs or mental health needs.

At the time of writing the latest results from the CoSpace study suggest that despite developmental differences in prevalent worries the pandemic is having different effects on the mental health of children and adolescents; whilst children's emotional difficulties are increasing over time, adolescents' emotional difficulties are decreasing. Children with existing needs may also be experiencing fewer emotional difficulties. As we settle into a new normal adolescents have the cognitive ability to make sense of the global situation, whereas smaller children are struggling to understand why somethings are now OK, and others are still not, and children who usually find school stressful and difficult are now benefitting from not having to go.

These early results demonstrate both how common worry is among children and adolescents and also how it can be relatively benign.

With a seven and an 11 year old in my own household I can watch these worries play out in front of me. The seven year old wants to know when she can play with her friends, when she can have sleepovers, and when we can go and visit Grandma and Grandad again. She doesn't know why she has to stay a long distance away from her friends when they do play, and she doesn't understand why playing outside is better than playing inside. However, if it means she can play with her friends she will just do it. Playing is better than not. On the other hand the 11 year old understands that the rules aren't absolute, but doesn't understand why some people don't seem to even try and follow them. She hates the uncertainty of it all and would rather know either way whether she will have normal school in September or not. She can link with friends virtually much more easily with facetime and Minecraft on her tablet or phone, so connection to others is less of an issue for her.

The evidence on the dangerousness of COVID-19 for children is beginning to emerge, and the early signs are good. It does appear that children are not at high risk of getting the virus and are also not at high risk of suffering greatly with it. What we know about helping anxious and worried children is that we need to use this information to be encouraging our children to leave their houses and to start, albeit slowly, returning to things they used to do and particularly starting to do the things they enjoy again. They will be worried about starting doing these everyday things again, as they have been told for a long time that they are not allowed because it is dangerous. But parents, siblings, and teachers can support these children to slowly, step by step, start to do them again. The adults can listen to the children's worries, but can reassure them that there are things that are safe and that they, the children, are brave enough and strong enough to do them. For the younger children, this may be simple reassurance and encouragement, but for older children the explanations might help.

This book isn't a therapy manual. It hasn't got the answers about how children's COVID-19 worries will change over the next months and years, but hopefully the insights into how developmental, systemic, and clinical psychology can help us understand worry in children will help us make sense of how these worries are changing and will prompt further research that will help us support those children who most need it.

CHAPTER ONE
What is worry?

DEFINITIONS OF WORRY

Geraldine was a 13 year old girl asking for help with her constant anxiety. When she met the clinical psychologist she explained that she worried all the time. When something unexpected happened her mind immediately leapt to all the different outcomes that might occur. Recently her father had been late home from work and she worried that he had been in a car accident and killed, she worried that he had lost his job and had just gone away, she worried that he didn't love her and her sister anymore and had decided not to come home. These worries kept coming until he walked in the door, a little late because a meeting had run over. Geraldine explained that this happened all the time.

The *Oxford English Dictionary* defines worry as

1. A troubled state of mind arising from the frets and cares of life; harassing anxiety or solicitude.
2. An instance or case of this; a cause of, or matter for, anxiety; *pl.* cares, solicitudes.

It is a familiar phenomenon; nearly all adults report worrying at least from time to time, with up to 70% of children as young as seven to eight years old reporting the same (Muris et al., 1998; Muris, Merckelbach et al., 2000). In popular parlance, worry is synonymous with anxiety, nervousness, concern, fear, and uncertainty. However, even when we start to pull apart the differences between these different phenomena certain things appear to be specific about worry. If I am worrying about something, then inevitably I am thinking about it. It also probably has that sticky feeling as the thoughts go round and round in my head. Unlike fear or nervousness, where I might know exactly what I am afraid of, when I am worried I can start somewhere in my worry and end up somewhere completely different. It is these features of worry that researchers noted when it started to become clear that worry could be a topic worthy of study in its own right, as separate from fear. Early definitions of worry in the academic literature emphasised the distinctions between the somatic and acute experience of fear, and the repetitive, iterative nature of worry (Tallis, Davey, & Capuzzo, 1994). Worry was conceptualised as part of anxiety, but differentiable to fear. In these early definitions of worry the construct was considered to be appropriate across the range of worry, with the same definition being appropriate for worry that was considered to be normal, and worry that was part of a clinical condition. In the early 1980s an interest in pathological worry started to flourish with the work of Tom Borkovec and colleagues. Indeed it is Borkovec and colleagues' 1983 definition of worry that persists in the literature on pathological worry. Borkovec defined worry as

> a chain of thoughts and images, negatively affect-laden and relatively uncontrollable; it represents an attempt to engage in mental problem-solving on an issue whose outcome is uncertain but contains the possibility of one or more negative outcomes; consequently, worry relates closely to the fear process.
>
> Borkovec et al. (1983, p. 10)

This definition highlighted several aspects of worry. It highlighted the function of worry as being one of problem solving. It highlighted the negative affect associated with worry. Further research from Borkovec (1994) found that worry was predominantly verbal-linguistic. These three factors have driven a research agenda that has led to multiple theories of worry, several different but effective treatments for pathological worry, and a greater understanding of the role worry may play in a variety of psychological disorders. In each of these domains the research involving children has lagged behind research involving adults, but increasingly worry as a separate phenomenon is being recognised and researched across the life span. This chapter focuses on the following three factors: worry as problem solving, worry and negative affect, and worry as verbal-linguistic – in order to highlight similarities and differences between adult and child worry. The chapter concludes with a review of the proposed functions of worry and ways of measuring it.

PROBLEM SOLVING AND WORRY

Worry has long been believed to have a problem-solving function, especially to those who engage in it regularly. Indeed there is a small but significant literature focusing on the role problem solving has in our understanding of adult worry. In one of the few studies of the content of everyday worry Tallis et al. (1994) found that both worriers and non-worriers report that problem solving is one of the main reasons they worry. Very little research has explored whether worry is an effective way of problem solving, but for those people for whom worry is problematic and interfering in their everyday life, it is clear that it isn't a good strategy for them to choose. Something is clearly going wrong with using worry to solve problems.

Different aspects of problem solving have been explored in relation to worry. Initial hypotheses focused on faulty problem solving. Problem solving involves several stages, including identification of the problem, identification of possible solutions, choosing a solution, and enactment of the solution (Figure 1.1) (D'Zurilla & Goldfried, 1971).

If this process has gone wrong for chronic worriers any, or all, of these problem-solving steps might be faulty. Davey (1994) explored this problem by looking at worry and problem solving in adults. He tested whether people's ability to use problem-solving steps to achieve a goal

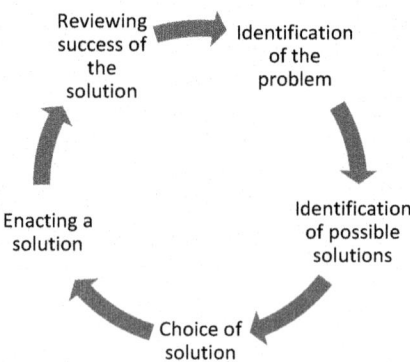

Figure 1.1 Problem-solving stages.

(using the Means End Problem Solving Inventory, MEPS; Platt & Spivack, 2006), and to find an effective solution were associated with their problem-solving confidence, approach-avoidance style in problem solving, and personal control (measured by the Problem Solving Inventory, PSI; Heppner & Petersen, 1982). Not only did Davey find that worry and anxiety were not related to problem-solving ability, he also found that problem-solving ability wasn't related to problem-solving confidence. However, those participants with high levels of worry and anxiety showed poor problem-solving confidence (Davey, 1992, 1994). Davey concluded that what was going wrong in problem solving in worriers was not that they were poor problem solvers but rather that they had poor confidence in themselves. However, when thinking about worry and problem solving in children there is good reason to question whether there are problem-solving deficits. Problem solving in general will be affected by cognitive development, and perhaps even social and emotional development. Furthermore, children with psychological difficulties may have specific difficulties with different aspects of problem solving. For example, Dodge and Crick (1990) reformulated the D'Zurilla and Goldfried model of problem solving within a social information processing framework in order to explain social problem-solving deficits in children with aggressive behaviour. Although some differences emerge in these deficits at different ages (Crick & Dodge, 1996), it does appear that aggressive children do struggle with misattributing hostile intent to others and failing to choose proactive solutions and predicting that aggressive solutions will work out well (Crick & Dodge, 1994).

A few years later Daleiden and Vasey (1997) saw the parallels between the struggles aggressive children had with problem solving and the struggles anxious children displayed. They developed a model of what difficulties anxious children might have with problem solving. They proposed that children who are anxious show attentional biases that lead them to judge neutral situations as threatening, or within a problem-solving framework see problems where there are none. They proposed that anxious children may struggle with distractibility and therefore may not be able to think about a number of different solutions or to see a solution through to the end. They propose that anxious children may choose more avoidant solutions rather than actively engaging with the problem and may struggle to enact the solution they do choose. Therefore, although the adult literature suggests that it is not problem-solving ability that is associated with anxiety and worry, it might be that, due to developmental factors, children with high levels of anxiety and worry have poor problem-solving skills. All of these hypotheses have some evidence to support them. Anxious children do indeed show biases towards threat in the face of neutral/ambiguous stimuli (Gifford et al., 2008), they do find threat more distracting (Bar-Haim et al., 2007) and they do choose more avoidant solutions (Barrett et al., 1996). The failure to enact solutions is harder to test as it needs naturalistic observations; however, it is commonly seen by clinicians treating anxious children. What remains unclear however, is whether this is due to anxiety or whether it is specifically due to worry. Derakshan and Eysenck (2009) argue that it is the worry component of anxiety that impairs problem solving, but only one aspect of problem solving-the efficiency of processing the information. They argue that worry and/or anxiety has much less impact on the effectiveness of the performance of the solution. This would tend to be consistent with the few studies that have specifically tested the relationship between worry, anxiety and problem solving in children. To date, two studies have explored this relationship. Wilson and Hughes (2011) explored social problem solving in 6–11 year olds using the Wally Problem Solving task (Webster-Stratton, 1990) developed for the Incredible Years programme (Webster-Stratton & Reid, 2003). Similarly to Davey, we found that there were no differences in children's ability to provide a number of appropriate solutions to social problems when comparing high and low worriers but that children who reported high worry also reported low confidence in their ability to solve problems. Efficiency of processing was not measured, but there was no impact of anxiety or worry on the effectiveness of the solutions provided by the children. Extending this to a sample of children with high and low worry, Parkinson and Creswell (2011) found that there were no differences in problem-solving skills between high and low worried children using the Alternative Solutions Test (Caplan et al., 1986). In contrast, children's confidence in their problem-solving abilities was significantly lower in the anxious group compared to the non-anxious group.

These studies do not allow a full exploration of real-life problem solving or of the efficiency of problem solving in anxious and worried children, but they do suggest that problem-solving confidence may be the key aspect of problem solving that is associated with high levels of worry in both children and adults. It could be hypothesised that this problem-solving confidence itself might be associated with poor processing efficiency: if problem solving feels hard to do, then this might impact problem-solving confidence more than finding a successful solution.

Negative problem orientation, a significant factor in several models of pathological worry or generalised anxiety disorder, is another aspect of problem solving that has been studied extensively in the context of worry. Given its role in models of pathological worry it is discussed in Chapter 4.

In conclusion, there may be more similarities than differences in adults and children when considering the relationship between worry and problem solving. It is likely that a high level of worry does not impact on how effective a problem solver someone is, but it might impact on the confidence they feel in their own problem solving and the efficiency of their problem solving. Worry may well function as a problem-solving strategy, but it may not be the best one to choose.

NEGATIVE AFFECT AND WORRY

Worry is often a problem because of the way it makes us feel. Even though the aim of worry may be to solve a problem, the fact we are thinking about potential threat increases our negative affect, and this relationship between worry and negative affect appears to hold across a wide range of cultures. However the relationship between worry and affect is somewhat more complicated than a simple linear relationship. Although worry orients us towards threat, the nature of worry as a verbal process (see below, this chapter) may serve to dampen the threat response. Indeed, in a review of five different models of pathological worry (generalised anxiety disorder) Behar and colleagues (Behar et al., 2009) propose that 'all models share an emphasis on avoidance of internal affective experiences' (avoidance models are discussed in Chapter 4). These avoided affective experiences include thoughts, beliefs, and feelings, but the common factor is that it is the affective experience that is avoided. Thus the contradiction within the worry process is that it makes us feel bad, but not as bad as truly engaging with the threat.

The evidence for the association between negative affect and worry is extensive in adults (Watson, 2005), but much sparser in children. Furthermore, some of the research in children's affect and worry addresses our understanding of the relationship between them indirectly, making it difficult to make strong conclusions. For example, Woodruff-Borden and colleagues (Affrunti & Woodruff-Borden, 2016; Gramszlo et al., 2018; Gramszlo & Woodruff-Borden, 2015) explored the temperamental dimension of negative affectivity in relation to worry in children. This construct of temperamental negative affectivity refers to a personality feature that leads the individual to view the world as more negative and to experience more negative emotions (Watson & Pennebaker, 1989) and in middle childhood is reliably measured using the Temperament in Middle Childhood Questionnaire (Simonds & Rothbart, 2004). In their three studies of 7–12-year-old children from the community, Woodruff-Borden and colleagues found that those children who reported higher levels of worry on the Penn State Worry Questionnaire for Children (PSWQ-C; Pestle, Chorpita, & Schiffman, 2008) also had higher temperamental negative affectivity as reported by their parents. This is an important finding, but it is limited in a number of ways. There have been criticisms of parent-reported temperament (Molfese & Molfese, 2014), but perhaps more importantly, these studies do not tell us much about the affective *experience* of worry for children. One study that has explored the emotional experience of worry focused on adolescents (Fowler & Szabó, 2013). A large sample of adolescents ($n = 340$) completed the PSWQ-C (Pestle, Chorpita & Schiffman, 2008) and the Depression Anxiety Stress Scale (DASS; Lovibond & Lovibond, 1995). Perhaps unsurprisingly worry scores from the PSWQ-C were highly correlated with all three scales on the DASS, namely depression, anxiety, and stress. What was surprising, however, was that in further analysis, stress scores accounted for more variance in worry scores than anxiety scores did. This result was also more marked for older adolescents compared to younger adolescents. For older adolescents, anxiety scores did not significantly predict worry, but stress did, whereas for younger adolescents both anxiety and stress predicted worry. In further analysis of individual symptoms of anxiety Fowler and Szabó found that PSWQ-C scores were most strongly associated with symptoms of tension, irritability, and problems relaxing and least strongly associated with symptoms of autonomic arousal, usually considered to be core anxiety symptoms, such as heart beating fast, difficulty breathing, and feeling dizzy. This may indicate that these two aspects of anxiety – the arousal/fear aspect of anxiety and the cognitive/worry aspect of anxiety – may indeed be separate. Below we explore whether this is true in terms of how children experience these different aspects of worry.

Fowler and Szabó's study is notable to be one of the very few studies directly assessing the affective experience of worry in adolescents. Clinical and research experience would suggest that there is a strong affective component to worry, but as indicated by Fowler and Szabó's results, this affective component does not necessarily map well onto autonomic symptoms of anxiety and may be impacted by developmental factors. An exploration of the verbal nature of worry may further start to explain both the affective experience of worry and some of the developmental differences between children and adolescents.

VERBAL-LINGUISTIC NATURE OF WORRY

The verbal nature of worry has been found in several studies of adults. If you ask adults about their worry, they report that they mainly worry in words (Borkovec & Inz, 1990). Furthermore, studies manipulating people into worrying in words or in images find that worrying in words maps more closely onto problematic worry (Behar, Zuellig, & Borkovec, 2005; Stokes & Hirsch, 2010). Borkovec has proposed that this may be one of the mechanisms by which worry is maintained (Borkovec, 1994). He proposes that worrying in words dampens down the emotional response typically seen with anxious responding and the emotional response that is seen with imagery-based thoughts (Sibrava & Borkovec, 2006). Therefore the choice to worry, or the automatic reaction to worry, in response to a feared stimuli helps regulate the emotional response. Borkovec proposes that this dampening of the emotional response directly reinforces worry as a strategy for managing threat. The problem is, however, that the problem doesn't ever get solved, or the individual never learns that there is no actual threat, and so the threat remains. Although a number of studies support this hypothesis (Thayer, Friedman, & Borkovec, 1996; Verkuil et al., 2009), it has proven hard to replicate, and even within the studies that do support it, the results suggest that the dampened response is complex (McLaughlin, Borkovec, & Sibrava, 2007; Thayer, Friedman, & Borkovec, 1996; Verkuil et al., 2009).

Research exploring the verbal nature of worry in children is much more limited. Exploratory studies asking children about their worries indicate that both the nature and the function of worry are more varied than are found in adults. Children do report that many of their worries are in words, but many report that their worries aren't exclusively verbal in nature, and several children report that the majority of their worries aren't verbal. We accidentally garnered further support for this observation (Burns & Wilson, 2016). Using an experimental paradigm we randomised children between the ages of 7 and 12 to worry in words or images in order to test whether one modality was easier to suppress. The experiment did not show that one modality was easier to suppress, nor that one modality was more associated with affect. However, in order to check the manipulation we spoke to the participants after the experiment and asked them to estimate how much time they spent worrying in words and how much time they spent worrying in images. Nearly all participants failed to do what was asked of them. Whether or not participants were asked to worry in words or to worry in images, they tended to reported worrying in words for approximately 50% of the time and in images for the other 50%. This suggests both that children struggle to change their natural way of worrying but also that their worry isn't specifically verbal.

Further research indicates that for children, worry may not be primarily experienced as verbal. After an initial study of a questionnaire measure of fear and worry where Spence and colleagues found that children were not differentiating fear and worry in their ratings (McCathie & Spence, 1991), Campbell, Rapee, and Spence (2001) went on to ask children aged 5–16 and adults to respond to a list of 24 items denoting negative outcomes. They were asked to rate each of these on how often they worried about them, how often they thought about them, and how bad would it be if they happened. The authors found that children rated the intensity or how bad the outcome would be as similar to how much they worried about it, whereas adults rated how much they thought about the outcome as similar to how much they worried about it. The adolescents in the study showed a pattern of responding somewhere between the two, suggesting a somewhat gradual change in this experience. Szabó (2007) followed up this study exploring aspects such as behavioural avoidance and affect. Once again, she found that children (aged 7–12) did not rate their worries as verbal, and the things they were worried about were also things that they experienced significant negative affect about, and that they avoided. Thus things that worried children appeared to be experienced very similarly to those things they were afraid of, unlike things that worried adults, which were experienced as predominantly verbal and not as affectively charged.

In a follow up to this study (Wilson, McEnaney, & Felekki, in prep.) we explored whether children's ability to distinguish between fear and worry was associated with whether they rated their worries as verbal or behavioural. In two studies, children from age seven were reliably able to differentiate between worry and fear based on vignettes of young children in anxiety provoking situations. In some vignettes the children were described as having thoughts going round in their head, and in some they were described as having a beating heart and feeling hot (Figure 1.2).

Story 1. Fear

This is Sam
Sam's mum is taking him to a birthday party
When Sam arrives at the party, his friend opens the door to invite him in.
Sam's friend has a big dog that starts to bark and run toward Sam as he goes into the house.
Sam's heart starts to beat fast and his tummy begins to feel wobbly.

Sam's friend thinks that Sam is scared.
Sam's mum thinks that Sam is worried.

Who do you think is light? Is it Sam's friend or is it Sam's mum?

Story 2. Worry

This is Sally.
Sally is at home with Mum and Dad.
Sally goes to the kitchen to get some lemonade?
As Sally is pouring the lemonade into a glass, her hand slips and the lemonade spills all over the kitchen table.
Sally thinks that her mum and dad will be cross with her for spilling the lemonade.

Mum thinks that Sally is worried.
Dad thinks that Sally is scared.

Who do you think is light? Is it Sally's Mum or is it Sally's dad?

Figure 1.2 *Example of story vignettes used to distinguish fear and worry.*

The four to six year olds were not as good at differentiating fear and worry based on these vignettes, with some suggestion that at this young age, girls were better than boys, but by age seven, most children were scoring the maximum score on the task. In the second of these studies we then used the same measures as Szabó (2007) to explore associations between fear, worry, and thinking. As found by Szabó and Campbell et al., there were significant correlations between worry, fear, and thinking across five- to ten-year-old participants. What we wanted to test, however, was whether there were any associations between an individual child's ability to distinguish between fear and worry and their tendency to rate worry as verbal, and the results were clear; there were not. This suggests that whether a child can differentiate between fear and worry in stories is unrelated to their experience of fear and worry and that at present we have very little understanding of the lived experience of worry for young children and how different this is or isn't to the lived experience of worry for adolescents and adults.

The strength of the evidence that children therefore do not experience worry as primarily verbal comes from the different nature of all these studies. Both in manipulated worry (Burns & Wilson, 2016) and in implicit relationships between worry and words (Campbell, Rapee, & Spence, 2001; McCathie & Spence, 1991; Szabó, 2007; Wilson, McEnaney, & Felekki, in preparation), children perform differently to adults. The questions therefore remain: what is the fundamental nature of children's worries, and how does this develop over time to become the primarily verbal worry we see in adults?

THE FUNCTION OF WORRY

The function of worry in adults has been studied in three primary ways: through clinical observation about what adults with GAD report about the function of their worry, through asking adults what their beliefs about worry are (often based on these clinical observations), and through the development of theories about the function of worry.

When adults are asked about why they worry they report a variety of functions for the process. For example, Borkovec and Roemer (1995) asked individuals with GAD why they worry. They found that the reasons generally split into six categories: to increase or maintain motivation, to problem solve, to be prepared, to avoid or prevent disaster, to distract from more emotionally laden topics, and superstitious beliefs. Borkovec and Roemer developed a brief questionnaire based on these six functions and found that adults with GAD reported all of these reasons for worry more than adults without GAD. Francis and Dugas' approached the question by interviewing adults about the reasons for their worry. In their interview about positive beliefs about worry (Francis & Dugas, 2004), only four factors emerged: worry to aid problem solving and motivation, worry protecting from the possibility of future negative emotions, worry that means you are a good person, and worry that is magical thinking. Another measure of these positive beliefs about worry is the positive beliefs sub-scale of the Meta-Cognitions Questionnaire (Cartwright-Hatton & Wells, 1997; Wells & Cartwright-Hatton, 2004). This questionnaire focuses on a sub-set of positive beliefs: particularly beliefs about problem solving (including coping and being organised) and about avoiding future problems, perhaps due to the measure also measuring a wide range of other meta-cognitive processes that maintain problematic worry (see Chapter 4). There is clearly overlap between the functions identified using different ways of assessing the perceived function of worry in adults, but different models/researchers emphasise different aspects of these.

In addition to consciously accessed functions of worry, a number of theories have emerged about the function of worry from clinical researchers' careful observation of their clients' experiences and processes. These have mostly emerged as clinical theories and include functions such as dampening the emotional response (Thayer, Friedman, & Borkovec, 1996), keeping everything at a low emotional level so the emotion does not escalate (Newman & Llera, 2011), and reducing uncertainty (Bottesi et al., 2016; Koerner & Dugas, 2006). These clinical theories are crucial to our understanding as these kinds of processes may not be obvious to someone experiencing them. There is value in accessing individual's conscious awareness of their worry, but there is complementary value in observing a wide range of people with problematic worry and determining more unconscious patterns of responding.

When exploring the function of worry for children a similar but somewhat different pattern emerges. We asked children aged between six and 12 years what they believed about worry (Wilson & Hughes, 2011), and approximately half of the six year olds, rising to approximately 70% of the 12 year olds, could report at least one positive belief about worry. The functions they ascribed to their worry included believing that worry helped them think things through, solve problems, motivated them, made them take care and kept them safe, and also they believed that worry showed they care about others. We also asked adolescents what they believed about their worries (Wilson, 2008). Adolescents showed a great deal of similarity to adults in the beliefs they reported, but it was notable that they also had beliefs that were related to peers and peer relationships (see Chapter 4). A number of studies have used questionnaires adapted from the adult questionnaires to assess these positive beliefs about worry, including the positive beliefs sub-scale of the MCQ (Donovan, Holmes, & Farrell, 2016; Kertz & Woodruff-Borden, 2013; White & Hudson, 2016) and the Why Worry II (Barahmand, 2008; Fialko, Bolton, & Perrin, 2012; Laugesen, Dugas, & Bukowski, 2003). These studies would suggest that children and adolescents hold a similar range of positive beliefs about their worry as those held by adults.

In terms of understanding the function of worry by exploring theories of worry, these have been much less well developed for childhood worry. Chapters 4 describes further the testing of the clinical theories developed for adult GAD in children, and many of the theories described earlier do hold some support, in adolescents at least (Reynolds, Cartwright-Hatton, & Wilson, 2012), but there are few theories that go beyond these.

What we are therefore missing in understanding the function of children's worry are theories, models, or explanations that go beyond either children's conscious appraisal of worry, or that go beyond an adult understanding of worry. There are indications that it might not be the same, and developmental considerations such as cognitive maturity or the importance of social relationships might impact on the possible functions, but it is unclear how different it might be.

MEASUREMENT OF WORRY IN CHILDREN

ASSESSMENT OF CHILDREN'S WORRY

A number of questionnaires, interviews, and experimental ways of assessing worry have been developed. Most of these have been developed for adults and adapted for children, but some were developed by clinicians and researchers working with children to assess some of the key aspects of worry. Many researchers have been interested in what children worry about, or the content of worry, and others are more interested in the process of worry. Clinicians on the other hand have focused more on the clinical aspects of worry, including the factors that make worry problematic: intensity, frequency, and uncontrollability, and other symptoms of worry-based anxiety disorders such as GAD. Different ways of assessing worry in children are reviewed below.

Assessing the content of children's worries: using checklists

There is an interesting literature tracking what children worry about. Indeed early papers on children's worry focused on the content of worries (Levy & Guttman, 1976; Pintner & Lev, 1940; Simon & Ward, 1974). This literature can help us track changes in worry over different generations (see Chapter 2) and can help us explore differences in the content of worry across children of different ages and genders.

There have been two main ways of assessing the content of worry in children: questionnaires and interviews, and it seems that these two methods might tap into different aspects of worry (Muris, Merckelbach, & Luijten, 2002). The questionnaires are often lists of different things children could worry about, and participants/patients are asked to tick off the things they worry about. One benefit of this approach is that children may not be very good at remembering their past worries if they are not worried at the time of completing a measure (see Chapter 2 for research into future thinking). Another benefit is that children may feel more able to report embarrassing or shameful worries by ticking a box than they would if they had to say the worries out loud. One disadvantage of this method is that unless you ask there is no measurement of how important the worry is to the child. A worry that is taking up hours of the child's time and gets in the way of their life may be endorsed the same way as a fleeting worry that a child had once, months ago, is. Clinically, what children are worried about seems to be less important than the other dimensions of worry, such as intensity and frequency. Checklist approaches can combine the two, with one measure combining both a checklist of worries, and also ratings of intensity, frequency, and uncontrollability for those items children endorse.

The Worries Inventory (Orton, 1982), was an attempt to replicate and extend one of the earliest studies of what children worry about from the 1930s (Pintner & Lev, 1940). After interviewing a small number of children about their worries to determine whether there were any items missing on the original inventory, Orton gave her 62 item inventory to 645 children aged 10–12 years. The items included worries about school, family, personal health and well-being, social adequacy, imaginary or unreasonable worries, personal adequacy, and economic and ornamental worries. She found interesting gender differences in this group, with girls reporting more worries across half of the domains, and although there were some changes in the content of worries when compared to the 1940 study, these were mostly in what the children were least likely to worry about, not what they were most likely to worry about. What is striking is that these categories are still relevant today and have been replicated in many other studies involving worry checklists. For example, Simon and Ward (1974) developed two Worry List Questionnaires of 100 items, derived from a pilot study. The categories for these questionnaires were family, school, economic, social, personal adequacy, personal health, animals, and imagination. Once again, in their study, Simon and Ward found that girls reported more worries than boys across a number of domains.

Since these early questionnaires there have been few specific questionnaires developed to explore the content of worries. One exception is the Worry Tendency Questionnaire for Chinese Adolescents (cited in Lin et al., 2017). This questionnaire was developed for adolescents and included categories of worries about learning, health, relationships, uncertainty about the future, and confidence. This is of interest as this measure was developed both more recently than early worry checklists but also in a different culture, and yet many of the categories overlap with the early worry checklists. This universality of different content of worry does suggest that although there may be differences, perhaps between boys and girls, in frequency of worries, there are more similarities in the content of worry across time and individual participants. Individual differences may be very important in working with worried children, but this universality may tell us something important about the nature of worry itself. Studies of worry in adults across different cultures suggest that there may be differences in personal worries depending on the circumstances of the person, but macro-worries, or those worries that are about issues in the wider world, do indeed seem universal (Boehnke et al., 1998; Suh, Schwartz, & Melech, 2000). As it is proposed that these macro-worries do not develop until adolescence, when abstract thought is fully developed, we might expect more differences in the content of children's worries depending on their personal circumstances. This is discussed further in Chapter 2.

There are therefore a number of questionnaires that can assess the content of children's worries. These are easily adapted for different generations and for different cultures by adding and removing categories or items. They can also be adapted to measure different aspects of worry such as frequency and intensity whilst maintaining generalisability across a large number of children. However, if resources allow interviewing children about their worries, they may give us similar levels of information about worry, whilst allowing children to talk about worries that the researchers or clinicians have not considered and therefore have not included.

Assessing the content of children's worries: interviewing children about their worries

One of the earliest studies where researchers interviewed children about their worries was Silverman, Greca, and Wasserstein (1995). Silverman and colleagues asked children about their worries in a number of domains: school, performance, classmates, friends, war, disasters, money, health, future events, personal harm, little things, appearance, and family. These domains structured the interview, but by asking children open-ended questions, rather than asking them to check their worries off on a checklist, they were able to capture additional worries that the researchers had not thought about. In addition to this, the researchers asked about the intensity of any worries, and also about whether the worrying event happened and how frequently it happened. Once again, gender differences emerged and children who were more anxious reported both more worries and also that these worries were more intense. One of the advantages of interviewing children about their worries is that the most currently important worry/worries to the child are likely to be reported as these are the worries the child will have recall for. In addition they can put their worries in their own words; this can be particularly helpful for accessing worries that would not usually be included on a checklist. Furthermore, interviewing children can be quite an easy way of including questions about intensity, frequency, and uncontrollability as they can be asked for any of the worries children spontaneously report. The disadvantages of interviewing children about their worries are the opposite of the advantages of having checklists: children may not recall all of their relevant worries and they may not feel able to talk about worries that they feel are embarrassing or shameful. It can be highly time-consuming for researchers to interview individual children and therefore it may be that in research it is a technique less used than checklists and questionnaires. This may contrast with clinical practice when getting to fully understand a child's worries is likely to involve conversations and gentle exploration of their experiences and the things that are distressing them. As a researcher pragmatic decisions have to be taken about what information is needed to answer the research question, but the clinician may have the luxury of time and the desire to fully understand an individual child. Combining different approaches may give us the richness of data that truly helps us understand worry in children.

> Megan was an eleven year old girl who had come to therapy for help with her anxiety. She struggled to talk about what was bothering her, just saying she felt nervous. Her mum talked about how Megan worried a lot about her friends and what they thought of her, and she felt that Megan was often asking her for reassurance. Megan

agreed with mum that she worried about what her friends thought of her, but struggled to explain further. The therapist offered Megan a checklist of different worries to see if any of them fitted for her. As she started to look down the list Megan became more clear about what worries she did and didn't have. She ticked lots of worries about school and tests, she also ticked lots of worries about friendships and being bullied. She was clear that she wasn't worried about her physical health so much, nor about wider social issues, such as climate change and politics. The therapist talked through the list with Megan. Her worries about friends were bound up with her worries about school. She thought that she was failing at school academically and worried that her friends might not want to hang around with her any more. She worried they thought she was stupid and one of two of the girls in her class had started to make fun of her when she got test results and they weren't good. The worries were all linked up together and combined to make Megan unhappy and constantly anxious in school and about school.

Measuring specific worries in children

Clinicians can be interested in the content of children's worries as indicators of different kinds of anxiety disorders; worries that are primarily about social situations may indicate a social anxiety disorders, whereas worries about specific stimuli such as spiders or heights, may indicate a specific phobia. Therefore some of the symptom-based measures of anxiety and worry include a number of questions about different types of worry. The Revised Child Manifest Anxiety Scale (RCMAS; Reynolds, 1980; Reynolds & Richmond, 1978) has a specific subscale for worry. Both the Spence Children's Anxiety Scale (SCAS: Spence, 1998) and the Screen for Child Anxiety Related Disorders (SCARED; Birmaher et al., 1997) have sub-scales for generalised anxiety disorder, and the relevant sub-scale items focus on worry. In the Multi-dimensional Anxiety Scale for Children (MASC; March et al., 1997) generalised anxiety disorder symptoms are measured with a harm avoidance subscale.

Similarly, a small number of questionnaires focus on just one kind of worry. The Social Worries Questionnaire for parents (Spence, 1995) and the Social Worries Anxiety Index for Young Children (Stuijfzand & Dodd, 2017) were specifically developed to assess social worries, such as worries about meeting new people or asking other children if they can play, in pre-school and school aged children.

There are a number of questionnaires that have been developed to assess children's worries in a specific context, for example worry about cancer or child surgery worries (Mendez, Quiles, & Hidalgo, 2001). Often these are developed by specialist teams by developing and validating items that are regularly brought up in clinics or research projects. They often do focus on specific content of worries and can help clinicians to understand specific aspects of the child's experience and to point to what the child might need help with.

The assessment strategy for the content of worries is therefore driven by the reason for the assessment. Researchers need their tools to be reliable and valid and therefore questionnaires and structured interviews are very helpful. Clinicians on the other hand need to understand the main concerns of children, whether they meet criteria for particular psychological disorders, and to have a focus for an intervention. This can be complemented by examining the processes involved in children's worry.

ASSESSING THE PROCESSES INVOLVED IN CHILDREN'S WORRY

As well as the two main ways of assessing worry – questionnaires and interviews – experimental procedures have been developed for assessing the process of children's worry. All three are reviewed below.

Questionnaires to assess the processes involved in children's worry

Questionnaires about the processes involved in worry have included specific questionnaires about the processes proposed in key models of worry, such as beliefs about worry or intolerance of uncertainty. These are reviewed in the relevant sections in Chapters 4 and 5. However, there are also questionnaires that assess more general worry processes. The most widely used measure of this is the Penn State Worry Questionnaire (PSWQ). The PSWQ was developed by Borkovec and colleagues to capture the problematic aspects of worry that the team saw being crucial to adults with GAD, namely the tendency to engage in excessive, generalised and uncontrollable worry. The adult version of the measure has 16 items about the nature of worry, such as 'My worries overwhelm me' and 'Once I start worrying I can't stop', which are scored on a five-point scale of not at all typical to very typical. This measure has been found to have good psychometric properties and has been widely used in studies of worry, both in clinical and non-clinical populations. Although there is some debate about whether it is best conceptualised as a single factor measure or a two-factor measure the two-factor structure mainly appears to be related to the negatively worded questions, rather than the questionnaire tapping into two different aspects of worry. Furthermore, there appears to be relative invariance in the factor structure across different cultures (e.g. Rodríguez-Biglieri & Vetere, 2011).

In 1997, the adult version of the PSWQ was adapted for use with children (Chorpita et al., 1997). In addition to changing the language (e.g. 'My worries really bother me') the number of items was reduced to 14. Since 1997 this has been extensively used to measure worry in children and has been shown to have good psychometric properties. Muris and colleagues (Muris, Meesters, & Gobel, 2001) explored the psychometric properties thoroughly and found that for younger children three reversed items (where high scores indicated low worry, rather than high worry) were confusing and removing them increased the internal consistency of the scale. This maps onto the difficulties found in determining the factor structure in adults and represents a clear way of resolving the difficulty. They therefore recommended using the 11 item version of the PSWQ-C for younger children. The PSWQ is by far the most widely used measure of worry and has been used by researchers and clinicians alike.

The catastrophising interview: an experimental paradigm capturing worry

One notable way of assessing worry within an experimental paradigm has been the catastrophising interview (Vasey & Borkovec, 1992). This was first developed for use with adults. The process involves generating a worry, either a real worry of the participant or researcher-generated worry, and asking the participant 'what is so bad about…'. When the participant gives an answer this then becomes the subject of the question 'what is so bad about…?'. For example, Davey and colleagues have used the original prompt of 'what would be bad about being the statue of liberty?' (Davey, 2006). When participants give responses such as 'I'd be cold' then this is added to the prompt question to give 'what would be so bad about being cold?'. The catastrophising interview is an iterative process and therefore the number of steps that a participant gives is recorded and in a few studies the content of these steps has been explored. Several studies have found that the number of steps in the catastrophising interview is associated with scores on the PSWQ and that these can be impacted by manipulating mood (Meeten & Davey, 2011). It also appears that the majority of worries generated by this process are related to social evaluation and many participants do end the process with a catastrophe such as death or madness (Davey, 2006).

The catastrophising interview has been used with children and adolescents across the age range (Figure 1.3). Muris and colleagues (Muris et al., 1998) asked children aged 8–13 years what their worries were and then what was so bad about their worries. Most children could come up with at least one iterative step, although it was only the older children who could generate more than a small number. In a study of young adolescents Turner and Wilson (2010) asked 11–13 year olds to generate a personal worry as the base worry for the catastrophising interview. There was a range of steps generated by the participants, but the mean number of steps was eight, suggesting that by this age young people are able to generate a significant number of worry steps. Furthermore, many of the young people could report on the process of their worry, and they often reported that their worries became worse across the iterative process.

Figure 1.3 Example of catastrophising interview from Osleger (2012).

An interesting developmental observation was that the end point of the process for these children was different to the end point found for adults. Children's catastrophic endings were less likely to be about death and madness, and more about social rejection and physical harm. Further studies have explored catastrophising in children using this process and are reviewed in Chapter 2.

The advantage of the catastrophising interview is that within a research setting it is a standardised way of measuring worry in a more 'live' way than simply getting children to report what they worry about. This taps into different thought processes than self-report methods can usually do, and yet it is standardised and so can be used across participants in a generalisable way. However, it is clear from the qualitative evaluation of the catastrophisation interview in children that it does not fully mimic the true process of worry (Turner & Wilson, 2010).

CONCLUSIONS ABOUT THE MEASUREMENT OF CHILDREN'S WORRY

Assessment of worry is a challenge because worry is an internal cognitive process that is not observable. However it might be a particular challenge in children because children are still developing language. Therefore it is hard to determine whether differences in the context and process of worry as reported by children are due to language or whether they are due to real differences in the worry process itself. Furthermore, by asking children to report on their worry or to talk about their worry it is likely that the worry process itself is interrupted. If children are simply asked to 'worry as they would usually do', then it is not clear that the process or experience will be similar across different children. Future research may be able to develop implicit measures of worry that have been developed for the assessment of fear-based responses, for example the implicit association test or IAT (Field & Lawson, 2003; Greenwald, McGhee, & Schwartz, 1998), or may be able to test hypotheses about children's worry more naturalistically. It is also clear that further qualitative studies of children's worry are warranted where the context and meaning of worry experiences can be described and our understanding of the experience deepened.

CHAPTER TWO
Children's worry and development

WORRY IN A DEVELOPMENTAL CONTEXT

The previous chapter explored the concept of worry and the definitions that have been used for adults and children. One of the criticisms that has been raised about our current understanding of children's worry is that it adapted from our understanding of adult worry. As Vasey and Daleiden noted back in 1994:

> While caution is necessary when applying adult-based models to children, their careful use can provide an important heuristic for initial research efforts. As research progresses, we expected that a more developmentally appropriate model of worry in children will emerge.
>
> Vasey and Daleiden (1994, p. 186)

Unfortunately, this model has not emerged. Applying adult models to children risks missing some of the key differences that may be present due to development. If we explore the different facets of worry we find that a number of these change across childhood and are predicated on cognitive, language, social, and emotional development. This chapter reviews these different facets of worry and details the literature to date that helps us understand the early development of worry.

DEVELOPMENT OF WORRY ACROSS CHILDHOOD

Throughout childhood there are changes and transitions that mark children's lives. These range from physical transitions such as growth spurts and puberty, to social transitions such as starting school, starting secondary school, dating, and making and breaking friendships. In addition to predictable transitions are those that are common but more individual and unpredictable such as moving house or moving school, childhood illnesses, and the arrival of siblings. All these events can prompt children's worries, but other aspects of children's development also appear to impact what children worry about.

The interest in how worry changes across childhood dates back to the earliest studies of worry in children. Writing in 1953 Angelino and Shedd report:

> Very broadly and only with reservation can we state that at age 10, 11, and 12 we find a preponderance of fears connected with animals. At 13 we find a shift to school-connected content. At age 15 this content appears to give way to economic and political interest which increases through age 18.
>
> Angelino and Shedd (1953)

Over 60 years later their findings are still relevant and represent a good description of what changes in children's worry over time. A number of studies have explored changes in children's worry, and these have used a wide variety of methodologies to determine such changes (see Chapter 1 for a review of these). Some studies have used lists of worries generated from pilot work and asked children to rate them on frequency and intensity (e.g. Brown et al., 2006). Others have used semi-structured interviews which combine open-ended questions with structured prompting about specific worries (e.g. Henker, Whalen, & O'Neil, 1995; Laing et al., 2009; Muris et al., 2000; Silverman, Greca, & Wasserstein, 1995). Only a small number of studies have used formal questionnaires of worry or worry processes to look at developmental changes (e.g. Barahmand, 2008; Chorpita et al., 1997; Pasarelu et al., 2017). From these studies it appears that there is some evidence that worry frequency increases to age ten (Caes et al., 2016; Muris, Merckelbach et al., 2000; Muris, Merckelbach, Meesters, et al., 2002) and then declines after that (Caes et al., 2016; Laing et al., 2009), but that the intensity of worries declines more in mid-childhood and increases after that (Caes et al., 2016; Silverman, Greca, & Wasserstein, 1995). However, the evidence isn't strong and with such varied methodologies, respondents, and age ranges it is hard to strongly support the idea of developmental changes in the frequency and intensity of worries (Cartwright-Hatton, 2006).

What is much clearer is that, as suggested by Angelino and Shedd, the content of children's worries changes over time. In young children the predominant worries, just like predominant fears, are physical and immediate. These include worries about animals, separation from parents, and bullying (Laing et al., 2009; Muris, Merckelbach, et al., 2000; Stevenson-Hinde & Shouldice, 1995). At older ages children become more worried about school, health, physical appearance, and personal harm (Brown et al., 2006; Caes et al., 2016; Henker, Whalen, & O'Neil, 1995; Muris, Merckelbach, et al., 2000), with only the oldest children worrying about social ills (Angelino & Shedd, 1953; Henker, Whalen, & O'Neil, 1995).

Alongside this development in the content of worry is development in children's ability to describe their worries with greater elaboration (Henker, Whalen, & O'Neil, 1995). Indeed, given the development of language and introspective capacity across childhood it is difficult to determine whether it is the experience of worry that changes or the ability to talk about it. Furthermore, given that worry is defined as primarily verbal it is difficult to determine whether it is increased language and cognitive ability that opens up the ability to think and therefore worry about different topics or whether the developmental shifts in the content of worry reflect children's widening experience of the world (Muris, Merckelbach, Meesters, et al., 2002). Given that many of our interventions for anxious and worried children are predominantly verbal exploring the inter-relationships between language development and worry development may be important. Examining whether there are developmental shifts in the components of worry and processes involved in worry may also help us understand whether the adult models of worry do really help us understand worry in children.

Another aspect of children's experience that is likely to impact the content of their worries is their cultural context. Several studies have concluded that anxiety symptoms in children do differ across different cultures (Essau et al., 2004; Silverman, Greca, & Wasserstein, 1995; Varela et al., 2008), with differences found in which anxiety disorders are most prevalent, which fear is most commonly reported, and which wider anxiety symptoms are reported. These of course represent different aspects of the experience of anxiety; the reporting, and even experiencing, of different symptoms is likely to be influenced by the social desirability of such symptoms in your society, with somatic symptoms being more socially accepted than emotional symptoms in some families and in some societies (e.g. Varela & Hensley-Maloney, 2009). The prevalence of individual worries also likely represents individual children's experiences. If you live in poverty with uncertain access to food and shelter, then your worries are more likely to be about hunger and safety. Whereas if you are wealthy and not living in precarious circumstances, your worries are more likely to be about friendships, school, and achievement. What appears to be the case, however, is that there are more differences between individuals in different cultures than there are between cultures. Furthermore, the content of worry does not appear to determine strongly whether it is becomes a problem. Chapter 4 will further review cross-cultural differences in the mechanisms involved in problematic worry.

COMPONENTS OF WORRY

As we saw in the previous chapter there are a number of different psychological processes involved in worry. Worry anticipates the future. This needs a child to be able to anticipate and think about the future and to think about hypothetical situations. Worry is iterative. This needs a child to be able to think repeatedly about one situation. This might involve sustained attention and might involve thinking about complex ideas where iteration of thought is possible. Worry involves or feels like problem solving and more often than not this will be social problem solving. This ability to solve social problems emerges throughout childhood and involves social and emotional skills, as well as cognitive and language skills. Problematic worry involves catastrophisation. This requires complex cognitive and language skills.

When worry is broken down into the different components, it is clear that all aspects of development are implicated, from cognitive and language development to emotional and social development. This chapter focuses on these four components, exploring what we know about how they develop across childhood and adolescence and then linking this to our understanding of the development of worry.

FUTURE THINKING

Future thinking has been described as one of the most important processes within human cognition, with some researchers suggesting that it distinguishes us from other species (Atance & O'Neill, 2005b). It is future thinking that allows us to prepare for and plan our own futures, whether explicitly or implicitly. Therefore, worry may be seen as future thinking that aims to prepare for and plan for the negative or catastrophic possible futures. Future thinking is a fundamental part of worry. Although you can worry about things past, it is usually the impact they may have on the future that is concerning. The focus on the future in worry may be one of the factors that distinguishes worry from rumination (Segerstrom et al., 2000), and therefore this future focus in worry needs consideration of the complex cognitive processes involved in putting ourselves into possible futures.

Much work has been done on children's ability to think about the future or mentally time travel. For example, Suddendorf (2010) asked three- and four-year-old children to say something that they would be doing tomorrow. Their parents were asked to rate whether these events were likely, and it was found that at four years of age, children almost always proposed realistic events, but younger than this, the ability was more unreliable. Across this age range (three to four years) a significant minority of children could not talk about something they would be doing tomorrow. In a slightly different paradigm, Atance and O'Neill

(2005) gave children a number options of what to take with them on a future trip. They chose from a pool of desirable and helpful options and then justified their choices. The determination of whether the child was thinking about the future or not was on the basis of how they justified their choice. They found that at age three, about 40–50% children were justifying their choices using future focused language. Extending this Atance and Meltzoff (2005) asked three, four, and five year olds about a possible future event, but this time the event called for a specific item; for example, one prompt involved a snowy scene, and the options children could choose were a winter coat, arm bands (water wings), or a towel. All children chose the correct item at a level better than chance, but this approached a ceiling level with the four and five year olds (91% and 97% correct, respectively). Differences between the different ages were even more marked for using future language in justifying the choices, with 35%, 62%, and 71% of three, four, and five year olds using future state language in their justification. We replicated these findings using a different scene involving a tropical greenhouse full of insects (Barrett & Wilson, 2019). Once again we found that children chose appropriate items more often than they used future uncertain terms to justify them. This ability to justify choices using these future uncertain terms was related to age but not to verbal ability (Figure 2.1).

Figure 2.1 *Items used in the future thinking task.*

The reliance on language for determining future thinking has some limitations, especially as these future thinking skills are developing at the same time that language is at a basic level but is quickly advancing. Therefore other experimental paradigms haven't relied on language. For example, Suddendorf, Nielsen, and von Gehlen (2011) showed children a puzzle that they couldn't complete because they didn't have all the parts. They then showed the children into a different room for a different task. However, in this second room was the part that the child needed to complete the puzzle in the first room, along with other desirable objects. As they left this second room children were asked to choose an object that they would like to take back into the first room. The reasoning was that children who were thinking about the future would choose the object that was needed to complete the puzzle, but those who weren't would just choose a more desirable object. At three years of age children chose the correct object at a chance level, but by four years of age children more often chose an object that could help them solve the problem.

A different but related body of research focused on children's thinking about the future is counterfactual thinking. Worries can typically be viewed as hypothetical thinking about the future, whereas counterfactual thinking is when future possibilities are in contradiction to what is currently happening or known. So, if worry is asking 'what if?' counterfactual thinking is asking 'what if that hadn't happened?'.

> Alice got her exam results and was disappointed. She was worried about whether it might impact on her future choices and her future career. Very soon she was thinking to herself, 'if only I had studied harder', 'if only the right question had come up on that test paper' 'if only I had eaten a proper breakfast the morning of the exam'.

There is debate about what age children start being able to think counterfactually (Beck et al., 2014) that mirrors the debate about hypothetical future thinking. There is some evidence that a certain kind of counterfactual thinking is present from about three years of age (Harris, German, & Mills, 1996; Robinson & Beck, 2000), whereas other researchers suggest that it starts a little later, from four years old (Riggs et al., 1998). It does appear, like hypothetical future thinking, to develop through childhood into adolescence, with greater complexity and capacity for abstraction (Beck et al., 2014; Rafetseder & Perner, 2012).

Therefore it suggests that the ability to think into the future does start early, from age four to five or so but that the nature of the task might significantly impact this. Therefore another interesting question is not when children develop this ability to mentally time travel but in what circumstances. Atance and Meltzoff (2006) found that children's current state significantly impacted on their ability to predict their future desires. They randomised 48 three-, four-, and five-year-old children into four groups: two groups got lots of salty pretzels during their task, and the other two didn't. The children were then asked to nominate what they would like, pretzels or water, with one group in each condition asked what they wanted right now, and the other asked what they would like to accompany a different task tomorrow. The children who had eaten the pretzels reported that they would want water, whether or not they were choosing for right now or to have tomorrow. This has been replicated in different age groups (Mahy et al., 2014) and we find that even adults find it hard to overcome their current emotion when thinking about the future (Kramer et al., 2017; Wilson & Gilbert, 2005). Furthermore, emotion valence appears to influence the presence of spontaneous counterfactual thinking in both adults (Roese & Olson, 1997) and children (Guajardo, McNally, & Wright, 2016).

This has significant implications both for worry and more generally for self-report of anxiety. Many clinicians have had the experience of children in the clinic room denying any difficulties with their anxiety and reporting very convincingly that they will be able to stroke the dog/go to school/go to bed in their own bed. Furthermore, several trials have found significant changes when parent or clinician report are used, but much smaller, and often non-significant, changes when self-report is used. Instead of concluding that children are not very good respondents, maybe we need to consider that young children are much more influenced by their current feeling and mental state than older children and adults and that their reports that things are fine and will be fine indicate this limitation of ability.

> Philippa, aged 13 was just starting therapy. She had not been into school for about 7 months. She had experienced significant bullying and had not been able to return after a summer break. Every morning her mother and father tried to encourage her to return to school and every morning she cried, shouted, and sometimes vomited. Her parents were on the point of giving up and school wanted to know when she was going to be back. Following an assessment it was considered that Philippa might benefit from cognitive behaviour therapy and so the therapist and Philippa sat down to plan some goals for the therapy. Philippa categorically stated she wanted to get back to school. She wanted to do well and get a good job and she missed her friends. The therapist set up a hierarchy of activities where getting back to school was at the top, and thinking about entering the school doors was at the bottom. In therapy Philippa was able to tolerate the anxiety of thinking about entering the school and found that the anxiety went down to low levels whilst thinking about this. This gave her great confidence and she told the therapist that she was ready to go back to school. She said she wanted to skip to the top of the hierarchy and go back into school on Monday. The therapist talked with her about the fact she hadn't been in since before summer. Philippa dismissed this and said she was ready and she felt strong enough to do it. She told her parents this was what was going to happen despite the therapist's suggestion that it seemed unlikely. Philippa didn't manage to get into school on the Monday and was upset and disappointed when she came back to therapy.

In a series of studies we have extended these findings to explore some additional issues in future thinking (Wilson, Curtin, O'Brien, Skelton, & Easton, in prep.). For these studies, we recruited 65 children of 5–6 year olds, 55 children of 7–9 year olds, and 60 children of 14–15 year olds. These children were given Atance and Meltzoff's trip task (Atance &

Meltzoff, 2005) along with measures of verbal ability and anxiety and worry. Half of the children in each age group were randomised into a negative mood induction condition, where they were played slow sad music, the lights were lowered, and the researcher spoke in a low quiet voice. It was predicted that children might choose more comforting options for the trip and that sad mood might make the children's justifications more present-focused. Results were complicated by the fact that the mood manipulation worked differently in each age group. In the youngest age group the mood manipulation did not work at all. The researcher reported that children did remain quiet during the sad music, but as soon as the researcher spoke to them afterwards, their mood lifted immediately. For the seven- to nine-year-old age group the mood induction was successful, but it was short lived, whereas for the older age group, the mood induction was successful and lasted throughout the experimental procedure. However, the mood induction did not impact on the choices made or the justifications given for choices in any age group. On further examination, however, some subtle differences emerged. In the two youngest groups there was an impact of verbal ability (as measured by the BPVS; Dunn & Dunn, 2009) on justifications, with uncertainty terms and references to the future being related to higher vocabulary. To explore the role of mood further we explored time taken to make choices (14–16 year olds), with the hypothesis that rumination or worry about choices may lead to longer choice times and also the number of words used to justify the answer (seven to nine year olds), with the hypothesis that perseveration might lead to an increase in words used. We could not find evidence that negative mood led to increased time taken to choose the objects to take on the trip; however, we did find evidence in the seven to nine year olds that children in a low mood condition used more words to justify their answers, perhaps suggesting some level of perseveration. Furthermore, when split by group, the association between vocabulary skills and future/uncertainty terms used in the justification could only be found in the neutral mood group, suggesting that other factors, not just verbal ability, were impacting on the responses when the children were experiencing low mood.

Echoing this finding, Mahy et al. (2014) make the important distinction between 'hot' and 'cold' reasoning processes, suggesting that thinking about the future when it requires inhibition of a current mood or physiological state may require more 'hot' processing, whereas thinking about the future more generally does not. They found that in the 'cold' processing condition, seven year olds out-performed three year olds, but this was not the case in the 'hot' processing condition. In order to fully determine whether the ability to think into the future is impacted by mood, we must design a condition in which the future event is in conflict with the current mood, perhaps anticipating a positive event or outcome.

When thinking about the future, we may also need to consider children's organisation of memory more generally. Vasey (1993) argued that young children do not have the organisational structures that are required to propagate worry, and therefore context dependency may be crucial to understanding distress and worry in younger children.

> Kae was 3 when she went on holiday. She was used to travelling, having moved countries on her 1st birthday, and was usually a happy traveller. But this time she wasn't happy in the airport. Her parents checked in the larger luggage and the airport staff asked them whether they had followed the guidelines with regards our hand luggage. They replied that they had. They reminded Kae that she would have to put her beloved Lucie-Bear through the scanner and she looked very concerned. Her mother asked her what was wrong. Kae couldn't tell her. Her mother asked whether it was putting Lucie-Bear through the scanner. She said it was. Her mother asked her what she thought might happen. She shook her head to tell her mother she didn't know. When they approached the security check Kae reluctantly handed over Lucie-Bear to be put in a tray to be scanned. She was very upset and concerned. Her mother asked again what she thought might happen and she again shook her head. Her mother asked whether she thought Lucie-Bear might get lost and her eyes widened, filled with tears and she nodded. A combination of reassurance and the few minutes it took to get Lucie-Bear back was enough to put things right.

Lagatutta has carried out a series of studies on young children exploring their tendency to use past information when thinking about the future or 'life history theory of mind' (Lagattuta, Tashjian, & Kramer, 2018). All the studies suggest that no matter how you measure children's use of the past to think about the future, some children as young as four years old use this life history information, with greater numbers of children using this information as age increases. This includes using past information to predict future emotions (Lagattuta, Wellman, & Flavell, 1997; Lagattuta & Wellman, 2001), to predict future worries and behaviours (Lagattuta, 2007; Lagattuta & Sayfan, 2011, 2013), and in their use of uncertainty ratings and language when thinking about the future (Lagattuta & Sayfan, 2011). The studies suggest that both general age-related development and executive functioning (EF) impact on children's ability to use past information to predict the future (Lagattuta, Tashjian, & Kramer, 2018), with children's verbal ability impacting on their use of language to talk about the future (Lagattuta, 2007; Lagattuta, Wellman, & Flavell, 1997). These studies also throw some light on the subtleties of future thinking. As well as differences across the age range, there were also some subtle gender differences, with female participants using uncertain ratings and using uncertainty in their language more than male participants (Lagattuta & Sayfan, 2011). There was some evidence that younger children required the past and the future to share exact details in order to be able to predict the future based on the past; however, older children managed to use this past information to predict the future even when it was only similar, rather than exactly the same (Lagattuta, 2007). Across the age range understanding the future emotion or behaviour of someone was easier when there was a contrast between the current emotion and the predicted emotion, for example, the predicted emotion being negative and the current emotion being positive, and in general negative emotions were easier to predict (Lagattuta & Wellman, 2001). Finally, there was a recency effect, with most recent past behaviours impacting more than behaviours previous to this (Lagattuta, Tashjian, & Kramer, 2018; Lagattuta & Sayfan, 2013).

This studies suggest that using past events to think about the future may be possible for even very young children, but that certain individual and environmental factors may impact on whether this occurs spontaneously. Children with greater verbal and cognitive ability, perhaps specifically with greater EF capacity, may be more likely to use past information to think into the future. Furthermore, if there is a mismatch between current emotion and predictions about the future, these may prompt future thinking more than if the current mood matches the predicted future mood. Given the impact of worry on EF, we may also predict that when children are worried their capacity to think accurately into the future may be impaired and they may rush to more certain judgements about what might happen.

Despite the importance of future thinking in understanding worry, we are only just beginning to determine the parameters that might impact on this relationship and to understand how individual differences might impact on the ability to worry and how worry might impact on the ability to think into the future. What is clear however is that children as young as four do have rudimentary capacities to think about the future and to talk about possible future events, although this may not occur spontaneously, and it may be limited in some ways. If this is the case, then children should have the ability to worry about future possible outcomes from at least four years of age, if not earlier.

PROBLEM SOLVING

Another body of literature that might be relevant here is research on problem solving. Chapter 1 reviewed the research on the relationship between worry and problem solving, but can the developmental psychology literature help us understand the development of worry by understanding the development of problem solving?

Developmentally, it appears that children start problem solving very early in life (Keen, 2011). From infancy babies appear to be exploring their environment in order to solve the problems it poses. From age six months babies appear to use simple problem solving such as putting an object in the other hand to free up the hand that is needed. From age nine months they use objects for things they are not designed for, but that achieve a different end (Lockman, 2000), for example, using a toy to push something along or hit something, or later, when infants are able to walk, using a toy kitchen as a set of ladders to reach high shelves. We also have evidence that children use social problem solving very early in life. It could be argued that social referencing, whereby an infant uses the affective response of a parent or caregiver to determine information about the safety of the situation (Emde, 1992), is one of the earliest forms of social problem solving. In situations of uncertainty the ability to use non-verbal information from a trusted caregiver may be crucial to the determination of the situation as safe. As children get older, they may look to others to learn about the environment. In her classic studies, Smetana describes how children develop their social order in relation to other children through play in nursery and pre-school settings (Smetana, 1985, 1993). Similarly, Dunn systematically observed and described the verbal interactions between pre-schoolers that provided good evidence that even young children show social problem solving (Dunn, 1988).

Both problem solving in general and social problem solving more specifically continue to develop across childhood (Figure 2.2). As children understand the intentions of others better, develop a larger range of strategies to solve inter-personal problems, and develop skills in carrying these out, their ability in successful problem solving

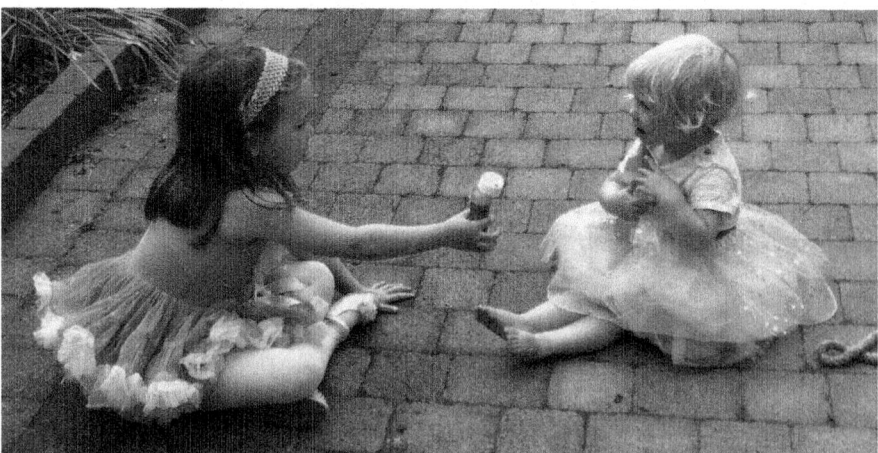

Figure 2.2 Learning from each other: social problem solving in action.

increases (Rubin & Rose-Krasnor, 1992). By adolescence, most young people are successfully negotiating complex social relationships, the emergence of romantic/intimate relationships, and developing into their adult identities (Blakemore, 2018). Indeed it has been suggested that in adolescence there is a rise in the importance of social relationships that can be seen in brain structures and function (Blakemore, 2008; Nelson et al., 2005; Steinberg, 2005).

A number of different processes are working concurrently to ensure the smooth development of these social problem-solving abilities. Some researchers (e.g. Leslie, 1994) have emphasised simple maturational processes whereby the development that occurs in brain structure and functioning allows for more complex information processing and behaviour to develop. These can also be framed within an evolutionary perspective (Belsky, Steinberg, & Draper, 1991), which highlights the key goals of the human organism at different life stages. Early life stages may be seen as aiming to understand when and how your needs are going to be met, with an early focus on survival, developing into a more generalised understanding of the availability and predictability of resources. These broad brush goals determine a variety of complex behaviours and it may be that a fine grained understanding of the mechanisms of social problem solving may need reference to behavioural or social learning models (Bandura, 1969, 2001). These learning models propose that we may learn much of our behaviour not only by differential reinforcement of our own behaviour – for example, being invited to play by being friendly, or being rejected by being loud and boisterous – but also that we learn by observing others. As Bandura notes 'learning would be exceedingly laborious, not to mention hazardous, if people had to rely solely on the effects of their own actions to inform them what to do'.

This developmental progression in the ability to socially problem solve is likely to be related to developments in metacognitive ability (Weil et al., 2013), which, in turn, is related to developments in executive functions (Roebers, 2017). It appears that all these functions predominantly involve the pre-frontal cortex (Dumontheil, 2014; Qiu et al., 2018). This is one of the later brain areas to develop, with significant changes occurring both in childhood and across adolescence (Dumontheil, 2014; Tsujimoto, 2008). It is also an area implicated in generalised anxiety disorder (GAD; Goossen, van der Starre, & van der Heiden, 2019), suggesting a link between problematic worry and deficits in social problem solving.

Finally, it is important to understand the impact of individual differences on these processes. For example, in her studies of pre-schoolers' social interactions, Hughes found strong associations between the ability to socially problem solve and other cognitive abilities, such as EF and theory of mind development (Astington & Hughes, 2013; Hughes & Leekam, 2004). Even if we are learning our social behaviour through our own experiences and by observing others, this is impacted by the cognitive capacity we have individually to do this.

> David was born with a significant learning disability and at eight years of age he had no spoken language. However, he used lots of different ways to communicate. In his family of origin there were many children and a lot of rough and tumble play which sometimes tipped over into aggression. On a school trip with a teacher David was keen to get the teacher's attention and started by pinching her arm. As he was safe, and he was not causing her pain she ignored this behaviour. He then tried to push her arm and started hitting her. Again, she ignored this behaviour. There was a short pause, and then David tried gently tickling her and making gentle vocalisations. David had observed how other children got attention, so started with the one that worked at home, moving through strategies he had seen other children try.

Much of the literature on social problem solving focuses on when it goes wrong. There are robust associations between problem-solving deficits and negative outcomes such as peer relationship difficulties (Warden & MacKinnon, 2003), aggression (Keltikangas-Jarvinen, 2002; Takahashi, Koseki, & Shimada, 2009), poor mental health such as anxiety and depression (Wright et al., 2010), and self-harm and suicide (Speckens & Hawton, 2011). These different outcomes interact with each other, with aggressive children having poor peer relationships and poor mental health (Werner & Crick, 2004), and young people who self-harm also showing poor peer relationships (Stallard et al., 2013). What these studies do not show is the direction of effect. Several studies indicate that poor problem solving leads to poor outcomes (e.g. Hawton et al., 1999; Spears et al., 2014), but few explore problem solving as an outcome. Given the cognitive capacity needed for successful problem solving, it might be expected that any psychological difficulty that takes up cognitive capacity, such as worry or rumination, might impact on problem solving. Indeed Guerreiro et al. (2013) call for more well-designed longitudinal studies to allow us to further explore the interactions between these mechanisms.

Therefore the developmental psychology literature on problem solving suggests that it does start very young, and interactive processes including simple maturation, social learning, and reciprocal reinforcement may play a role in its development. Furthermore, individual differences will impact on the child's ability to problem solve across a wide range of situations. Problem-solving deficits may well lead to a variety of poor outcomes for children and may interact with other processes, such as the development of peer relationships to mediate or moderate these outcomes.
However, poor problem solving is associated with difficulties with peer relationships, behaviour, and mental health, and therefore if worry is a poor way of problem solving, the reliance on worry to solve problems is likely to cause children further difficulties. Chapter 1 suggested that worried children may indeed not have problem-solving deficits, but rather may have poor confidence in their own ability to problem solve. Exploring the problem-solving theories may well help us explain how this poor confidence develops and how worry might impact on poor long-term outcomes for young people.

EXECUTIVE FUNCTIONS

By examining future thinking and problem solving it becomes clear that children's cognitive ability is important in our wider understanding of the development of worry. The aspects of cognitive ability that might be particularly important for understanding worry are those aspects of worry that allow us to sustain our attention, reflect on our own experiences, and our ability to iterate our thinking by following logical thought processes. Many of these cognitive abilities come under the umbrella of executive functions.

Like many cognitive abilities executive functions appear to develop throughout childhood. EF has been split into different components by different researchers, but it is widely accepted that inhibition, working memory, and cognitive flexibility are key components (Diamond, 2013). We know that these all develop across childhood, with a basic working memory ability being the first to mature, and certain aspects of inhibition being latest to mature. There is a significant literature on the relationships between anxiety and EF, testing, and developing Eysenck's attentional control theory (Eysenck et al., 2007). In this theory, and much of the empirical work supporting it, anxiety is seen to impair EF. This occurs across both adult and child populations (Kertz et al., 2016; Ursache & Raver, 2014; Visu-Petra, Miclea, & Visu-Petra, 2013), and in populations that do not have typical neurodevelopment (Hollocks et al., 2014; Ng-Cordell et al., 2018).

However, there is much less research that links these components to worry. In order to explore these links it might be relevant to draw on an adult model of worry. One of the key models that considers executive functions in worry has been developed and tested by Colette Hirsch and colleagues. Hirsch and Mathews (Hirsch & Mathews, 2012) detail a cognitive model of worry in adults. It draws strongly on cognitive psychology as well as being driven by a wealth of clinical experience. Hirsch and Mathews propose that it is both controlled or voluntary attentional processes and uncontrollable or involuntary attentional processes that contribute to the representation of the threat. These attentional processes can be considered part of the wider construct of executive functions. In the model if someone is unable to ignore or override a negative representation of a threat then the top-down controlled attentional processes are allocated to dealing with the threat and this inevitably leads to prolonged worry. The model is built on evidence about cognitive biases in worriers. These biases include attention towards threat, with worriers more likely to attend to threat in their environment, and also more likely to have difficulties disengaging from thinking about threat. Research with both anxious adults and children suggest that anxiety is consistently associated with biased attention to threat (Bar-Haim et al., 2007; Dudeney, Sharpe, & Hunt, 2015). Furthermore, these biased attentional processes are specifically associated with worry and GAD in adults (Goodwin, Yiend, & Hirsch, 2017), with less evidence that they are specifically associated with worry and GAD in children; Waters, Bradley, and Mogg (2014) find evidence for increased attention towards threat in young people with GAD. Hirsch and Mathews also propose interpretation biases in GAD, with worriers more likely to interpret a situation as threatening. These interpretation biases are seen both in adults (Feng et al., 2019) and young people (Stuijfzand et al., 2018) with GAD and high levels of worry (for a review of the Hirsch and Mathews model in young people see Songco, Hudson, and Fox (2020)).

It appears then that cognitive biases are associated with anxiety and worry in children, but how do these relate more broadly to executive functions? One of the paradoxes of worry described by Hirsch and Mathews is that worry itself reduces our capacity for controlling our attention. Attention towards threat and negative threat interpretations' impact deplete our attentional processes (Hirsch, Hayes, & Mathews, 2009), but this process may be highly relevant to children. In young children attentional control is only just developing, and therefore there may be bi-directional relationships between attentional control and worry. Children who are just developing attentional control or have naturally poor attentional control may therefore struggle to inhibit worry, and in addition worry-prone children may have impaired attentional control due to their worry. Attentional control abilities do appear to be highly associated with worry in children (Gramszlo et al., 2018; Gramszlo & Woodruff-Borden, 2015) and may interact with meta-cognitions in predicting higher levels of worry (Reinholdt-Dunne et al., 2019), but there is less evidence about which directions of effect may be present.

Geronimi and colleagues (2016) explored the links between worry and EF in 7–12 year olds using parent report of their children's EF. Higher levels of worry were associated with increased difficulties in EF across all the different facets of EF measured. However, age acted as a moderator for some of these. For working memory, planning, and moderating there were stronger relationships between EF and worry for younger children, suggesting that as children get older, the impact of their EF on their ability and tendency to worry decreases. This fits with cognitive models of worry, where worries become over-rehearsed with time and therefore do not require as much cognitive capacity as they do when they are not familiar cognitive processes (Hirsch & Mathews, 2012).

One of the ways in which EF might impact worry is by changing how children use past information to predict the future. In a series of experiments with children aged four to ten years of age Lagattuta and colleagues have shown that not only does children's ability to predict the future from past events develop over time (see earlier discussion) but also that EF affects that relationship. Children with better EF appear to be able to use the past information, or current ambiguous information, to predict future events and emotions (Lagattuta, Sayfan, & Harvey, 2014; Lagattuta, Tashjian, & Kramer, 2018). We would therefore expect complex relationships between EF, age, and worry. In young children the ability to predict the future from past events might increase worry, particularly for those who have had difficult early lives. However, for older children EF might protect against problematic worry by allowing children more access to possible alternative futures that are not negative or catastrophic. However, the picture is likely to be even more complicated than this. As well as age, temperamental factors impact the relationship between worry and executive functions. Gramszlo and Woodruff-Borden (2015) found that children aged 7–10 who were difficult to soothe had higher levels of self-reported worry. However, this relationship was fully mediated by parent-reported attentional and emotional control aspects of EF.

Further exploration of different aspects of EF, especially attentional control, in relation to worry is warranted to further delineate the impact age and other aspects of cognitive development have on the relationships between these two. In order to determine whether certain kinds of children are especially as risk for developing worry, and whether our adult cognitive model of worry maintenance is appropriate for younger population, we need to determine whether attentional control leads to increased worry or whether increased worry decreases attentional control abilities or both.

CATASTROPHISATION

One of the key processes in pathological worry is catastrophisation (Davey, 1994a; Wilson, 2010). This is the process whereby the iterative nature of worry leads to increasingly negative potential outcomes as people ask themselves, 'What if?' (Davey, 2006; Vasey & Borkovec, 1992). Catastrophisation is one of the processes that might distinguish problematic and non-problematic worry (see Chapter 4), and several studies with adult participants have found that people with high trait worry are able to produce more steps in a catastrophising interview (Davey, 2006). The catastrophising interview involves identifying a possible worry, either by asking the participant to identify one or by giving the participant a common situation that causes worry for many people, and then asking the participant what would be so bad about the situation or example given. This answer is written down and the participant is then asked what would be so bad about that?

> The participants were given the situation of starting a new school. So each of them were asked "what would be bad about starting a new school?". Mary's first answer was "I wouldn't know anyone." The researcher then asked "what would be bad about not knowing anyone?" Mary replied "I might be lonely." The researcher asked "what would be bad about being lonely?" Mary thought "I wouldn't have any friends" she answered. The researcher asked "what would be bad about not having any friends?" "It would mean I wouldn't want to go to school" Mary said quickly. What would be so bad about not wanting to go to school was that she wouldn't go to school, this would lead to not getting good grades, getting a bad job and being poor, sad, and lonely as an adult.

In contrast Luke replied to the first question "I wouldn't know where to sit?". When the researcher asked "what would be bad about not knowing where to sit Luke replied "nothing really, I'd just ask the teacher and then I'd know."

To date several studies have used a catastrophising interview with children and adolescents. In one of the earliest studies using a catastrophising interview with children, Vasey and colleagues (Vasey, Crnic, & Carter, 1994) interviewed 76 children between five and 12 years old. In the youngest age range (five to six years) children struggled to produce a number of steps in the catastrophising interview, but by age eight to nine, they could produce about four steps. Vasey and colleagues suggest that verbal ability might impact on the ability to produce worry steps, as when they controlled for the number of words in the answer there was no longer an effect of age on the worry steps. Osleger (2012) tested this directly in 9–11 year olds. She found that both verbal ability, as measured by the similarities subtest on the Weschler Abbreviated Scale of Intelligence (WASI), and verbal fluency predicted the number of worry steps in the catastrophising interview. We replicated this finding in 7–10 and 6–11 year olds (Wilson, Bourne, & Cuddy, in prep.) except using the vocabulary subtest of the WASI. Across these studies, we also replicated Vasey's results about number of worry steps produced. The younger children produced three to four worry steps on average, but the older children produced seven to eight. This relationship with verbal ability suggests that the catastrophising interview may not necessarily tap into worry processes and may instead be a test of verbal ability. This is also supported by the findings that in two of these three studies, and also in Turner and Wilson (2010) there were no associations between worry steps produced and measures of worry and anxiety. Furthermore, Osleger found evidence that the interview may not be particularly reliable in this population; there was a very low correlation between number of steps on two consecutive catastrophising interviews.

What might be more relevant to our understanding of worry is analysis of the content of the worries produced and interviews with participants after the interview. Vasey, Crnic, and Carter (1994) found that the worries reported by children across the wide range of ages showed a predictable developmental progression with worries about physical harm decreasing in older groups and social concerns increasing across this time-frame. Other studies have tested a much narrower age range of children and therefore cannot show this same pattern; however, different studies have explored different aspects of the worry steps. Turner and Wilson (2010) explored why participants stopped and didn't stop producing worry steps in the catastrophising interview. There appeared to be three patterns in the catastrophising interview: (1) children came to a catastrophic conclusion very quickly, (2) children ended up with a repeating circle of negative outcomes that weren't so catastrophic, or (3) children ended up after several elaborations slowly getting more and more catastrophic. Typically, it is this third group that appear to be worriers as they can produce lots of iterations. However, we may also be clinically concerned about the first group. Indeed this group also reported high levels of worry. Osleger also qualitatively examined content. Using inductive thematic analysis, she coded the pattern of responses across the interview. The worries were coded into standard worries, long term worries (about long term future), circular responses and extreme responses. Exploring the characteristics of high and low worriers, she found that long term worries were more likely in a low worry group, and circular (perseverative) and extreme (catastrophic) responses were found in the high worry group.

Number of steps in a catastrophising process may be more representative of verbal ability in children, in contrast to the studies on adults, where it does appear to be reliably associated with trait worry. However, there may well be particular processes in catastrophising that are associated with trait worry, such as perseverative patterns and extreme end points. These extreme or catastrophic end points might occur relatively quickly, bring a worry bout to an end quickly, but with a high level of emotion, or might occur slowly, encouraging perseveration.

To date no studies have examined catastrophising patterns in children with anxiety disorders. It would be very interesting to see whether the patterns are indeed different to children with normal levels of anxiety and worry. It would also be very interesting to examine whether certain patterns of catastrophising are risk factors for later anxiety or mood difficulties and in particular whether certain patterns are risks for certain anxiety disorders.

CONCLUSIONS

What is clear from reviewing the developmental literature across a number of domains is that whilst some aspects of development do change dramatically at certain time points in a child's life, most complex aspects change somewhat throughout childhood, with children gaining ability to pass developmental tasks more easily, to justify their responses verbally, and to understand and work with complexity as they age. Some of these abilities are largely intact in their adult form by early adolescence, whilst others are developing into adulthood, and possibly beyond.

Worry can be seen as one of these complex phenomena and so it is perhaps unsurprising that the trajectory of the development of worry, considering factors such as the number of iterations in a worry chain, the types of things children worry about, the ability to represent worry in words and understand it as different from fear, develops similarly across childhood into adulthood. The parallels are clear. From this perhaps we should conclude that worry is a normal and somewhat inevitable aspect of human cognition. That once we are able to iterate thought, and once we are able to look into the future and think about what it might bring, it is then inevitable that we engage from time to time in worry processes. Can then developmental psychology add to our understanding of worry and its development across childhood into adulthood? At present the literature does not allow this question to be fully answered, but a number of hypotheses might be developed. Perhaps understanding how developmental psychology can inform the study of children's worry will allow us to look for anomalies of development that might lead to certain children being at risk for developing problematic worry. It might also lead to a greater understanding of different presentations of worry.

At present our definition of worry is adapted from adult definitions. Exploring development, especially when certain aspects of it are delayed or enhanced, may help us develop a definition of worry that encompasses different presentations of worry, such as what worry looks like if someone is non-verbal, and what it looks like when following a train of thought (iterative thought) is hard.

Finally, understanding that the presentation and experience of worry is likely affected by our developmental stage may lead to different and new interventions for those whose worry interferes with their daily life. This may be especially true for children but may also be true for other populations whose development is atypical, such as those with specific learning disabilities or more global intellectual disabilities, neuro-developmental conditions, or those with acquired brain injury or cognitive degenerative conditions.

CHAPTER THREE

Children's worry and the family

Unlike several features and consequences of anxiety, you cannot see worry. When a child is anxious you might get behaviours such as reassurance seeking, avoidance or withdrawal from situations and safety behaviours such as holding on to a particularly loved object or clinging to a parent. If the anxiety is intense enough it is possible to see somatic aspects of the anxiety such as sweating and shaking. The sequelae such as poor sleep and changes in appetite might also be noticeable. The problem with recognising that your child is worrying is that none of these behavioural indicators are necessary for worry to be present. The most obvious sign that a child is worrying might be a sense that they aren't paying attention or do not respond quickly to a request or to their name. These can easily be misinterpreted as the child ignoring you or misbehaving. This private nature of worry makes the systemic aspects of worry particularly important to understand (Lagattuta, Sayfan, & Bamford, 2012). If a parent cannot see worry within the child how can they respond to their child compassionately and effectively to resolve or contain the worry? This chapter focuses on what we know about worry in the context of the family. There is very little research that focuses solely on worry, and therefore studies of anxious children are important to produce further hypotheses about worry in the context of the family.

CONCORDANCE BETWEEN CHILD AND PARENT ANXIETY AND WORRY

We know from studying anxiety disorders that they run in families (Vasey, Crnic, & Carter, 1994). We can see this in genetic studies where heritability of anxiety disorders is quite high (Eley et al., 2015), but not as high as other disorders (Gregory & Eley, 2007). We can see this when we look at studies of parents with anxiety disorders and the risk their children have of developing the same (Beidel & Turner, 1997), and vice versa, looking at studies of children with anxiety disorders and determining from these how many parents have anxiety disorders (Clefberg, Liberman, & Öst, 2016; Last, Phillips, & Statfeld, 1987).

However, we also know that there is not always homotypic continuity. Children are somewhat likely to have the same disorder as their parents (Ferdinand et al., 2007); however, anxiety disorders also seem to be related to emotional symptoms more generally, suggesting there is some heterotypic continuity (Bittner et al., 2007). Therefore it has been suggested there might be a general factor that leads to concordance between childhood and parental anxiety disorders. It could be something temperamental, or biological/genetic, like behavioural inhibition (Lahat, Hong, & Fox, 2011), but it could also be something symptomatic like worry (Weems, 2008).

There is a significant body of research that has explored the concordance between parental anxiety and child anxiety as measured by continuous measures. Correlations between self-report measures of child and parent anxiety are usually small to moderate. The association between parent and child anxiety may vary depending on the measures used for the parent and child; very few measures of anxiety have parallel versions for children and adults, which means many studies have to use different measures of anxiety, and these may measure different types or aspects of anxiety. For example, the Beck Anxiety Inventory for adults (BAI; Beck, Brown, & Steer, 1988) is one of the most widely used anxiety scales in clinical practice and yet is not suitable for individuals with co-morbid physical health conditions because of its focus on the somatic symptoms of anxiety. Scales for children's anxiety, such as the Spence Anxiety Scale (Spence, 1998), have great face validity, but have poorer ability to distinguish between different types of anxiety/anxiety disorders, compared to newer measures such as the Screen for Child Anxiety and Related Emotional Disorders (SCARED) or the Multi-dimensional Anxiety Scale for Children (Muris, Merckelbach, Ollendick et al., 2002). One exception to the lack of similar measures for adults and children is the Revised Children's Manifest Anxiety Scale (RCMAS; Reynolds, 1980). This measure of anxiety was developed for different populations concurrently, with a child version, a student version, and an adult (AMAS) and older adult version. To our knowledge only unpublished studies have looked at the associations between parent and child anxiety using the RCMAS and AMAS. In our own study of parents and their 6–12-year-old children the correlation between father and child anxiety was higher than the correlation between mother and child anxiety and both were small or very small associations ($r = 0.24$ for fathers vs $r = -0.03$ for mothers; Errity, 2013). This points to another factor that might significantly impact the concordance between parent and child anxiety, namely the gender of the parent. Many studies of parenting focus solely on mothers, or recruit both mothers and fathers, but end up with a sample that is mainly mothers. Despite a clinical and theoretical interest in the role of fathers in childhood anxiety (Bögels & Phares, 2008), relatively few studies have distinguished between mothers' and fathers' anxiety, and our study, amongst others, suggests that it might be important. In addition, in exploring the concordance between parent and child anxiety there is little focus on the wider context such as sociodemographic factors such as age, culture, SES, and family composition when exploring these relationships.

There is therefore a broad, but limited, literature that explores the concordance between child and parent anxiety. However, fewer studies have explored associations between parent and child worry. In this literature there are fewer issues concerning measures because there are so few widely used measures. Every study we found tested the association between parent and child worry using the Penn State Worry Questionnaire (PSWQ; Meyer et al., 1990). As reviewed in Chapter 1, the PSWQ focuses on features of worry, rather than the content of worry. However, it would perhaps be foolish, given what we know about the developmental progression of worry, to expect the content of worries to be the same in children and their parents and therefore measures of worry that focus on content do not allow us to measure concordance between parent and child worry.

When we look at the concordance between parent and child worry using the PSWQ and PSWQ-C we find similar results to those found in studies of the concordance between parent and child anxiety. Often the correlations are relatively small. For example, Wilson et al. (2011) found that there was a small to moderate correlation between parent and child worry ($r = 0.27$) with participants who were largely mothers (86%) and largely white-British (95%). In a sample of Australian parents, most of whom were mothers (90%), a slightly higher correlation was found between parent and child worry ($r = 0.3$). In one of the only studies to explore differences in parental worry between two groups of children – anxious and not-anxious – Donovan, Holmes, and Farrell (2016) found that there were no differences in maternal worry between the two groups.

It may be that worry and anxiety have different explanatory roles in our understanding of concordance between parent and child anxiety. Fisak and colleagues (Fisak et al., 2012) found that parent worry *about their child* predicted child anxiety better than the parent's own anxiety level, and indeed parent worry mediated the relationship that was present between parent anxiety and child anxiety. Furthermore, Triantafyllou and colleagues (Triantafyllou et al., 2012) found that mothers of young people with internalising difficulties (anxiety and depression) catastrophised more than mothers of young people with externalising difficulties or no psychological difficulties. The mothers' anxiety was not statistically significantly higher, nor was it related to their catastrophising, suggesting that there may be a unique relationship between parental worry and child anxiety.

What is clear, therefore, is that although anxiety and worry do run in families to a certain extent, parental anxiety/worry does not explain much of the variance in child anxiety/worry; therefore, we need to look to other factors in the environment (individual factors will be considered in Chapter 4).

PARENTING BEHAVIOURS AND WORRY

A number of models have been developed to explain how parenting might be associated with childhood anxiety. In these models anxiety-specific parenting behaviours have been proposed. These include over-protection, lack of autonomy granting, over-involvement, and rejection. McLeod, Wood, and Weisz (2007) conducted an early meta-analytic review exploring the links between these parenting factors and childhood anxiety. Even in 2007 they found 47 studies reported in 41 papers that explicitly measured child anxiety and parenting. There were a number of conclusions drawn from their analysis. They found that effect sizes were larger for studies where the children had been diagnosed with anxiety disorders, compared to general population studies. They also found stronger results for observational data and for studies with an independent report of parenting. They concluded that although the evidence was mixed and there were different factors that impacted on the relationship between parenting and child anxiety, there was strong evidence for a small to moderate association between child anxiety and controlling parenting, and weaker evidence for an association between child anxiety and parental rejection.

More recently Yap and colleagues have conducted a couple of systematic reviews, examining parenting associations with both childhood anxiety and depression (Figure 3.1), focusing on studies where the children were under 12 years of age. This approach allows us to explore whether there are specific parenting factors associated with childhood anxiety, rather than with emotional disorders more generally. Yap and Jorm (2015) systematically reviewed the literature on associations between parenting and childhood anxiety (ages 5–11 years) and classified the evidence as sound, emerging, or equivocal. In contrast to the evidence for childhood depression (Yap et al., 2014), they found that the evidence for parenting factors in children's anxiety was emerging at best, despite a similar number of studies for anxiety and depression being included in the review. The emerging factors were similar to those found by McLeod et al. and included over-involvement, autonomy granting, and modelling of anxiety, as well as aversiveness and inter-parental conflict. However, these parenting factors may not be specific to anxiety. Several of these factors were also found to be associated with depression in children such as aversiveness, inter-parental conflict, and over-involvement (Yap et al., 2014). Indeed, although for depression in children there was

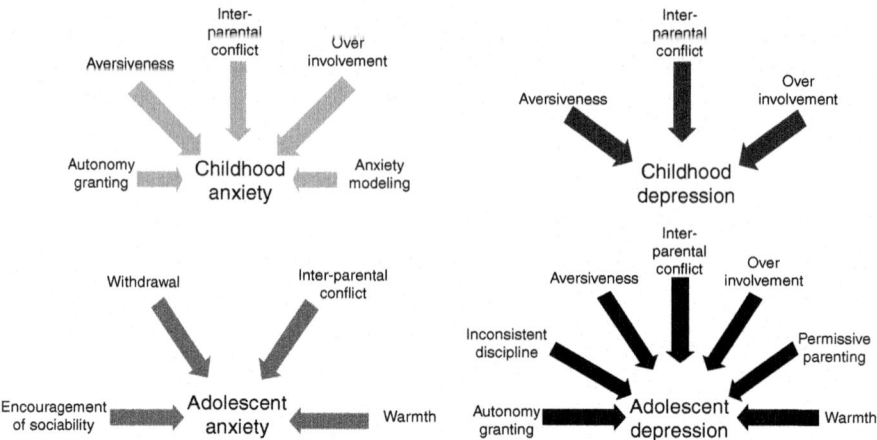

Figure 3.1 Parenting factors that predict child and adolescent anxiety and depression, from Yap et al. (2014) and Yap and Jorm (2015).

a lack of evidence for associations with poor autonomy granting and anxiety modelling, this was mainly due to the lack of studies, rather than null findings. Just as McLeod et al. noted, there was still a paucity of longitudinal studies looking at these associations between parenting and child anxiety and depression, but this also seems to be worse in the anxiety literature. Compared to approximately 20% of the studies in depression, only 12% of the studies focusing on childhood anxiety were longitudinal.

Yap et al. (2014) also reviewed the literature on *adolescent* anxiety and depression and their associations with parenting (Figure 3.1). What is striking about this review is the low number of studies that have explored adolescent anxiety in relation to parenting. Compared to 140 articles that tested the associations between parenting and adolescent depression, only 17 tested the association between parenting and adolescent anxiety, with an additional 27 testing the association between parenting and both anxiety and depression. Results also suggested that there is something different happening in parent-child relationships when children are reaching adolescence. Some of the well-established findings in younger children, such as the associations between over-involvement and autonomy granting and anxiety, were not found or were found to have a small effect. Warmth and inter-parental conflict were also only found to be minimally associated with adolescent anxiety. One important parenting factor that appears to emerge in adolescence is encouragement of sociability, which appears to be associated with lower levels of adolescent anxiety.

It is likely that these studies represent a predominantly Western relationship between parenting and childhood anxiety. Considering other cultures may change these conclusions. Varela has explored anxiety and worry in Latino populations, largely in the United States. Although he concludes that many aspects of anxiety in children are similar for white-American children and Latino children, there are some notable differences. For example, it appears that controlling behaviours may not be as influential in the development of anxiety in Latino youth (Luis, Varela, & Moore, 2008; Varela et al., 2009). This has also been found in other cultures, notably Eastern cultures (Mousavi, Low, & Hashim, 2016), and indeed in a comprehensive review of parenting in the context of internalising disorders more generally, Pinquart and colleagues found that harsh control was less predictive of internalising disorders when the study had a higher proportion of ethnic minority groups in its sample (Pinquart, 2017).

All of these reviews focus on child anxiety in general, with few focusing in on specific types of anxiety. Indeed, McLeod et al. report that although they wished to distinguish types of anxiety in their meta-analysis, they were unable to as most studies used generic anxiety measures. To date, only four studies have specifically looked at parenting factors associated with children's worry. All the studies have used models of child anxiety to develop their hypotheses and therefore this has influenced their choice of measures. Muris et al. (2000) examined children's perceptions of how they were parented using the EMBU (Swedish for 'My Memories of Upbringing'; Castro et al., 1993) and found that children who reported that their parents were more rejecting and anxious reported higher levels of worry. In contrast, in a follow up study of adolescents, participants reporting higher levels of over-protection and anxiety in how they were parented scored more highly on a measure of worry (Muris, 2002).

Brown and Whiteside (2008) extended these studies to explore the same relationships in children with anxiety disorders (aged 7–18 years) and again found that child reports of parental rejection were significantly associated with child worry. There were also small correlations between worry and anxious rearing ($r = 0.23$) and over-protection ($r = 0.21$), but these did not reach significance due to the small sample size. One study that did not find such associations is Wilson et al. (2011) who found no associations between adolescent reported worry and adolescent or parent reported parenting in a non-referred sample ($-0.05 < r < 0.08$). With such a small number of studies it is as yet unclear whether these differing results reflect developmental differences, differences between clinical and community participants, or whether they are due to another, as yet unknown, factor.

Other studies have focused on parenting in the context of GAD symptoms in children (see Chapter 5 for a review of GAD as a diagnosis in childhood). Hale, Engels, and Meeus (2006) explored GAD symptoms and perceived parenting in adolescents and found small to medium associations between GAD symptoms and rejection ($r = 0.27$) and alienation ($r = 0.31$) and small associations between GAD symptoms and parental psychological control, over-involvement and trust ($r < 0.18$). Hale et al. (2006) suggested that these two factors of rejection and alienation might also have different developmental impacts, with parental alienation particularly impacting on older adolescent girls and parental rejection particularly impacting on younger adolescent boys. However, it may be important to consider directions of effect. Hale et al. (2013) specifically question whether worry and GAD symptoms in children might prompt parents to behave in certain ways, rather than the parental behaviour increasing or causing worry. Other studies have explored parental behaviour and child anxiety over time and have found evidence for both directions of effect (Allmann, 2018; Wijsbroek et al., 2011; Williams et al., 2012). There appear to be interactive effects whereby overcontrolling parental behaviour can exacerbate anxiety in children, whose behaviour then exacerbates controlling behaviour in the parents. In one of the only studies to explore parenting in the context of

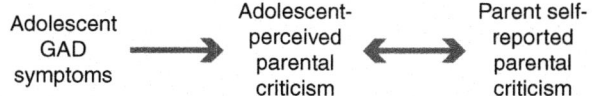

Figure 3.2 Longitudinal relationships between GAD symptoms and parenting from Nelemans et al. (2014).

childhood GAD longitudinally, Nelemans et al. (2014) found that over a six-year period, there was substantial evidence that GAD symptoms in adolescents increased their perceptions of being criticised by their parents, and higher levels of perceived parental criticism predicted higher levels of parental self-reported criticism. Furthermore, maternal-reported criticism increased adolescent perceived criticism over time, but not GAD symptoms (Figure 3.2). Thus, it appears that GAD symptoms in adolescence may be driving changes in parental behaviour, rather than the other way around.

One hypothesis is that the parenting behaviours of mothers and fathers may have differential effects and therefore separating out the effects of each may be important. For example, Grüner, Muris, and Merckelbach (1999) found associations between GAD symptoms, and child reported parental control, anxious rearing, and rejection, although different factors were somewhat important for mothers and fathers. Although parental rejection was the greatest predictor of child GAD symptoms for both mothers and fathers, paternal anxious rearing was more important than paternal control in predicting child GAD symptoms, whereas maternal control was more important than maternal anxious parenting in this prediction (Figure 3.3).

This gendered finding may be even more pronounced in other developmental periods. In a study of infants, Möller, Majdandžić, and Bögels (2015) found that neither mothers' nor fathers' self-reported challenging behaviour was associated with infant anxious temperament (10–15 month olds), but that maternal over-protection was highly associated ($r = 0.55$), and paternal over-protection was not ($r = 0.06$).

Furthermore, there may be cultural differences in the specific role of fathers. A number of studies have found that paternal warmth in Chinese

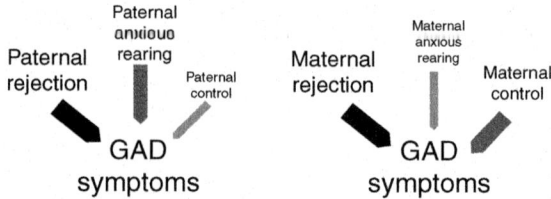

Figure 3.3 *Relative relationships* between paternal and maternal factors in predicting GAD symptoms in children from Grüner, Muris, and Merckelbach (1999).*

* The size of the font is only for illustration purposes; the darker thicker lines represent greater contributors than thinner lighter lines. However, the areas of the arrows are not directly related to the size of the effect.

families is particularly protective for young people at risk of developing anxiety disorders (Quach et al., 2015; Xu et al., 2017). There is little cross-cultural work exploring the different mechanisms by which mothers and fathers might influence children's anxiety, but it is clear that considering both parents is crucial.

A different approach to exploring transmission of anxiety from parent to child is to consider parents who themselves have anxiety disorders. The literature exploring the impact on parenting of having an anxiety disorder is very mixed. Some early studies found that anxious parents were more controlling, more critical, and less autonomy promoting (Hirshfeld et al., 1997; Whaley, Pinto, & Sigman, 1999). However, others found no differences between anxious parents and non-anxious parents (Ginsburg, Grover, & Ialongo, 2005; Turner et al., 2003). A number of factors may explain the differences including whether the behaviour is observed or self-reported (Drake & Ginsburg, 2011), the type of task used in an observation (Ginsburg et al., 2006), the age of the children (Kaitz et al., 2010), and whether or not the child has an anxiety disorder themselves (Creswell et al., 2013). However, there may also be some crucial differences in parents themselves that determine whether anxiety impacts parenting behaviour. A number of researchers have suggested that maternal and paternal anxiety have different roles to play (Bögels & Phares, 2008; Liber et al., 2008; Möller, Majdandžić, & Bögels, 2015), mirroring the research suggesting paternal and maternal behaviour have a different impact on GAD symptoms in children and adolescents. Perhaps most importantly studies have suggested that the nature of the anxiety disorder itself is important. Several studies have focused on mothers with a single anxiety disorder, such as panic disorder (Schneider et al., 2009), or social anxiety disorder (Crosby Budinger, Drazdowski, & Ginsburg, 2013), but these studies either look at parenting in general or observe parenting behaviour in a task that might be particularly difficult for the parent in the context of the kind of anxiety they experience; for example, observing socially anxious mothers in a socially demanding situation with their child. Lynne Murray and colleagues have tried to look more specifically at this issue. Following their work exploring the impact maternal social anxiety has on infants (Murray et al., 2007, 2008), they further determined that training non-anxious mothers to behave in a socially anxious way had a similar effect on the infants in that it led to them being more avoidant and more fearful (de Rosnay et al., 2006). This was particularly marked in infants who already showed risk factors for anxiety, particularly behavioural inhibition. In these studies it appeared that mothers were modelling an anxious response in a social situation that was then repeated by the infant. The challenge therefore was to develop a task where parents with GAD might model anxious behaviours. Murray and colleagues chose a task where there was uncertainty involved. Instead of interacting with a stranger or performing a task in public – typical tasks that prompt social anxiety – dealing with uncertainty was considered something that people with GAD find particularly difficult (see Chapter 4 for discussion of intolerance of uncertainty). Murray and colleagues (2012) compared mothers with social anxiety disorder to mothers with GAD interacting with their children in three tasks: the child preparing and giving a speech, the child interacting with a potentially scary object, and a neutral task of playing together with play dough. On many of the parenting variables that were coded the anxious parents were different from their non-anxious counterparts; they were more passive and less encouraging than non-anxious mothers. However, there were few behaviours that distinguished the two anxious groups. Displaying anxiety in the situation was more prevalent in the socially anxious mothers compared to the mothers with GAD. What was notable was that for nearly all maternal behaviours coded there were group by task interactions whereby the socially anxious mothers showed more anxious behaviours in the speech task and the mothers with GAD showed more anxious behaviours in the interactions with the potentially scary object.

It appears that exploring specific anxiety disorders in parents and the impact they have on parenting may help us understand better how anxiety disorders are transmitted. However, there is less focus on the impact on the child. Murray and colleagues show that modelling social anxiety can increase socially anxious responses in infants, but it isn't clear how anxious responding to uncertain events leads children to worry more. Stein and colleagues propose that it might be through worry acting as a prime. In their comparison of mothers with GAD, mothers with depression, and mothers with no emotional disorders, they found that a worry prime caused mothers with both GAD and depression to talk a lot less, despite their infants vocalising more, compared to a neutral priming situation (Stein et al., 2012). This is an interesting mechanism to consider. If parents change their behaviour based on what is happening internally, which is what was happening with the worry prime, then the behaviour is going to appear more variable to their children, and therefore perhaps, children will find their parents more uncertain and predictable. It may be that it is in this context that parents who have a history of worrying can pass on a need to resolve uncertain situations by inadvertently creating them for their children. However plausible this mechanism is, there is not enough research to be able to determine its validity.

Overall the conclusions that can be drawn about the role of parenting in childhood worry and generalised anxiety disorder are, at best, very tentative. The associations that have been found are similar to those found in the child anxiety literature, perhaps unsurprisingly because worry is an important aspect of childhood anxiety. However, most of the studies specifically looking at worry have been guided by a theoretical model, either a model of childhood anxiety with a focus on rejection, over-protection/over-involvement, and control, or a more general model such as expressed emotion (criticism). Without more open-ended studies of parenting in the context of worry we may be missing important parenting components that may play a role in the development and maintenance of children's worry. Furthermore, without longitudinal and experimental studies we cannot simply focus on the role of parents in the development of children's worry, but we have to consider the role worry plays in the development and maintenance of particular parenting behaviours. It is likely that many effects are bi-directional, with children impacting on parents and vice versa. Finally, it is important that future studies consider gender, both of the children and the parents, and that they also consider cultural variation in mothering and fathering. There are some indications in the sparse literature that already exists that gender may be important in understanding specific relationships between child worry and parenting behaviour.

ATTACHMENT AND WORRY

Another prominent systemic factor in the literature is attachment. Attachment is proposed to be a primary biological drive that an infant has towards a primary caregiver. A number of 'attachment behaviours' lead to the infant maintaining proximity to the caregiver (Bowlby, 1969). It has long been accepted that insecurely attached children, or those who have a particular pattern of distress and resistance to soothing by the caregiver, have a higher risk of anxiety disorders, especially those who display an anxious-ambivalent type attachment, and this has been supported by cross-sectional, longitudinal, and intervention studies (Colonnesi et al., 2011). However, there may be specific links between insecure attachment and worry in children. For example, it has been proposed that that the kinds of environments that insecure children grow up in may specifically lead to worry (Cassidy, 1995). If your early environment is inconsistent with uncertain threat, not only is your attention drawn to actual threat, but you are encouraged to scan the environment for possible threat in order to be prepared. This early scanning of the environment for possible future threat may be the earliest precursor of worry (see Chapter 6). Poor attachment has been found to be greater in adults with severe GAD (Cassidy et al., 2009) and in students with GAD (Eng & Heimberg, 2006). Furthermore attachment type has been found to differentially predict response to treatment for adults with GAD (Newman et al., 2015). However, there are several problems with asking adults about how they were parented. Retrospective reports are notoriously inaccurate. Indeed, in the field of attachment it has been found that early measured attachment status may not be reliably associated with later attachment status (Waters, Hamilton, & Weinfield, 2000), with environmental factors impacting on individual's perceptions of their past attachment status (Roisman et al., 2002). It may therefore be important to study attachment and worry in children specifically. Only a couple of studies have specifically explored the attachment status of worried children. Both Muris et al. (2000) and Brown and Whiteside (2008) used child self-report of attachment and found that children who rated themselves as insecurely attached reported higher levels of worry. However, these studies are limited by the self-reported nature of the attachment status. Cross-sectional designs, using a single informant and using questionnaires, all lead to greater associations between attachment and anxiety, compared to longitudinal, multiple informant, experimental designed studies (Colonnesi et al., 2011). Therefore, despite theoretical links between insecure attachment and worry, there is a dearth of research exploring this.

Where attachment theory may play an important role in our understanding of children's worry may be in its relation to other variables. Several studies have found that attachment and parenting variables contribute independently to anxiety in children (Brown & Whiteside, 2008; Mothander & Wang, 2014; Muris, Meesters et al., 2000; Roelofs et al., 2006), or predict anxiety via mediational models (Breinholst, Esbjørn, & Reinholdt-Dunne, 2015; Breinholst, Tolstrup, & Esbjørn, 2019). Other authors have proposed that attachment might be associated with anxiety via its effect on children's emotional regulation (Bosquet & Egeland, 2006; Esbjørn et al., 2012). The majority of the work has been on anxiety disorders in general, but one study has focused on GAD specifically. Marganska, Gallagher, and Miranda (2013) tested a number of emotional regulation variables as mediators in the relationship between insecure attachment and GAD symptoms in adults. They found that poor emotional regulation strategies, poor impulse control, and non-acceptance of negative emotions all mediated the relationship between insecure attachment and GAD symptom severity. These factors are reviewed later in Chapter 4, but it suggests that attachment might not have a very strong independent impact on GAD and worry in children but might have an impact on certain psychological processes that themselves impact worry.

What we find therefore is that there are few candidates for specific parenting behaviours that lead to increased anxiety but that there are consistent, albeit small, associations between a number of parenting factors that appear to confer greater risk of developing emotional disorders. It is probably worth noting however that many of these factors have also been found to confer additional risk of children developing externalising disorders, including behavioural difficulties, aggression, and conduct disorder (Buschgens et al., 2010; Forslund et al., 2016; Jager et al., 2016; Okado & Bierman, 2015; Vahedi et al., 2018; Xing & Wang, 2017). If we want to find specific pathways whereby parents influence their child's anxiety, we may need to look to other parenting factors.

WORRY PROCESSES IN PARENTS AND CHILDREN

In order to explore possible causal processes between parent and child worry, research has begun to examine whether it is not only the child's level of worry that is associated with the parent's level of worry but also whether particular processes involved in worry are similar across parents and children. Research has explored whether cognitive biases in anxiety are similar in parents and children (for example see Creswell & O'Connor, 2006; Lester, Field, & Cartwright-Hatton, 2012; Lester et al., 2009). However, when studying worry it may be more beneficial to focus on those cognitive processes involved in worry, such as meta-cognition and intolerance of uncertainty.

META-COGNITIONS IN PARENTS AND CHILDREN

In thinking about concordance between parent and child as related to phenomena such as anxiety and worry there are two main issues: what are the processes that lead to this concordance and does one influence the other, especially in a negative direction, for example does parental worry make child worry worse? As we have seen earlier, the concordance between parent and child worry and anxiety is only modest, although robust; however, factors that have been widely examined, such as parenting behaviours, offer only a partial explanation for possible processes linking parent and child worry. Within cognitive behavioural models of psychological difficulties both behaviour and cognitions are important. Therefore it makes sense to explore the cognitions that have been implicated in worry processes to see if these may help us understand the processes involved in concordance.

Chapter 4 outlines many of the different cognitive processes involved in worry becoming problematic, but the two that have garnered most support are meta-cognitive beliefs and intolerance of uncertainty. A small number of studies have explored associations between worry meta-cognitions in parents and children. In the first study to do this, Jacobi and colleagues (Jacobi, Calamari, & Woodard, 2006) explored these relationships in older adolescents in the context of obsessive-compulsive symptoms. The correlations between parent and child beliefs were small to medium, ranging from $r = 0.06$ for correlations between parent and child cognitive self-consciousness to $r = 0.19$ for the importance of thoughts and need to control thoughts. Wilson et al. (2011) found similar results in a slightly younger sample of 11–16-year-olds. The correlations ranged from $r = 0.03$ for uncontrollability and danger beliefs to $r = 0.13$ for superstition punishment and responsibility beliefs, but there was a larger correlation for positive beliefs: $r = 0.27$. In two studies of even younger children, aged 7–12 years, Esbjørn and colleagues (Esbjørn et al., 2016; Lønfeldt et al., 2017) found similar correlations between parent and child positive beliefs about worry ($r = 0.27$ and 0.29, respectively). However, unlike the very small correlations found for other kinds of beliefs in the studies of adolescents, there were also medium correlations found for other dimensions of beliefs about worry. Across the two studies correlations ranged from $r = 0.14$ to $r = 0.30$. There appeared to be better concordance between parent and child cognitive self-consciousness and cognitive confidence in these younger dyads compared to the parent-adolescent dyads. The authors suggest that this may be an important age to explore concordance between parent and child meta-cognitions as parents might still be a significant influence on their children's thinking. However, it is notable that there are so very few studies exploring this, and further research may highlight further developmental, cultural, or socio-economic factors that impact on these relationships.

INTOLERANCE OF UNCERTAINTY IN PARENTS AND CHILDREN

If there are few studies examining meta-cognitive processes across parents and children, there are even fewer studies exploring concordance between parental intolerance of uncertainty and child intolerance of uncertainty (IU). Jacobi, Calamari, and Woodard (2006) did have a partial test of this in their study of adolescents' OCD symptoms. The correlation between parental and adolescent perfectionist and intolerance of uncertainty beliefs was only $r = 0.13$, and the measure used was not a pure measure of IU. More recently, Sanchez, Kendall, and Comer (2016) used the Intolerance of Uncertainty Scale (IUS; Buhr & Dugas, 2002) to explore whether maternal and child intolerance of uncertainty mediated the relationship between maternal and child anxiety in children aged 7–13 years. There was a moderate correlation ($r = 0.42$) between maternal and child intolerance of uncertainty, but IU only partially mediated the association between child and mother anxiety. One major difficulty with this study is that mothers reported on their own and their child's intolerance of uncertainty. Although mothers are quite good at reporting behaviours that result from IU, it is likely that they have not got a true understanding of their children's experience of IU. Clearly, many more studies are required before we understand the role of intolerance of uncertainty in the concordance between parent and child worry.

PARENTS' INVOLVEMENT IN THE TREATMENT OF WORRIED CHILDREN

One of the main reasons for exploring associations within these worry processes is to try and understand what role parents might have in the development and maintenance of problematic worry and what role children might have in eliciting certain responses from their parents. Understanding these processes are crucial to designing appropriate and effective interventions for children who struggle with their worry and anxiety. Clinically, observations support the research findings, namely that there are specific characteristics of parents of anxious children; they appear to be more controlling of their children's behaviour, they appear to grant their anxious children less autonomy, and in some clinical examples they appear to sabotage their child's therapy.

> John was doing very well in therapy. He had identified his main fears and worries and had developed a hierarchy of things he wanted to achieve. He was working through this well and had realized that most of the things he was worried about were not going to come true. He was coming to the last of his goals; being able to go to the shops by himself. This was developmentally appropriate, and the therapist had checked that it wasn't likely to be dangerous where John lived. This goal needed John's mother to be on board. John himself explained to his mother that this was his last goal and he really felt he could do it. The therapist explained to his mother that she also thought he could do it, but if there were any factors that might get in the way it was absolutely fine if he didn't manage this last goal this week, he could continue the work they had already been doing and they would simply review the following week and try again. John's mother looked relieved and turned to John explaining to him that it meant that if John went down to the shops and the bigger lads were there and if they threatened him or tried to take his money or his bike, that he didn't need to go into the shop, he could just return home. Luckily, John had had so much success with doing the things he was worried about that he smiled at his mother and told her not to worry.

Clinically therefore it seems clear that parents can influence the treatment of their child's anxiety disorder. This message was reinforced by one of the earliest trials that directly compared child-only CBT with family CBT (cCBT vs fCBT). Barrett and colleagues, back in 1996 (Barrett et al., 1996), found that after a 12 week treatment the children with separation anxiety, overanxious disorder (see Chapter 5 for a review of overanxious disorder in relation to worry), and/or social anxiety who experienced fCBT did better than the children who experienced cCBT. However, soon after that a similar study found no differences in outcomes for children whether they received cCBT or fCBT (Cobham, Dadds, & Spence, 1998). However, the results turned out to be even more complicated than that. Following up their original participants six years later, Barrett et al. (2001) now found no differences between the two groups, and yet following up their children three years later Cobham et al. (2010) did now find fCBT to be superior! Over the years this equivocality has been grown. Studies of both group and individual CBT with and without parental involvement have shown cCBT and fCBT to have similar outcomes across a wide age range: 7–18 years (Barrett, 1998; Nauta et al., 2001; Siqueland, Rynn, & Diamond, 2005), whereas other studies with a slightly more restricted age range – 6–14 – have found either a significant benefit of fCBT or a trend towards that (Heyne et al., 2002; Mendlowitz et al., 1999; Wood et al., 2006). Only one study of note has found a benefit of cCBT compared to a family based alternative (Bodden et al., 2008). A number of reviews have aimed to explore why research might have given us these mixed results. Breinholst et al. (2012) suggest six factors that may be worth exploring: differences in treatment delivery, differences in parental factors targeted, lack of an explicit model of change, differences in outcome measures, individual differences, and treatment flexibility. In particular, Breinholst and colleagues propose that this mixed evidence about the benefits of involving parents may partly be due to poor alignment between models of parental involvement and of change, and the intervention targeted at the parents. They also suggest that the outcomes that clinical trials focus on – namely how many children become free of their anxiety disorder diagnosis – might not map onto the changes that occur as a result of including parents. If parents are involved it may be that parent-child relationships improve, or that parents themselves become less stressed or anxious. Certainly there is evidence that parents are impacted by interventions whether or not they are involved (Esbjørn et al., 2014). There may also be more general differences, perhaps in satisfaction and engagement with the service.

We may also be looking in the wrong place for differences. If we look within the parent, or even with the family, we risk ignoring some wider cultural differences. As we saw earlier, there may be important cultural differences in which parental behaviours put children at greater risk, or protect children from, the development of anxiety. It also appears that cultural factors may impact on whether parental involvement is helpful for children. Vaclavik and colleagues (2017) randomised Latino children and adolescents in the United States into group CBT or parent-involved CBT. Both interventions showed positive results, with reductions in anxiety symptoms, but parental acculturation impacted which intervention had the largest effect. When the parents scored low on a measure of acculturation the group-based CBT was more effective, whereas when parents had high scores on a measure of acculturation the parent-involved CBT was more effective. In a direct comparison of Latino parents with non-Latino white parents in the United States, Seligman and colleagues (Seligman et al., 2019) found that parent-involved CBT for anxious youth was equally effective for both groups but that there were additional barriers in accessing the therapy for the Latino parents. It is an interesting question as to whether cultural differences in beliefs about anxiety and mental health drive beliefs about seeking support for these difficulties, or whether there is something important in immigrant status that impacts both help seeking and the services that children and parents receive when they do seek help.

More recently meta-analyses and studies combining datasets have aimed to clarify the issue of parental involvement. For example, Silverman, Greca, and Wasserstein (2019) looked at different types of outcomes measured in treatment trials. In the first study they found that there was some specificity in terms of outcomes depending on who was involved in the intervention; when children were the sole receivers of a group intervention as well as a decrease in their anxiety, there was an increase in their social skills – a result not found for family focused CBT. In contrast, when parents were involved in the intervention their parenting was improved, a result not found when only children received the intervention. In the second study they found bi-directional relationships between change in parents and change in children. These factors together perhaps explain results of a meta-analysis completed by Manassis and colleagues (Manassis et al., 2014). These researchers looked at both immediate and longer-term outcomes for anxious children and their families. It appeared from their data that there was no benefit of involving parents/families in immediate outcomes, but that in the longer term there were further improvements in the group of families who received family focused interventions, whereas in the group of families that received child-only interventions the outcomes were simply maintained. Having parents change their parenting and also be influenced by their children's improvements over time might have a positive effect long term on the improved outcomes for anxious children.

What we don't know is which children may particularly need this kind of extra intervention. It is suggested that children of parents with anxiety disorders may benefit more from parental involvement in therapy. A number of researchers have suggested that some parental anxiety disorders might be particularly risky with respect to the child having a negative outcome in therapy (Cooper et al., 2008). In particular, it appears that if a parent has a diagnosis of social anxiety disorder the child is at much higher risk of psychological distress symptoms, of anxiety symptoms, of not responding as well to therapy, and to develop anxiety disorders themselves (Creswell & Cartwright-Hatton, 2007; Hudson et al., 2015a; Ollendick & Benoit, 2012). This is interesting in the context of worry, as social anxiety disorder is not a disorder of worry, but it does involve worry. Furthermore, fear of social evaluation is important in social anxiety disorder, and many adolescent worries are about social evaluation. How much of this is true for children with worry-based disorders such as GAD? When we explore the literature that specifically looks at the role of parents in the treatment of worry or GAD, we find a very small number of studies. Certainly there do not appear to be any studies of generic CBT for children with GAD (Oldham-Cooper & Loades, 2017). Chapter 5 details five studies testing interventions specifically designed for children with GAD, with a further two testing interventions for worry. All of the programmes for children with GAD involve parents in some way from inclusion in the initial session and in the end of sessions where possible (Payne, Bolton, & Perrin, 2011), to a full parallel programme for parents lasting seven (of the ten) sessions (Holmes et al., 2014). The two programmes to target worry (Meagher, Chessor, & Fogliati, 2018; Topper et al., 2017a) did not involve parents, perhaps unsurprisingly as the focus was on prevention and early intervention, rather than on intervention for a child with an anxiety disorder.

It appears from these studies that there is clinical recognition that involving parents in intervention may be useful for children with GAD. Indeed, Hudson et al. (2015b) found that in their clinic data, children with GAD benefitted more from broad-based family interventions than children with social anxiety disorder. However, in an analysis of an even larger set of intervention data, McKinnon et al. (2018) found that children with GAD benefitted equally from individual, group, and family CBT.

Involving parents therefore may present some benefits for worried children, but at the present time we cannot really make any strong conclusions as to what these might be. Indeed, it might be that all paths lead to Rome; a number of studies have found that working solely with parents teaching them CBT models that they can then use to help their children face their fears and manage and overcome their anxiety are highly effective (Cartwright-Hatton et al., 2011; Cobham, Filus, & Sanders, 2017; Esbjørn et al., 2019; Evans et al., 2019; Lebowitz et al., 2014, 2019; Salari et al., 2018; Thienemann, Moore, & Tompkins, 2006; Thirlwall et al., 2013), and just as effective as working with the child or the child and parent together (Smith et al., 2014). Few of these studies focus solely on children with GAD, but for nearly all of them there are a significant proportion of children with GAD in the trial.

CONCLUSION

It is clear that a number of processes are interacting when we try and understand worry in the context of the family. Parenting behaviours are likely to impact on levels of anxiety and worry, and parenting cognitions might also impact children's worry cognitions and cognitive processes. However, there are a number of provisos to consider; these relationships are most likely to be bi-directional, with children's worry impacting parental behaviour and cognitions as well as the other way around; the overall variance in children's worry accounted for by parenting factors is likely to be relatively small; and although for some, involving parents in therapy for worried children might be beneficial, it is likely that not including parents will not necessarily lead to more negative outcomes.

If this is the case, if we are to understand why some children are more worried than others and if we are to try and help those children with high levels of worry, we need to look to factors beyond the family. We need to look at more complex relationships between childhood worry and parenting behaviours and cognitions, perhaps exploring external factors such as culture, social circumstances, and life events, and perhaps exploring child factors such as temperament and cognitive processes.

CHAPTER FOUR
When children's worry becomes a problem

Although worry is a normal experience with some people experiencing worry regularly, and the majority of people worrying from time to time, for some adults and children worry becomes problematic. Worry may become problematic when it becomes excessive, intense, or uncontrollable (Ruscio, 2002; Wilson, 2010). Indeed, two of these parameters – excessiveness and uncontrollability – are part of the diagnostic criteria for Generalised Anxiety Disorder (GAD) (American Psychiatric Association, 2013), an anxiety disorder whose key feature is worry. Over the past 30 years there has been a concerted effort to understand the processes involved in GAD and problematic worry in order to design effective treatment programmes for those affected by it. In addition to considerable burden on the individual, GAD has a significant economic burden on society, with the impact on quality of life, and economic burden being similar to other mental health conditions such as depression, other anxiety disorders, and substance use disorders (DiBonaventura et al., 2014; Hoffman, Dukes, & Wittchen, 2008; Rovira et al., 2012). Thus, there are societal pressures to effectively support and treat those who experience problematic worry, and therefore a need to understand the processes involved in this. This chapter focuses on what we know about these processes in both adults and children.

PROCESSES INVOLVED IN PROBLEMATIC WORRY

There are a number of models that aim to explain pathological or problematic worry in adults. These have been widely tested on adults with GAD, adults with high levels of worry, and adults in the general population. One strategy in understanding problematic worry in children has been to take the processes involved in these models and to see whether they work the same in children. As this research is somewhat in its infancy much of the research has been on typically developing or non-clinical children and adolescents. When models have been found to be relevant, they have then occasionally been tested on children with anxiety disorders and clinically referred children. This chapter describes a number of relevant models of problematic worry and GAD and synthesises and critiques the research applying these models to children and adolescents.

The most prominent models of GAD in the literature are cognitive-behavioural. Cognitive-behaviour therapy has long been held to be an evidence-based intervention for both children and adolescents and there is a trend in Europe for these interventions to be based on our models of the disorder and the processes that maintain the symptoms. There are a number of cognitive-behavioural models of worry that emphasise different aspects of it and the processes involved in its maintenance, but they share some common themes. In a comprehensive paper on GAD Behar et al. (2009) reviewed the five main models of GAD (Koerner & Dugas, 2006; Mennin et al., 2002; Roemer & Orsillo, 2002; Sibrava & Borkovec, 2006; Wells, 1995). They isolated specific factors that were implicated in GAD within the individual models and found five factors that were common to two or more models, and two factors that were specific to one model (Table 4.1). Beliefs about worry, cognitive/experiential avoidance, problems with strategies for managing difficulties or emotions, problematic relationships with internal experiences, and heightened internal experiences/hyperarousal were common to at least two models. Intolerance of uncertainty (IU) and attachment/trauma were the factors found to be specific to only one model. Some of these factors have been investigated in both children and adults, but some have only really been considered for adults. These seven factors are reviewed below. The adult literature is briefly reviewed to provide the context, followed by the literature on children and adolescents.

BELIEFS ABOUT WORRY

Most people hold beliefs about worry. These may be positive: worry helps me be prepared, worry helps me solve my problems, and worry warns me that I need to do something; and they may be negative: worry can harm my health, worry is a huge waste of my time, and worry will cause me to go mad. People with problematic worry may hold different

Table 4.1 Shared and unique components of five key models of GAD in adulthood, from Behar et al., (2009).

	Intolerance of uncertainty model	*Meta-cognitive model*	*Avoidance model*	*Emotional dysregulation model*	*Acceptance model*
1. Beliefs about worry	Beliefs about worry (positive more important)	Positive and negative beliefs about worry	Positive worry beliefs		
2. Cognitive/experiential avoidance	Cognitive avoidance		Cognitive avoidance		Experiential avoidance
3. Problems with strategies for managing difficulties or emotions	Negative problem orientation	Ineffective coping	Ineffective problem solving	Poor understanding of emotions Maladaptive emotion management Negative cognitive reactions to emotions	Behavioural restriction
4. Problematic relationships with internal experiences			Interpersonal problems		Problematic relationships with internal experiences
5. Heightened internal experiences/hyperarousal				Emotional hyperarousal	Internal experiences
6. Intolerance of uncertainty	Intolerance of uncertainty				
7. Attachment and trauma			Attachment and trauma		

beliefs about worry, or hold more beliefs, or may hold them more strongly. Furthermore, beliefs about worry might play a different role in the development or maintenance of worry in problematic worry when compared to everyday worry. In each of the models of GAD these beliefs play a different role in the process of worry becoming problematic. Similarities and differences in this are reviewed below.

Beliefs about worry in adults

In most models of pathological worry and GAD there is some role for individuals' beliefs about worry. Borkovec adapted his initial model of GAD, which focused on avoidance of emotion, to include positive beliefs about worry (Borkovec et al., 1999). In Borkovec's model these positive beliefs reinforce and are reinforced by worry; Borkovec proposes that worry dampens the emotional experience, providing good evidence to the individual that it is helpful, thus reinforcing the beliefs, and these beliefs about worry being positive make worry more likely, reinforcing worry itself. Positive beliefs about worry are also a key part of Dugas et al.'s model (Dugas, Marchand, & Ladouceur, 2005), but in this model positive beliefs about worry make worry more likely in the context of uncertainty, where people believe that worry will help them cope with the uncertainty.

Despite the role beliefs about worry play in these early models it is perhaps Wells who has pioneered the research on beliefs about worry (Wells, 1995) and their role in the development and maintenance of GAD. In Wells' meta-cognitive model of GAD positive beliefs about worry prompt worry as a coping strategy in the face of threat. However, once worry has been activated negative beliefs about worry prompt worry about the worry itself, which increases negative affect.

There is significant research evidence that these processes are present in people with GAD. A number of studies have found that positive beliefs about worry are associated with excessive worry and GAD (Borkovec, Hazlett-Stevens, & Diaz, 1999; Borkovec & Roemer, 1995; Hebert et al., 2014; Ladouceur et al., 1998; Wells & Carter, 2009). Indeed, positive beliefs about worry have been found to predict unique variance in worry (Voon & Phillips, 2015) and moderate the relationship between stressful events and later worry (Iijima & Tanno, 2013). Furthermore, McEvoy et al. (2015) found that positive beliefs about worry reduced after successful therapy for adults with GAD.

However, other research has suggested that these positive beliefs about worry may be implicated in the development of worry but that negative beliefs are more important for understanding problematic or pathological worry. For example, Penney et al. (2013) found that only negative beliefs about worry, not positive beliefs about worry, predicted GAD symptoms, and furthermore negative beliefs about worry mediated the relationship between trait worry and GAD symptoms. This suggests that for those individuals who are high in worry, having negative beliefs about worry may lead to the worry being perceived as problematic and thus lead to greater GAD symptoms. In one of the few experimental studies of beliefs about worry Prados (2011) manipulated positive and negative beliefs about worry in a non-clinical group of adults and examined the effect they had on later worry and affective reaction. Contrary to the prediction, manipulating beliefs about worry in a positive direction did not increase worry or negative affect. However, manipulating beliefs about worry in a negative direction did lead to a smaller affective response, suggesting that negative beliefs about worry do inhibit the affective response initially, although perhaps leading to problems later in the process. Understanding negative beliefs about worry may also be important in the treatment of GAD. Although McEvoy et al. (2015) did find changes in positive beliefs about worry following treatment, they found much greater changes in negative beliefs.

We know very little about whether these relationships hold across different cultures. Worry meta-cognitions appear to be important across different cultures (Ghafoor et al., 2019), with invariance in the structure of Meta-Cognitions Questionnaires (Dai et al., 2019; Yılmaz, Gençöz, & Wells, 2008), but research in this area is very much in its infancy.

In summary, both positive and negative beliefs about worry have been found to be important in our understanding of worry, but there may be different processes involved in everyday worry and problematic worry/GAD. Exploring these in younger populations is important because the ability to think and form beliefs about ones only thinking is something that develops through childhood. Flavell (1979) pioneered work into children's meta-cognition. In a number of studies he showed that children's awareness of their own thinking develops from about age seven onwards. Whereas pre-school-aged children have little awareness that cognitive processes are continuous and occur even when resting (Flavell, 1999), by the time children enter school they have some consideration of their own cognitive processes. For example, from age seven children are quite good at estimating their own memory capacity (Flavell, Friedrichs, & Hoyt, 1970). If children are to be able to reflect on and, more importantly, report their beliefs about their worries, they require these meta-cognitive abilities. Thus, we need to review the research on measuring children's meta-cognitive beliefs about worry in order to put into context what is known about them in relation to worry itself.

Measuring beliefs about worry in children

There have been two main ways of assessing beliefs about worry in children: bottom up and top down. Bottom-up approaches have asked children open questions about their beliefs and then classified them into appropriate categories. Top-down approaches have taken the measures used to assess meta-cognitive beliefs about worry in adults and adapted them for use with children. There have been more top-down approaches, with at least three different adaptations of the Meta-Cognitions Questionnaire being available. The first adaptation was by Cartwright-Hatton and colleagues (2004) who adapted the shorter Meta-Cognitions Questionnaire, the MCQ-30, for use with adolescents. This largely involved changing the language of the measure, with no major change to the content or structure. Indeed, in their factor analysis of their data from over 160 adolescents, they found that five factors emerged that mapped very well onto the five factors in the original measure.

However, these studies have focused on adolescence. Due to cognitive maturation, it is likely that adolescents' meta-cognitive processes are more similar to adults' than children's are. There have been two independent attempts to adapt the MCQ for use with younger children. Bacow and colleagues (Bacow et al., 2009) attempted to develop the measure for children aged 7–17 years. Their version has only 24 items, following the decision to remove items related to cognitive confidence. Psychometric properties for the measure were found to be good, with good internal consistency and concurrent validity with measures of worry and depression. Unlike the MCQ-A, the MCQ-C was largely validated on children with diagnoses of anxiety disorders, and the authors surprisingly found that these children did not have higher scores on the MCQ-C when compared to a non-clinical group. Indeed, for one of the subscales, the cognitive monitoring scale, the non-clinical group evidenced higher scores. This suggests that criterion validity was not good for this measure. Furthermore, in a follow up study comparing meta-cognitions in children with and without anxiety disorders, only one difference was found: cognitive monitoring was higher in the non-clinical group. It is possible that this indicates that with younger children the relationships between meta-cognitions and anxiety symptoms such as worry and obsessions are not yet established or that the measure isn't tapping into the construct in the way it does in adults.

Esbjørn and colleagues also tested an adapted MCQ-A (Gerlach et al., 2008) for use with children aged 9–17 years (Esbjørn et al., 2013). In a large study of 974 children and adolescents drawn from a community sample, this version of the MCQ was found to have good psychometric properties. These authors retained all five subscales and thus 30 items, and the measure was found to have good factor structure with all five factors represented. It also demonstrated good internal consistency and good concurrent validity with measures of GAD and OCD. Furthermore, this 30 item version appears to have validity in even younger children, aged seven to eight years (White & Hudson, 2016).

We have taken the alternative, bottom-up, approach in exploring beliefs about worry in children. In a number of studies we have asked children open-ended questions in order to determine their beliefs about worry. In Wilson and Hughes (Wilson & Hughes, 2011) we asked children from 6 to 11 to report their beliefs about worry by asking them what they thought was good and friendly about worry and what was bad and unfriendly about it. We found that children as young as six years old could report on their beliefs about worry using this format and that the beliefs were largely similar to those found in adults. One significant difference was the presence of the family in the beliefs. For example, one child reported that worry was helpful sometimes because it told her mummy that she needed some help. This may not represent a significant category of positive beliefs about worry, but it does demonstrate some differences between children and adults in their beliefs. Further studies exploring children's beliefs about worry in the context of what it means to their family are warranted.

When we explored the answers to these open-ended questions in older children (Wilson, 2008) aged 12–16 similar themes were found, with all ages reporting positive beliefs about worry such as worry keeps you safe and shows you care and negative beliefs about worry such as it makes you feel bad or sick and interferes with sleep. In contrast to the younger children however, the older children reported more effects on friendships, with reported positive beliefs such as worry helps you tell your friends what is bothering you and reported negative beliefs such as worry can get in the way of friendships. We found a similar pattern of spontaneously reported beliefs about worry in a different sample adolescents with no differences between those who experienced chronic pain and those who didn't (Madhavakkannan et al., in prep; see Chapter 5 for more details about this study). Clinically these developmentally appropriate beliefs may well emerge within a clinical interview or using these open-ended questions, but using standardised measures of beliefs about worry, adapted from adult measures, may miss these important differences.

Beliefs about worry in children

We appear therefore to have a number of ways in which we can assess beliefs about worry in children and adolescents, but the evidence suggests that those beliefs are likely to be similar to beliefs held by adults, with some small but notable differences. Therefore, it is worth asking whether those beliefs are related to worry in the same way they are in adulthood. Two reviews in 2010 synthesised the relevant literature available at that time (Ellis & Hudson, 2010; Wilson, 2010).

Ellis and Hudson synthesised the available studies in 2010 and concluded that at that time, there was enough evidence to suggest that both positive and negative beliefs about worry were associated with higher levels of worry in children and adolescents. At that time only one study (Bacow et al., 2009) had a clinically-referred sample of children with anxiety disorders. This study showed interesting results, with some of the sub-scales on their adapted MCQ showing lower levels in children with anxiety. Since that time a few studies have explored meta-cognition in children with anxiety disorders, and it appears that just like in adults, children with higher levels of excessive worry and anxiety disorders have more positive beliefs about worry and also more negative beliefs about worry. Furthermore, they appear to work in similar ways to the mechanisms proposed for adults.

> Lucy wanted help with her worry. She felt like it was taking over her life and it was stopping her doing the things she enjoyed. It had got worse recently due to exams, but she described herself as having always been a worrier. Lucy was keen to explore what she could do to worry less, but some strategies such as controlled worry periods, and distraction weren't working for her. When setting homework after another therapy session Lucy looked sad and hopeless so the psychologist asked her about this. Lucy explained that once again she did not think the therapy would work because she just couldn't do the tasks designed to help her reduce the time she spent worrying. They talked about this together and eventually Lucy explained that if she did manage to stop worrying, that would mean that she no longer cared about the things she worried about, and as many of these were things that were important to her; her family, her friends, her exam marks and her future, stopping worrying would mean she had become a nasty, mean person.

Since 2010 a handful of papers have explored meta-cognitions in adolescents and children. Many of these find medium correlations between the different sub-scales of the Meta-Cognitions Questionnaire, and worry and anxiety (Esbjørn et al., 2013, 2015; Smith & Hudson, 2013; Wilson et al., 2011; Wolters et al., 2012). However, there may be a different role of positive beliefs about worry when comparing children and adolescents. In three studies of adolescents, positive beliefs about worry not only correlated with worry but also significantly predicted worry in regression models (Fisak, Mentuccia, & Przeworski, 2014; Thielsch et al., 2015; Wilson et al., 2011), whereas studies that included younger children (from age seven upwards) found that either there was only a small contribution of positive beliefs to a prediction of worry (Esbjørn et al., 2013) or anxiety (Wilson et al., in prep.), or there was no role for positive beliefs (Esbjørn et al., 2015; Fialko, Bolton, & Perrin, 2012; McMahon, Duane, & Wilson, in preparation).

In our open-ended questions there was also a developmental trend for negative beliefs about worry to be present prior to positive beliefs about worry (Figure 4.1), and for more negative beliefs about worry to be reported as children got older, suggesting that it is not just the role

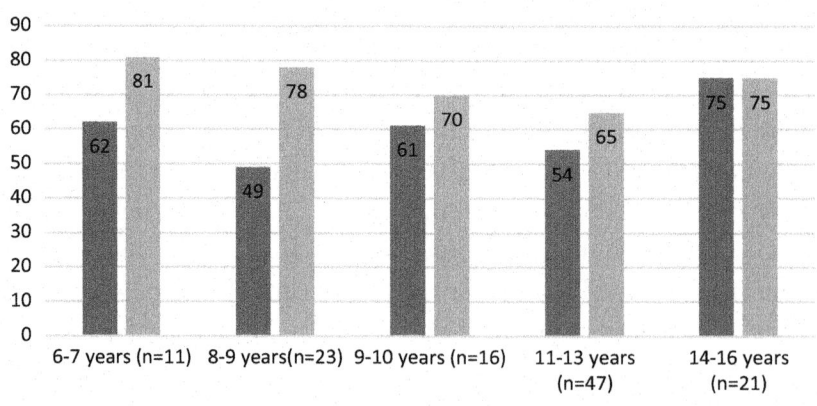

Figure 4.1 Percentage of children reporting positive and negative beliefs at each age, from Wilson (2008).

positive beliefs have in the maintenance of worry that is developmentally sensitive but also the development of these beliefs in the first place.

Understanding the developmental progression of meta-cognitive beliefs about worry may also help us understand meta-cognition in children more broadly. Most meta-cognition research in children focuses on learning and classroom strategies and skills. This requires children to focus on non-emotional topics, such as maths or language. Little is known about how meta-cognition changes when the process is about emotional or 'hot' topics, such as worries and anxiety. It appears that more emotionally salient beliefs about worry, namely the negative beliefs that worry can harm you and interfere with your life, are present earlier and contribute to problematic worry earlier than positive beliefs, with positive beliefs about worry contributing more in later adolescence and adulthood. If this is the case, it may be that positive beliefs about worry represent some kind of post-hoc rationalisation of worry for frequent worriers, which then paradoxically leads to maintenance of worry. This suggests that early intervention may be useful in stopping problematic worry from developing in the first place.

COGNITIVE/EXPERIENTIAL AVOIDANCE

Cognitive avoidance plays a key role in two of theories of GAD/worry in adults: the avoidance model of worry developed by Borkovec and colleagues, and the IU model of GAD/worry developed by Dugas and colleagues. In the Borkovec model worry itself is an avoidance strategy. By worrying in verbal thoughts the emotional response is dampened and thus negative affect is avoided. In the Dugas model additional strategies – such as distraction, thought substitution, and thought suppression– as well as the worry itself are used to avoid cognitive arousal. A number of studies have supported the links between cognitive avoidance and worry in adults (Dugas et al., 2007; Roemer et al., 2005; Sexton & Dugas, 2009), with additional studies showing that cognitive avoidance reduces in effective treatment for GAD (Dugas & Robichaud, 2007; Treanor et al., 2011).

Experiential avoidance features in the acceptance model of GAD (Roemer et al., 2005; Roemer & Orsillo, 2002). In this model adults with GAD have problematic relationships with their internal experiences and thus avoid several different aspects of these, not just their cognition or cognitive arousal. As this model is relatively new, there is less empirical evidence supporting this factor in relationship with GAD, although studies do suggest that experiential avoidance is higher in individuals with GAD compared to individuals without anxiety disorders, and that the avoidance is related to levels of worry (Lee et al. 2010; Roemer et al., 2005). Furthermore, cross-cultural studies suggest that experiential avoidance is relevant across a wide range of cultures and may have very similar relationships with anxiety across these cultures (Borgogna et al., 2020; Monestès et al., 2018).

In children there are a few studies exploring cognitive avoidance and worry. The earliest of these found a clear association between worry and cognitive avoidance, with those young people with high levels of worry also reporting higher levels of cognitive avoidance (Laugesen, Dugas, & Bukowski, 2003). Since those early studies researchers have endeavoured to explore the associations between worry, cognitive avoidance, and other factors. Fialko, Bolton, and Perrin (2012) found that cognitive avoidance was associated with anxiety and worry in young people but that worry fully mediated the relationship between cognitive avoidance and child anxiety. In a number of studies Donovan and colleagues (Donovan, Holmes, & Farrell, 2016; Donovan et al., 2017; Hearn et al., 2017) have found that children with a diagnosis of GAD have higher cognitive avoidance than those with no diagnoses. They also found that cognitive avoidance predicted worry and that both parent worry and parent cognitive avoidance predicted child cognitive avoidance. This small body of research suggests that cognitive avoidance is important in our understanding of pathological worry and that it might be a process that is specific in understanding worry, compared to understanding anxiety more generally.

In contrast there are no studies to date of experiential avoidance and worry in younger populations. There is plenty of evidence that experiential avoidance is importance in the development and maintenance of other kinds of distress in young people such as stress (Ishizu, Shimoda, & Ohtsuki, 2017), social anxiety (Lee, Kim, & Park, 2014; Papachristou et al., 2018), and trauma (Kroska et al., 2018; Shenk, Putnam, & Noll, 2012). This literature on experiential avoidance suggests that it often mediates between life events (Kroska et al., 2018) or temperamental factors (Papachristou et al., 2018) and anxiety symptom outcomes. It would therefore be interesting to test not only whether highly worried children and adolescents report higher experiential avoidance but also whether this kind of avoidance mediates the relationship between life events, temperament, and later worry.

Specific studies exploring the avoidance of emotional experience are discussed below.

PROBLEMS WITH STRATEGIES FOR MANAGING DIFFICULTIES OR EMOTIONS

As described in Chapter 1, one of the key drivers of worry is the need to problem solve. Therefore, both clinical and non-clinical researchers have sought to explore problem solving in relation to worry. Within the Dugas model a negative problem orientation (NPO) comprises four different components: lack of confidence in problem solving, a bias towards seeing all problems as threats, pessimism about the outcomes of problem solving, and frustration during problem solving itself. In adults negative problem-solving orientation has been found to be higher in people diagnosed with GAD, and in people with high pathological worry scores (Ladouceur et al., 1998), and has also been found to predict GAD severity amongst those with GAD.

Several studies have explored the concept of an NPO as a whole and in children the findings are equivocal. Whilst some researchers have found that children with GAD have higher NPO than children without GAD, and NPO predicts worry in community samples (Laugesen, Dugas, & Bukowski, 2003), other studies have found that when all the different aspects of the IU model are included NPO does not uniquely predict worry or GAD symptoms (Barahmand, 2008; Kertz & Woodruff-Borden, 2013), and most authors conclude that IU is more important (Donovan et al., 2017; Kertz & Woodruff-Borden, 2013; Laugesen, Dugas, & Bukowski, 2003).

However, it isn't just NPO that has been proposed in models of GAD. Borkovec and colleagues propose that people with GAD have interpersonal problem-solving deficits. Studies by Davey and colleagues suggest that it isn't the problem solving per se that is problematic but the confidence in problem solving (Davey, 1994b) and this appears to be true for children as well (Parkinson & Creswell, 2011; Wilson & Hughes, 2011; see Chapter 2). In the meta-cognitive model of GAD Wells proposes not generic problem-solving deficits but rather a set of strategies for managing unwanted thoughts that are counterproductive. For example, Wells found that adults with GAD were more likely to choose worry as a strategy for dealing with unwanted thoughts and furthermore were more likely to punish themselves for having unwanted thoughts (Wells & Carter, 2009). These ways of managing unwanted thoughts are often captured using the Thought Control Questionnaire (TCQ; Wells & Davies, 1994). This questionnaire asks people about a variety of strategies that they could use to manage unwanted thoughts, from distraction and social control (talking to others) to reappraisal, worry, and punishment. There have been two independent adaptations of the TCQ for adolescents so that these interesting strategies can be explored in younger populations. Gill and colleagues (Gill et al., 2013) adapted the original TCQ in a sample of 589 adolescents between the ages of 13 and 17. They found that, similar to adults, distraction, social control, and reappraisal were the most commonly used strategies for managing unwanted thoughts, but worry and punishment were most strongly associated with anxiety, low mood, and obsessions. Whiting and colleagues (Whiting et al., 2014) also adapted the TCQ for use with adolescents on a sample of 212 12–18 year olds. They don't report the frequency of use of different strategies but also found that worry and punishment were most strongly associated with anxiety, low mood, and obsessions. A further study found similar results in relation to obsessions, with the most frequently used strategies being distraction and social control, and punishment and worry predicting obsessions in 13–16 year olds (Wilson & Hall, 2012).

We have attempted to use assess thought control strategies in younger children, adapting only the language of the TCQ-A, and specifically exploring the relationship they have with worry. Mullen explored thought control strategies in 179 children aged between 8 and 13 (Wilson et al., 2019). We found that four of the five sub-scales of the TCQ were significantly associated with worry, anxiety, and obsessions: social control, worry, punishment, and reappraisal. The only strategy that wasn't associated with worry and anxiety was distraction. It is interesting therefore that distraction is the most commonly used strategy to manage unwanted thoughts, suggesting that in general both children and adults are drawn to adaptive ways of managing thoughts. McKinney further explored thought control strategies in even younger children. Seventy-six children aged 5–11 completed an adapted version of the TQS using visual prompts. In this younger age group there were no significant associations between thought control strategies and anxiety (rho < .2). However, these children were also asked to report their own ways of managing unwanted thoughts. As well as reporting control strategies similar to those asked about by the TCQ-C, these young children also reported strategies such as fidgeting, withdrawing, expressing their thoughts out loud, and deliberately calming themselves. These children could also report more concerning outcomes of unwanted thoughts with some children reporting that they had no strategies to cope, and that they just had to sit with the unwanted emotional response and that they felt that they could not always cope (Figure 4.2).

This lack of strategies was also found in one of the few qualitative studies of control of worry (Normann & Esbjørn, 2018). Once again, there

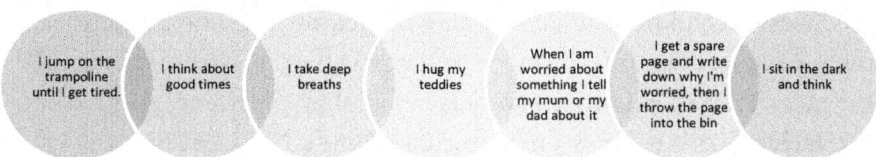

Figure 4.2 Examples of young children's reported thought control strategies, from Wilson, Mullen, et al. (in preparation).

may be differences found in the processes involved in worry between adolescents and younger children, although there are too few studies to confirm this at the present time. Given that meta-cognitive processes emerge from about age seven onwards it isn't surprising that younger children have not got a wide range of strategies for managing internal experiences. They are only just becoming fully conscious of their thoughts and internal experiences, and so being able to reflect on this and choose ways of managing these must occur after this age. At this age children have already got a good set of strategies for managing interpersonal problems but perhaps have not yet developed relevant strategies for managing their own internal thoughts and feelings.

We know so very little about young children's experiences of thinking and of experiencing thoughts as wanted or unwanted. Further research can not only uncover possible ways of helping children with problematic worry, it may also help us understand how children experience, relate to, and understand their internal worlds.

PROBLEMATIC RELATIONSHIPS WITH INTERNAL EXPERIENCES

Problematic relationships with internal experiences are important in models of GAD, but they are also important developmentally. Throughout childhood, children have to learn about their internal experiences, make sense of them, and through interactions with these and with others understand when internal experiences are normal and when they are not normal and something needs to be done about them. Meta-cognitive development has been described earlier in relation to beliefs about worry, and there is also a large body of research exploring children's understanding of emotions in others. However, there is much less on children's understanding of their own emotions. Some interesting work on mixed emotions suggests that children understand the idea of mixed emotions in others before they experience them themselves (Larsen, To, & Fireman, 2007; Smith, Glass, & Fireman, 2015), with understanding of mixed emotion in others being present in more than 50% of children as young as three years old. This pattern of children understanding an internal experience in someone else prior to experiencing it themselves might therefore impact on their understanding of their own internal experiences.

In the emotional dysregulation model of GAD (Mennin et al., 2002, 2005) negative reactions to emotions are due to poor understanding of emotions, and this results in poor management or regulation of emotions. In this model not only are emotions felt more strongly but also the response to them is dysfunctional and can maintain the problem. These problematic responses include emotional avoidance (Cooper, Miranda, & Mennin, 2013) and over-reactivity (Mennin et al., 2009), both in self-report and in observational/behavioural studies (Cooper, Miranda, & Mennin, 2013; Kerns et al., 2014; Mennin, McLaughlin, & Flanagan, 2009). However, within this model, it is poor understanding of one's own emotions and how they differentiate that is key to understanding worry and GAD (Mennin et al., 2005).

In the acceptance model of GAD (Roemer et al., 2005; Treanor et al., 2011) problematic relationships with internal experiences are further delineated into two components: negative reactions to emotional experiences and fusion with internal experiences. As these are relatively newer models of GAD there is less evidence for these processes. However, there is evidence that adults with GAD are more afraid of emotional experiences (Mennin et al., 2005; Salters-Pedneault et al., 2006; Turk et al., 2005), and, in non-clinical adults, negative reactions to emotions are associated with GAD symptoms (Roemer et al., 2005).

In children there are very few studies of problematic relationships with internal experiences. We know that children with high levels of anxiety can have poor understanding of the emotions of others or poor general understanding of how emotions work (Southam-Gerow & Kendall, 2000). They also demonstrate poor regulation of emotion (Suveg & Zeman, 2004). However, perhaps due to developmental factors, research has only just started to explore how they feel and react to their internal experiences. We have started to explore what children feel about their worries, but we don't know much about what children feel about other internal experiences. In a study aiming to develop and validate a measure to explore this Kennedy and Ehrenreich-May (Kennedy & Ehrenreich-May, 2017) explored the psychometric properties of the Emotional Avoidance Strategy Inventory for Adolescents in a sample of 261 11–19 year olds. Kennedy and Ehrenreich-May found three clear dimensions of emotional avoidance: avoidance of thoughts and feelings, avoidance of emotional expression, and distraction. They found that both kinds of avoidance, but not distraction, predicted scores on an anxiety measure, but only avoidance of emotional expression predicted depression scores. In a parallel study, McMahon, Duane, and Wilson (in preparation) asked young people about how they manage unwanted experiences and found that there were different kinds of distraction. Some young people reported very active distraction techniques involving other people or actively engaging in an activity, whereas others tried to distract themselves by thinking about other things. It wasn't possible in this study to explore the associations between the different kinds of distraction and levels of anxiety and depression, but it is possible that just as different kinds of avoidance are associated with anxiety and depression, certain aspects of distraction may well relate to anxiety and depression in different ways.

By adolescence then, young people with higher levels of anxiety are avoiding their internal experiences. We simply do not know, however, which leads to which: do young people who avoid their internal experiences have more problems with worry, or do young people who worry more avoid their internal experiences more? Furthermore, avoidance is only part of the picture of understanding internal experiences, and much more research is required to determine how young people make sense of these and why, for some, it goes wrong.

HEIGHTENED INTERNAL EXPERIENCES

Kennedy and Ehrenreich-May's study demonstrates that young people with higher levels of anxiety want to avoid their internal experiences more. This may be because these internal experiences are more intense and therefore harder to experience. In both of the models that emphasise emotional experience – the emotional dysregulation model and the acceptance model of GAD – it is proposed that adults with GAD have heightened internal experiences or hyperarousal, and research supports this proposition (Mennin et al., 2005; Roemer et al., 2005; Salters-Pedneault et al., 2006). When applying this to childhood and adolescence, studies have also found that children with anxiety disorders have more intense emotional experiences (Carthy et al., 2010a, 2010b; Suveg & Zeman, 2004), perhaps due to an exaggerated amygdala response (Thomas et al., 2001). This relationship also holds in non-clinical samples, with intense emotions being associated with anxiety symptoms (Suveg et al., 2009; Weems et al., 2005). However, intensity of the anxiety response is unlikely to account for worry fully, as worry appears to be mediated by lack of activity in the prefrontal cortex and the anterior cingulate cortex (Goossen, van der Starre, & van der Heiden, 2019) during emotional regulation tasks. An exaggerated amygdala response, however, may be a useful consideration for understanding worry in very young children as the communication and networks between the amygdala and other affective parts of the brain may not have yet developed.

Research exploring systemic and environmental factors involved in the development and maintenance of children's anxiety disorders has also found some interesting relationships between anxiety and intense emotions. Suveg and colleagues (Suveg et al., 2009) found that it was the combination of frequent emotional experiences with strong somatic/emotional reactions predicted anxiety levels and also that children who did experience intense emotions but were reluctant to express emotions had poorer social outcomes (Jacob, Suveg, & Whitehead, 2014). It might be that reluctance to express emotion might be part of family patterns: children with anxiety disorders have parents who are more likely to discourage emotional discussion and emotional expression, as well as talking about emotion less often themselves (Suveg et al., 2005). More recently Benoit Allen et al. (2016) have explored interactive effects between child and parent factors. This study assessed children's experience of emotions, their perceptions of control, and their parents' autonomy granting in a sample of 106 9–14 year olds with anxiety disorders. The study found that these children showed the greatest levels of emotional arousal when they perceived themselves to have low control, but their parents were autonomy granting. There were also indications that when children perceive themselves to be low in control, then autonomy granting may not be helpful, as this was related to children's low acceptance of emotions.

Despite a handful of these relevant studies, there is a lack of literature on children's experience of emotion in the context of anxiety and in particular in the context of children's worry, however, there is a significant literature exploring basic temperament, including dimensions of felt experience, in relation to later anxiety and worry. One temperamental factor, behavioural inhibition (BI) may provide a useful conceptual bridge between early intense emotional responses, and later anxiety disorders. BI refers to a biological predisposition to inhibit behavioural responses in the face of threat (Kagan et al., 1984; Kagan, Reznick, & Snidman, 1987). This can include infants and children inhibiting emotional responses to new situations, strangers, as well as aversive stimuli such as loud noises, unexpected movement, or physical threat. Children who have high BI are usually shy and timid with others, and thus it has been suggested that BI may be a risk factor for later anxiety disorders, including panic disorder (Hirshfeld-Becker et al., 2008) and social anxiety disorder (Clauss & Blackford, 2012). Infants with high BI have been shown to have higher heart rate, and less heart-rate variability (Coll et al., 1984), similar to anxious children (Weems et al., 2005). Furthermore, BI appears to be quite stable over time (Kagan et al., 1984).

Although behaviourally inhibited children show these blunted responses to novel stimuli, these may be consistent with having more intense emotional responses. A number of studies have found that children and infants with high BI show increased startle responses to threat (Figure 4.3). For example, Schmidt and Fox (1998) found that infants who showed negative affect and high motor activity in their startle

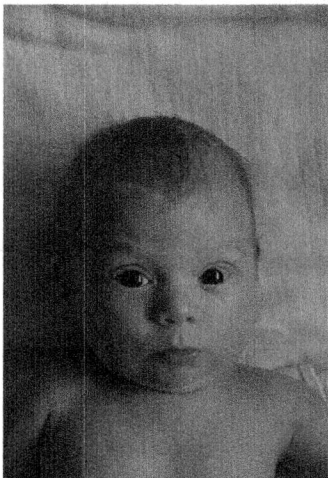

Figure 4.3 *A startled baby!*

response at four months had greater fear-potentiated startle responses at nine months.

Barker and colleagues went on to explore the impact of BI on later startle responses. In their first study they found that children with high BI had increased and faster startle responses than children with low BI (Barker, Reeb-Sutherland, & Fox, 2014). In a follow up study they found that this startle response at seven years moderated the relationship between early BI and later anxiety symptoms. Those children with high BI in infancy and high startle responses at seven years were more likely to have high anxiety scores at nine years old. This is consistent with an early review by Turner and Beidel (1996). This review concludes that there are many methodological difficulties with the research in BI and that to fully understand the role it plays we need to consider systemic and environmental factors. It may be therefore that BI plays some role in the development of anxiety disorders for some children, but it is unlikely to be a primary cause.

What the construct of BI does, however, is to provide a link between these early intense emotional experiences that some infants experience, through childhood experiences of increased startle, but decreased emotional expressiveness, to later development of anxiety disorders. Poor emotional expressiveness (Jacob, Suveg, & Whitehead, 2014) or poor emotional regulation strategies (Bender et al., 2012; Suveg et al., 2010), as described earlier, may be some of the key factors that determine whether or not a behaviourally inhibited child develops later anxiety.

INTOLERANCE OF UNCERTAINTY

IU has been defined as

> an individual's dispositional incapacity to endure the aversive response triggered by the perceived absence of salient, key, or sufficient information, and sustained by the associated perception of uncertainty.
>
> (Carleton, 2016)

Although a transdiagnostic construct pertaining to anxiety in general, IU is viewed as the core component of GAD in one of the most researched models of this disorder (Koerner & Dugas, 2006). Worry in this model is viewed as a mechanism or strategy that aims to resolve uncertainty in a variety of ways, such as thinking through lots of possible outcomes, or to move off the experience of uncertainty, to the certainty of catastrophic outcomes. It appears to be relevant across a variety of different cultures (Norton, 2005; Zainal, Newman, & Hong, 2019) and related to worry in similar ways (Rucker, West, & Roemer, 2010). Initial studies of this construct in relation to worry identified that adults with GAD had higher scores on measures of IU (Dugas et al., 2007). Further studies showed that successful treatment of GAD was not only associated with reductions in IU (Dugas et al., 2003; Dugas & Ladouceur, 2000) but also that these reductions mediated the impact of the intervention (Bomyea et al., 2015). Also, despite its role transdiagnostically, it appears that IU might have some specific relationship with GAD (Gentes & Ruscio, 2011). The evidence is therefore strong that IU has a significant role in our understanding of problematic worry in adults, but is the same true for children?

Intolerance of uncertainty in children

There are now a number of studies that have explored whether children show the predicted relationships between IU and worry. In the earliest study of IU in younger people, Laugesen and colleagues (Laugesen, Dugas, & Bukowski, 2003) showed that in a non-referred sample of 528 children aged 14–18, there were strong correlations between IU and worry. Indeed of all the four variables predicting worry (derived from the Dugas model), IU showed the strongest association. In the one treatment trial using the IU model as the basis for therapy, Payne, Bolton, and Perrin (2011) showed that children aged 7–17 years who addressed their IU using exposure and cognitive restructuring demonstrated significant reductions in their worry and other GAD symptoms (see also Perrin et al. 2019). Therefore IU shows promise for being important in our understanding of adolescent worry. This promise perhaps explains the recent explosion of studies exploring IU in children. Osmanağaoğlu, Creswell, and Dodd (2018) completed a meta-analysis of studies that explored IU in relation to anxiety and worry in children and adolescents. This meta-analysis identified an additional 30 studies since the Laugesen study that assessed IU and anxiety and/or worry. Of these 31 studies ten were completed in the ten years following the first study (2003–2013), with the remaining 21 being completed in the years 2014–2018. The strong finding was that IU was robustly and strongly associated with both anxiety and worry with mean effect size of $r = 0.6$ for IU and anxiety, and $r = 0.63$ for IU and worry. The studies were relatively evenly spread across different age groups: seven studies had a mean age of participants of <11 years, 14 studies had a mean age of participants of 11–14, and ten had a mean age of participants of 15+; however, age was not found to be a moderator of the relationship. Gender and type of study also did not moderate the relationship, despite considerable heterogeneity within the studies. The conclusion therefore is that IU is strongly related to worry and anxiety in younger populations. However, this is only the beginning of understanding its role in the development and maintenance of worry in children and adolescents. The authors note that most of the 31 studies were cross-sectional, with only one longitudinal study and one treatment trial meeting inclusion criteria for the meta-analysis. The longitudinal study (Dugas, Laugesen, &

Bukowski, 2012) suggests that the relationship between worry and IU is bi-directional, and the treatment trial suggests that IU is amenable to intervention and that changing IU can change worry.

IU is perhaps the best candidate for a core process in worry and GAD. It has been argued (Sankar et al., 2017) that IU plays both a specific role in GAD and a general role in anxiety. If this is the case, then understanding the overlap between IU and worry and how they both develop across childhood and adulthood could significantly improve our treatment of worry in childhood. Weems (2008) suggests that worry might be an underlying factor of all anxiety disorders, and BI has also been proposed as an underlying factor (Lahat, Hong, & Fox, 2011). IU may be a linking factor between these core risk factors and therefore deserves further evaluation.

ATTACHMENT AND PREVIOUS TRAUMA

The final factor to consider in this chapter is attachment and childhood trauma (see also Chapter 3).

Only one model, the avoidance model of GAD, proposes that adults with GAD and high levels of worry may be more likely to have experienced attachment difficulties or trauma in childhood. Cassidy (1995) proposes that adults with GAD are more likely to have insecure and disorganised attachment than adults without GAD and a few studies have supported this association (Cassidy et al., 2009; Marganska, Gallagher, & Miranda, 2013). Research discussed in Chapter 3 suggests that this relationship might also hold for children, although the research is mixed and there might be a more complex relationship between attachment and problematic worry that includes other variables. For example, the gender of the parent might be important. Many studies of attachment focus only on mothers, and it has been suggested that poor mother-child relationships might be particularly important in the development of childhood anxiety disorders (Viana & Rabian, 2008). However, it might be that both mothers and fathers are important, but in different ways. Indeed, a study by van Eijck et al. (2012) highlights the importance of looking at the relationship between attachment and GAD symptoms

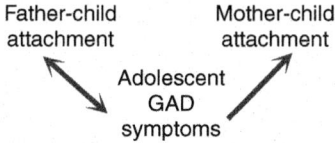

Figure 4.4 Longitudinal directions of influence between parent-child attachment and adolescent GAD symptoms, from van Eijck et al. (2012).

bi-directionally and measuring attachment between children and both parents. This large longitudinal study of 1313 adolescents found that there were bi-directional relationships between father-adolescent attachment and GAD symptoms, and in contrast mother-adolescent attachment was impacted by GAD symptoms in the adolescent, but not the other way around (Figure 4.4). This supports some of the research discussed in Chapter 3 that although there are robust associations between parental factors and childhood anxiety and worry, some of these are bi-directional and some of them work in the opposite direction to the one proposed in the research literature.

MODELS OF GAD: SIMILARITIES AND DIFFERENCES FOR CHILDREN AND ADULTS

It appears inevitable, and mostly sensible, that if we have well researched models for adults, then we are going to examine these same factors to test whether they are relevant for children with the same kinds of difficulties. If we examine the adult models of GAD we see that, at present, some of the proposed factors are more well researched than others in both children and adults, but some provisional conclusions can be drawn.

Overall, it does appear that once children get to adolescence, the factors in the models are both present in children and relate to anxiety and worry in similar ways. When we look at the research in children the results are more confusing. It does look like from even a young age children do report beliefs about worry, they can reflect on their own experiences, and they are aware of having to manage unwanted thoughts. However, these core experiences do not appear to be related to problematic worry in predictable ways. A key question to be answered in future research is to determine whether these factors are only important in the maintenance of problematic worry and GAD or whether they are risk factors for worry becoming more problematic over time. In Chapter 6 it is proposed that the experience of worry is primary and that other factors such as beliefs about worry result from experiencing worry and reflecting on it. If this is the case, then preventing worry getting worse becomes a different task from intervening with children who already have problematic worry.

One factor that might be different is IU. IU seems to be very robustly associated with worry from an early age. It is perhaps a prime candidate for a temperamental factor that underlies infants' responses to uncertainty from very early in their life. How these responses are responded to by caregivers may well determine how much of a problem uncertainty becomes for a child, but these are likely to interact with other factors both within the child, such as executive functioning capacity and language ability, and outside of the child such as life events. The models of problematic worry and GAD in adults focus on the intrapersonal factors, as these are often the factors that are amenable to intervention and therapy. However, it would be foolish to ignore the interactions between these intrapersonal factors and the wider context in which people live.

In order to properly understand both normal worry and problematic worry in children there is still a great deal of research to be done further testing these important constructs. There are only a few studies where the participants are children with significant psychological difficulties and diagnosed anxiety disorders, but there is a striking lack of research in adolescents with anxiety disorders. There is a similar striking lack of research into whether these models are appropriate across different cultures, different social-economic levels, and for both girls and boys. The research using community samples and those using clinical samples do appear to show similar results, but further research will determine whether our adult models of problematic worry can truly help us to understand and treat problematic worry in children.

CHAPTER FIVE
Children's worry and psychological disorders

Worry has an interesting place in our understanding of psychological disorders in childhood. Worry is the key symptom of one psychological disorder, generalised anxiety disorder (GAD); it is a diagnostic criterion in other anxiety disorders such as separation anxiety disorder and panic disorder; and it has also been recognised as a symptom across all anxiety disorders. However, in recent years there has been an increasing understanding that worry may play a role in maintaining symptoms in a wide variety of psychological disorders. The overlap between rumination and worry suggests that exploring worry in the context of depression is important, but researchers have also suggested that worry may be important in our understanding of eating disorders, psychosis, and insomnia. As well as playing a role in the maintenance of particular psychological disorders, worry may also play a role in certain pathological processes, such as chronic pain. Finally, although worry doesn't play a central role in our understanding of neurodevelopmental conditions such as autism spectrum conditions (ASC) and attention deficit hyperactivity disorder (ADHD), exploring worry in these groups of children may aid our overall understanding of the development of worry and the role it plays in different individuals' distress.

This chapter starts by exploring the role of worry in different anxiety disorders, starting with GAD, but goes on to explore what role it may have in other psychological disorders and how it may differ for neurodiverse children.

GENERALISED ANXIETY DISORDER IN CHILDREN

To understand the current diagnosis of GAD and its relevance in childhood it is worth exploring its history. Prior to the *DSM IV* children did not usually get diagnosed with GAD; instead, children who had 'generalized and persistent anxiety or worry' (Spitzer, 1980) met criteria for a diagnosis of over-anxious disorder (OAD). Over-anxious disorder shared many criteria with GAD at that time, but had less focus on worry, and a broader base of possible symptoms such as reassurance seeking, competence concerns, as well as somatic complaints and marked feelings of tension. The problem with OAD as a diagnosis, however, was that it lacked specificity. It appeared that the variety of key symptoms and the reliance on judgements that they were unrealistic or marked or excessive meant that many children could meet criteria for the disorder. This led to criticisms that the diagnosis was rather meaningless and perhaps just represented anxiety in children in a general way. In *DSM III* criteria for OAD it was explicit that if children met diagnostic criteria for GAD, then they should be given that diagnosis, suggesting that there was some understanding that the two diagnoses were different. However, in the development of *DSM IV* the lack of specificity of the diagnosis of OAD became a problem. Researchers and clinicians clearly needed a diagnosis that got at the key aspects of OAD, namely anxiety and worry, but that had tighter criteria. GAD appeared to fit this bill. Indeed studies that tested the diagnosis of GAD in children found that the diagnostic criteria were more discriminating with greater specificity and sensitivity (Tracey et al., 1997). However, the move from OAD to GAD did subtly change the nature of the disorder, and thus the children who met criteria for it. With the focus on worry in conceptualisations of adult GAD it became more crucial to understand worry from a developmental perspective when children now were being diagnosed with this disorder. However, our understanding of worry, and therefore of childhood GAD, hardly progressed (Cartwright-Hatton, 2006). In adolescents it appeared that the cognitive-behavioural mechanisms involved in maintaining worry, and thus maintaining GAD symptoms, were very similar to those found in adults (see Chapter 4); however, the same could not be same about children. It may be that the differences seen between children and adolescents and adults may make the diagnosis of GAD somewhat meaningless in younger children, and re-consideration of the diagnosis of OAD may be warranted.

A number of lines of research help us develop this argument. Costello, Egger, and Angold have explored in detail the epidemiology of childhood psychological disorders, with a number of studies of childhood anxiety (2004). By using large epidemiological databases they have been able to explore the phenomenology, co-morbidity, and developmental outcomes of children with different anxiety disorder symptoms. These databases mostly span the time when the diagnosis was changed from OAD to GAD, but as they have records of individual symptoms it has been possible to go back and determine which children meet criteria for OAD, which meet criteria for OAD, and which meet criteria for both. First, it is notable that there is not a great deal of unique overlap between the two. Of the 67 children who met criteria for GAD and/or OAD but did not meet criteria for depression, only 12 met criteria for both disorders. Large percentages of children who met either OAD or GAD criteria also met criteria for depression, 34% and 42%, respectively, and 30 children out of 182 who met criteria for any one of these diagnoses (GAD, OAD, and depression) actually met criteria for all three. Second, and perhaps most important, however, are the developmental outcomes of these different sets of symptoms. Not only was the age of onset of GAD much younger than OAD, children who met criteria for OAD were at higher risk of later OAD, panic attacks, depression, and conduct disorder, whereas the children who met criteria for GAD were only at higher risk of conduct disorder (Bittner et al., 2007). This longitudinal, epidemiological approach suggests that at best GAD and OAD might describe distinct clusters of symptoms in children and that they might relate to different phenomenology. Clinically this fits with how children present with overwhelming anxiety. For some the anxiety appears to be mostly somatic, but almost anything can trigger it. In others there is clear evidence of worry and of cognitive biases and of significant behavioural avoidance as you would expect to see in adults with GAD. From the outside these can look similar with reports of feeling bad, seeking reassurance from family, and avoidance of friends or previously enjoyed activities.

> Shane is a twelve year old who has a diagnosis of GAD. Shane's parents report that he finds everything overwhelming. They report that even as a baby he reacted strongly to sounds, smells, strangers, being apart from them and new routines. As he got older these changed, but he always had a strong emotional reaction to the

particular stimuli that he is scared of. Shane gets comfort from being near his parents, and he prefers to be apart from others, especially if they are loud and unpredictable. Shane talks about being worried and scared, but doesn't recognise what is going on in his head when he gets anxious, he reports that he simply feels awful and needs to get away.

In contrast Susie, also 12 with a diagnosis of GAD, reports that her head is always full of thoughts. She doesn't react very much to things that scare her, but they stay with her and go round and round in her head. She thinks about all the things that might go wrong and this makes her feel bad. She talks to her parents about her worries, but this only works for a short time. When she is feeling very worried she avoids her friends because she feels she can't talk to them.

Research and clinical practice have long left behind the diagnosis of OAD in favour of GAD; however, the differences identified between these two diagnoses may help us to understand any specific effect worry has on our understanding of anxiety disorders in childhood. Indeed, identifying these interesting differences may encourage us to think transdiagnostically about individual symptoms, rather than focus solely on different diagnoses.

WORRY IN ANXIETY DISORDERS IN CHILDHOOD

In their work on epidemiology, Costello, Angold, and Egger differentiate between worry-based disorders, which they propose are related to functioning of the septohippocampus, conditioned fear disorders, such as specific phobias and trauma reactions, which are controlled by amygdala functioning, and unconditioned fear disorders, such as panic disorder and obsessive compulsive disorder, which have a biological pathway in the brainstem and hypothalamus. They suggest that the overlaps between different disorders, in terms of both diagnostic criteria and observed co-morbidity, may suggest that in childhood there may not be the proposed distinctions between different anxiety disorders. Weems (Weems, 2008; Weems & Stickle, 2005) goes further than this and proposes a model of continuity and change in anxiety disorder symptoms that explain the co-morbidity and the lack of homotypic continuity in anxiety disorders in childhood. Weems proposes that underlying all anxiety disorders is a maladaptive anxiety response that is dysregulated and leads to distress. He suggests that aspects of this dysregulated response represent core features of anxiety disorders and that the features that differentiate between different anxiety disorders are secondary features. Secondary features of anxiety disorders may map onto normal developmental fears, worries, and concerns (see Chapter 2) and therefore do not represent different disorders, but more likely different stimuli for the anxious response.

This can also be found when examining different models for different anxiety disorders. We have already seen that meta-cognitive processes and intolerance of uncertainty appear to be transdiagnostic processes across different anxiety disorders (see Chapter 4), and similarly, systemic factors such as parenting appear to influence the development of a wide variety of psychological disorders in childhood, including anxiety disorders (see Chapter 3). What is perhaps unique about Weems' proposal is the centrality of worry as a core feature of anxiety. Given what we saw in Chapter 2 about the cognitive skills needed to worry, and the age at which these individual skills develop, it makes sense that from a young age children can and do worry. However, we see differences in anxious responding in children before they can talk, and therefore if worry is a primary process, then we may need a radically different model of worry to understand this (see Chapter 6).

A few studies support this notion. Weems, Silverman, and La Greca (2000) interviewed a number of children with GAD/OAD and specific phobias, as well as children with no disorders. They found that the frequency and intensity of worry distinguished those with psychological disorders from those without, but it was much harder to find differences in worry between those with different anxiety disorders. There was some suggestion that the intensity of worry might distinguish those with anxiety disorders, from those children with other disorders, but this was not a strong effect. Reviewing the literature Wilson (2010) does suggest that it is the intensity of worry that distinguishes those with anxiety disorders from others. However, this begs the question, what does the intensity of worry consist of? And how is some worry more intense than others. Intensity is measured through self-report, where children are asked how bad their worry is. Thus the finding seems to mean that children who have worry that needs clinical help find their worry more 'bad'. There is still much research to be done to determine what physiological or psychological factors lead to us experiencing our worry as 'bad' worry. Perhaps it is the strength of the emotional or somatic response. It perhaps is how fearful we are of the stimuli that has prompted worry, or perhaps it is our own appraisals of worry (see Chapter 4 for studies on beliefs about worry).

When we look at studies that compare these appraisals in children with different anxiety disorders we also find that there are few differences. Hearn et al. (2017) explored differences between eight- and 12-year-old children with social anxiety disorder and GAD and children with no anxiety disorders on key variables associated with worry, including intolerance of uncertainty, negative and positive beliefs about worry, cognitive avoidance, and negative problem orientation. Although the children with anxiety disorders differed from the children without, there were no significant differences between those children with SAD and children with GAD.

It therefore appears that the diagnosis of GAD, which in adults is the diagnosis of worry, may not be as distinct from other anxiety disorders when we consider these diagnoses in children. Furthermore it may be very difficult to distinguish worry across different anxiety disorders in childhood. It appears that we may need different classification systems for younger children, and worry may be an important contender for a key psychological process underlying such a system.

WORRY IN DEPRESSION AND MOOD DISORDERS IN CHILDREN AND ADOLESCENTS

Whereas the mean age of onset of anxiety disorders is childhood (prior to age 12) for most anxiety disorders, the mean age of onset of depression is in adolescence (Lewinsohn, Clarke et al., 1994; Lewinsohn, Duncan et al., 1986). Thus studies of worry and depression are predominantly in adolescence.

Although there is interest in repetitive negative thinking in depression, the focus has typically been on rumination rather than worry. However, despite efforts to distinguish worry and rumination in the literature, it remains difficult to do so completely in people's experience. Rumination is typically considered to be repetitive thinking about the self, especially in the context of negative thoughts about the self (Smith & Alloy, 2009), whereas worry is repetitive negative thinking about possible future outcomes. Distinctions have also been made between normal and pathological rumination, sometimes expressed as brooding and reflection (Verstraeten et al., 2011). Brooding comprises a passive focus on symptoms and past failures, whereas reflection comprises an active focus on gaining insight into such problems. This distinction maps onto normal and pathological worry, where normal worry focuses the mind on solutions to problems, whereas pathological worry does not resolve the problem; rather it maintains it. What is clear from client reports of repetitive negative thinking is that people who are depressed both worry and ruminate and that each one can lead to the other. People who are anxious similarly worry and ruminate with an interaction between the two. Also, within Beck's hypothesised cognitive triad, negative thinking about the self, the future, and the world is key to all emotional disorders, and therefore it would be hypothesised that negative thinking about the future would be an important maintenance factor in depression.

Several studies have aimed to determine whether there is symptom specificity across worry and rumination, with worry predicting anxiety disorders and rumination predicting depression. This seems to be the case in young adults (students) (Calmes & Roberts, 2007; Hong, 2007) and some studies find this is also the case for younger populations (Muris et al., 2004; Verstraeten et al., 2011). Others do not find a differentiation (Young & Dietrich, 2015) or find that worry or rumination independently predict both anxiety and depression (Broeren et al., 2011). Therefore, there does appear to be a role for worry in understanding both the onset of depression in adolescents, but also in the experience of depression. Folk et al. (2014) found that in a sample of high-risk youth poor worry regulation predicted later anxiety symptoms, but poor coping with worry predicted later depression symptoms. Furthermore, Klemanski et al. (2017) recruited young people with single diagnoses of depression or anxiety disorders, and those with both. There were no differences in levels of worry between those young people with anxiety and those with depression. However, the mean level of worry of those with both disorders exceeded the mean levels of worry with only one of these difficulties.

If worry does indeed predict depression as well as anxiety, then this suggests it is an important transdiagnostic process. More than this, though, it suggests that limiting our clinical research in worry to children and young people with GAD will limit our understanding of worry as a process in itself.

WORRY IN PSYCHOSIS

Worry has relatively recently been proposed as an important process in psychosis. The role of anxiety in psychosis has a long history, but in 1999 Freeman and Garety determined that people with persecutory delusions had high levels of worry, comparable with people with anxiety disorders. Furthermore, adults who experienced delusions held similar beliefs about worry and control of thoughts to adults with anxiety disorders and that in their participants who experienced delusions, worry predicted delusional distress (Freeman & Garety, 1999). Following this surprising finding the same authors went on to find that 68% of people with persecutory delusions had worry levels similar to those found in adults with GAD and that worry predicted persistence of delusions over a three month period (Startup, Freeman, & Garety, 2007). With this increased evidence for a role for worry in understanding and helping people who experienced distressing delusions it made sense to develop an intervention to deal with this. Indeed, two randomised controlled trials have showed promising results for treating worry in the context of persecutory delusions (Foster et al., 2010; Freeman et al., 2015).

When we apply this understanding to younger populations we find that the research is truly in its infancy. A number of studies have confirmed a link between delusions and anxiety in adolescents (Galbraith et al., 2014; Ronald et al., 2014; Wong, Freeman, & Hughes, 2014), but only one study to date has explored worry in the context of young people with psychotic symptoms. Bird et al. (2017) followed up 33 young people who had presented to services with paranoid thoughts. A wide variety of psychological factors predicted the persistence of paranoia, but these included both anxiety symptoms and worry as measured by the Penn State Worry Questionnaire.

Therefore, it does seem like worry may be important in understanding the distress caused by certain psychotic symptoms. As these symptoms are very unusual in childhood, and usually start in adolescence, then in order to understand them further we must focus on worry in adolescence. By adolescence beliefs about worry, and beliefs about thinking more generally are well established (see Chapter 4) and thus further investigation of the processes involved in worry in young people with psychotic experiences is warranted.

WORRY IN EATING DISORDERS

Although there is a common perception that all girls are worried about their weight, shape, and how they look, in studies of adolescent worries, these often are quite far down the list, after worries about school, achievement, and careers, with those adolescents and young people at high risk also worrying about money (Brzezinski, Millar, & Tracey, 2018; Esters, 2003). Worries about shape and weight are crucial in understanding eating disorders, and increased social media contact might be increasing these kinds of worries (Sharpe et al., 2013), although the research is equivocal and mostly cross-sectional (Saiphoo & Vahedi, 2019). It is clear that concerns about shape, weight, and personal appearance are part of eating disorders, and may well precede them. The relationship between them is less clear.

Diagnosed eating disorders are more common in later adolescence compared to childhood and early adolescence, with full eating disorder diagnoses being very rare before the age of 13 (Smink, van Hoeken, & Hoek, 2012). Thus it is perhaps unsurprising that studies of anxiety and eating disorders suggest that anxiety disorders, which are often diagnosed before the age of 13, can be a risk factor for later eating disorders, but not the other way around (Bulik et al., 1997). When we focus in on worry, similar results are found. Worry has consistently been shown to be higher in young women with eating disorders (Sassaroli et al., 2005; Startup et al., 2013; Sternheim et al., 2012) and levels of worry also correlate with higher levels of eating disorder symptoms (Sala & Levinson, 2016; Sassaroli & Ruggiero, 2005). Few studies have explored these associations longitudinally, but in one study that did, Sala and Levinson (2016) found that worry did predict eating disorder symptoms over time but that this prospective association may be somewhat specific. In their study of 300 young women, worry predicted drive for thinness two and six months later, but not bulimia or body dissatisfaction. In addition, drive for thinness did not predict later worry. Just as in predictions of paranoia or delusions, there may be specific kinds of experiences, beliefs, and behaviours that worry does predict that are different to those anxiety, the more general phenomenon, predicts. Further exploration of these relationships may help us understand the role of worry within a wider context of distress.

To date no studies have explored relationships between worry and disordered eating in younger populations, but the emerging evidence about the specific relationships between worry and the development of eating disorders suggests that further understanding of worry in childhood and adolescence and how to help young people with problematic worry may well be able to prevent onset of eating disorders.

WORRY IN INSOMNIA

Worry has long been an important part of our understanding of insomnia. In Harvey's cognitive behavioural model of insomnia (Harvey, 2002), worry about sleep is the entry point to a set of cyclical processes that maintain wakefulness and distress. This has led to a specific intervention for insomnia – Cognitive Behaviour Therapy for Insomnia (CBT-I) – which has shown to be effective in a number of trials (see Koffel, Bramoweth, & Ulmer, 2018; van Straten et al., 2018, for meta-analyses). However, more recent work has questioned the type of negative thinking that is related to sleep quality. In a study of adults with insomnia, Carney et al. (2010) found that it wasn't worry, but rumination, that was related to sleep quality. This is in contrast to most research that has found that worry is related to sleep quality (e.g. McGowan, Behar, & Luhmann, 2016; O'Kearney & Pech, 2014). In the literature there appears to be a distinction made between worry about sleep and night-time worries, and general worry and daytime worries, with each of these playing a different role in insomnia. More general worry and worry during the day appear to be associated with subjective sleep quality, whereas night-time worries and worry about sleep itself appear to be associated with objective sleep measures, both in community samples (Lancee et al., 2017) and in people selected for being high in worry (Weise et al., 2013), or for having insomnia (O'Kearney & Pech, 2014). A number of studies have explored possible mediators or interactive factors in the relationship between sleep and worry. It appears that impaired sleep might impact the ability to focus attention, which then increases worry (Cox et al., 2018), and high worry might interact with dispositional factors, such as heart rate variability, to lead to poor sleep (MacNeil et al., 2017). It might also matter how study participants are chosen. In a study of 53 students selected for being high or low worriers McGowan, Behar, and Luhmann (2016) found that worry predicted sleep disturbance in the high trait worriers, but not the other way around, whereas Thielsch et al. (2015) found a bi-directional relationship between sleep quality and worry in 56 adults with diagnosed GAD. This suggests that the bi-directional relationship may develop over time. By exploring these associations in childhood we might be able to determine which is primary.

The association between worry and sleep is also robust for children and adolescents across the age range from pre-schoolers to late adolescents (Clementi & Alfano, 2014; Fletcher et al., 2018; Steinsbekk, Berg-Nielsen, & Wichstrøm, 2013). However, the direction of effect is not clear in the age groups too. Roberts and Duong (2017) found that sleep disturbance impacted on later anxiety in a longitudinal study of adolescents drawn from the community, and Alvaro, Roberts, and Harris (2014) in a similar population found that insomnia predicted GAD, but not the other way around. In contrast, Shanahan et al. (2014) used an epidemiological database to explore the relationships between sleep and anxiety disorders in children and adolescents (9–16 years) and found bi-directional relationships between GAD and sleep disturbance. Cross-sectional studies have explored possible psychological factors that might influence the relationship between anxiety and worry, with negative beliefs about sleep (Alfano et al., 2009), intolerance of uncertainty (Lin et al., 2017), and catastrophisation (Danielsson et al., 2013; Hiller et al., 2014) all playing a role in our understanding of how worry and sleep interact. Blake and colleagues (Blake, Trinder, & Allen, 2018) propose a bio-psycho-social model of the associations between anxiety, depression, and sleep in adolescence. In this model a number of factors that are specifically important in adolescence – such as biological changes in sleep architecture and mesolimbic dysregulation, the importance of social interaction (especially impaired social interaction), and the role of parents – interact with psychological factors, such as pre-sleep behaviours and cognitions, and executive dysfunction to produce significant overlaps between sleep dysfunction and internalising disorders. Although CBT for insomnia (CBT-I) does appear to be effective in adolescence (Blake et al., 2017), there are few high-quality studies, there is no standardised way of measuring sleep and there are very few studies that test durability using follow up assessments. Furthermore, there may be significant barriers to the implementation of insomnia interventions (Koffel, Bramoweth, & Ulmer, 2018), suggesting that further work on how interventions can target both anxiety and sleep disturbance are needed.

> Steph was a high achieving high school student. She did well at school, worked hard, had a few good friends, and a few hobbies she really enjoyed. She had been an anxious child in her early years, but had found that she could really concentrate well on her school work and this would distract her from any worries she had. The problem was Steph had started to sleep badly. Whenever she awoke in the night she would start to think about all the work she had to do at school, and would think about what might happen in the future if she didn't do well. If she caught herself thinking these kinds of thoughts she often then started worrying about her worry. She would think that it meant she would never get back to sleep, and that if she didn't sleep she would never be able to concentrate in school the next day. Steph often found her thoughts going round and round in her head until the early hours.

WORRY IN PAIN

Pain is another phenomenon of childhood and adolescence that is both normal and yet can become pathological. It has been estimated that up to 25% of children and adolescents experience chronic pain (Perquin et al., 2000; Stanford et al., 2008), with few of these children seeking or receiving help for it until it impacts severely on their everyday life (Gauntlett-Gilbert & Eccleston, 2007). Anxiety is known to be associated with pain in both younger (Simons, Sieberg, & Lewis Claar, 2012) and older populations (McWilliams, Cox, & Enns, 2003), and it may be one of the factors that leads to increased help-seeking. Co-morbid anxiety and pain are associated with poorer social and physical functioning in children (Cohen, Vowles, & Eccleston, 2010). What is less known is the specific role worry may play in determining these outcomes. Only a small number of studies have explored worry in childhood and adolescent pain. In a study of young people presenting with chronic pain, Simons, Sieberg, and Lewis Claar (2012) found elevated levels of worry in children and adolescents who experienced regular pain as measured by the Revised Children's Manifest Anxiety Scale (RCMAS), with high levels of worry being associated with pain-related disability. In a study of children in the community, Wurm et al. (2018) found that worry mediated the relationship between earlier peer-related stress and later musculo-skeletal pain. These quantitative studies suggest a role for worry in the development of pain and pain-related disability, but examination of the content and frequency of children's worries might show a different pattern. Fisher, Keogh, and Eccleston (2017), in a diary study of pain, found that older adolescents (16–18 year olds) who experienced chronic pain did not report more worries, and the content of the worries was largely similar for adolescents with and without pain.

Eccelston et al. (2012) have however proposed that there may be important aspects of the process of worry that mirror similar psychological mechanisms that can be found in pain. One major process that might be similar for worry and pain is catastrophisation. As described in Chapter 2 catastrophisation is one of the mechanisms by which normal worry becomes problematic worry. Catastrophisation is the process by which thinking about possible negative futures leads to thinking about the worst that can happen. In worry this leads to increased negative affect and the perseverance of worry. Pain catastrophisation is common in young people who experience chronic pain, and it is the process whereby pain and its consequences are appraised particularly negatively, and in an exaggerated way. Pain catastrophisation has been shown to be associated with greater pain severity (Crombez et al., 2003), anxiety, and depression (Eccleston et al., 2004), and pain-related disability (Vervoort et al., 2006); however, it isn't clear what processes might link worry catastrophisation and pain catastrophisation.

Heffernan et al. (2020) interviewed 12 adolescents with chronic pain aged 12–17 about their experience of worry and of pain. Worry was described as a ripple effect, starting small and permeating out to other worries and to physical experiences. In contrast the focus in pain was on uncertainty, both daily, as the young people didn't know how they would be affected day to day by their pain, and also longer term, where diagnoses and effective treatments were uncertain. Interestingly, pain catastrophising was only present in the accounts of the young people when specifically asked about, and there was no sense that the catastrophising that occurs within pain was associated with worry-related catastrophising.

In a parallel mixed methods study of worry and pain, we asked similar questions to 90 young people aged between 14 and 19 (Mullen et al., in preparation). Although there were few quantitative differences in young people's worry and anxiety, qualitative differences did emerge between young people who experienced chronic pain and those who didn't. The contents of worries were very similar, in that the focus was on social relationships, exam performance, and the health of themselves and family, but the worries of young people in chronic pain were subtly different, with these typical worries being linked to pain and chronic illness. With this larger sample, catastrophising, both of pain and of duration and intensity, and also about the origins of the pain was described more often. Again, uncertainty about origins of pain and about what each day is going to be like was prominent in the accounts of young people experiencing chronic pain.

It may be that worry and pain are linked through complex mechanisms involving bi-directional relationships. The research exploring the possible linking mechanism of catastrophisation has only recently been explored, and a further avenue, of intolerance of uncertainty, may also hold promise for a mechanism that links the two. What is clear however is that worry is an important phenomenon within young people who experience pain, as it leads to more negative outcomes. Therefore a better understanding of worry in childhood may well inform a better understanding of pain.

WORRY IN AUTISTIC SPECTRUM CONDITIONS

There has been increasing interest in the phenomenon of anxiety in autistic spectrum conditions (ASC), with some suggesting that anxiety might even constitute a diagnostic criterion for these conditions. It has been estimated that up to 40% of autistic children and adults have an anxiety disorder, with a significant proportion of these having more than one anxiety disorder (Hollocks et al., 2019; van Steensel, Bögels, & Perrin, 2011). It is unclear whether there are particular anxiety disorders that autistic people develop or whether it might be that anxiety in general is different.

A number of explanations have been proposed for this high level of anxiety in autistic people, including social difficulties leading to social anxiety (Russell & Sofronoff, 2005; Spain et al., 2018), sensory sensitivities leading to increased anxious arousal and fear (South & Rodgers, 2017), and the need for sameness leading to intolerance of uncertainty (Glod, Riby, & Rodgers, 2019; Hodgson et al., 2017). One thing that is interesting about this research is that although some of these factors, such as IU, have been proposed to be important in anxiety in neurotypical populations, some of them, such as sensory sensitivities, are widely overlooked.

There are therefore a number of reasons why worry might be particularly important in autistic people. First, anxiety disorders are more prevalent, and therefore it might be expected that worry is more prevalent. Second, unusual language development and unusual use of language are key features of ASC. Given that worry is defined to be largely verbal (words), rather than imaginal (pictures), it is reasonable to propose that worry might be different in people with ASC. Third, as IU has been proposed to be key in GAD, and GAD is considered to be a disorder of worry, the fact that IU is important also for understanding autistic people, it might be that worry and IU are associated in an interesting way for autistic people.

There are surprisingly few studies of worry in autistic people. Settipani et al. (2012) explored different anxiety disorder diagnoses and different anxious symptoms in a series of 100 children reporting to a University anxiety disorder clinic. Of the 100, 42 had elevated ASC symptoms (not diagnoses). Although there were very few significant differences in the prevalence of different anxiety disorders between the group with elevated ASC symptoms and those without, when symptoms were explored interpersonal worry was the best predictor of a child having elevated ASC symptoms, suggesting the importance not only of worry but specifically of interpersonal worry. In another study of ASC symptoms, Liew et al. (2015) explored pathways between ASC traits and high worry. They found that the best mediator between these two were indeed aversive sensory experiences in daily life: the outcome of sensory sensitivities.

Although these studies indicate that worry might be important in ASC, they did not recruit people with diagnosed ASC. Hare, Gracey, and Wood (2016) used an experience sampling technique with nine autistic adults and found that worrying thoughts were the most prevalent kind of thought these adults experienced, and these were more likely to occur in times of anxiety. Ozsivadjian, Knott, and Magiati (2012) interviewed parents of autistic children about their views of anxiety in their children. Parents did report that their children worried, but the main finding about verbal worries was the problems the children had reporting their worries and fears, sometimes due to poor verbal skills and sometimes due to poor ability to determine the source of the fear or worry.

Given that parents report that children struggle to verbalise worries, we thought it might be interesting to ask young people directly about their worries to see if they can verbalise them and reflect on them when asked to do so. We interviewed 27 autistic adolescents and 23 neurotypical adolescents about their experiences of worry and anxiety (Flynn & Wilson, submitted). Both groups were able to describe their worries, both in terms of the content of worries but also in terms of how they experienced worries. The common finding across both groups of adolescents was that they reported that worry was less intense than anxiety. Some autistic participants did experience worry and anxiety as different, with worry being related to repeated thoughts and anxiety being a bodily experience, whereas other participants did not experience them as different, except in intensity. One of the key differences was the extremity with which the most anxious adolescents experienced anxiety. The neurotypical adolescents with the most extreme anxiety reported severe anxiety experiences, whereas the autistic adolescents with the most extreme anxiety reported panic attacks, self-harm as a result of anxiety, and greater disability associated with the anxiety. Furthermore, they reported more physical sensations of anxiety, suggesting that sensory sensitivities and misinterpretation of bodily sensations might be key features that lead to greater anxiety levels.

WORRY IN ATTENTION DEFICIT HYPERACTIVITY DISORDER

Traditionally researchers and clinicians working with people with ADHD have been interested in co-morbid behavioural difficulties, such as conduct disorder and oppositional defiant disorder. This is warranted because ADHD is highly co-morbid with these kinds of difficulties (Jensen, Martin, & Cantwell, 1997; Reale et al., 2017). However, more recently there has been interest in anxiety in the context of ADHD. Co-morbidity of anxiety disorders and ADHD is significant (Shekim et al., 1990; Van Ameringen et al., 2011), leading Jensen and colleagues back in 1997 to call for two different diagnoses of attention: ADHD aggressive subtype and ADHD anxious subtype (Jensen, Martin, & Cantwell, 1997). Research suggests attention to this co-morbidity is warranted; young people with high levels of anxiety and ADHD symptoms have poorer social skills (Bishop et al., 2019), poorer executive functions (EF) (Sørensen et al., 2011), and poorer academic outcomes (Cuffe et al., 2015); they also respond worse to medication (Bedard & Tannock, 2008) and to Cognitive Behaviour Therapy (Halldorsdottir et al., 2015). Exploring this co-morbidity further suggests that worry might be a significant aspect of anxiety for both children and adults with ADHD. In a qualitative study of students with significant ADHD symptoms, one of the key factors they identified as a difficulty was worry (Kwon, Kim, & Kwak, 2018). This worry was about past events and current situations and was characterised by repeated thoughts rather than anxious responding. College students with ADHD also show higher worry about tests and test performance than their peers, despite similar actual performance (Lewandowski et al., 2013), and have more intrusive thoughts and more meta worries and social worries (Abramovitch & Schweiger, 2009).

Fewer studies have focused on children with ADHD, but those that have also suggest that worry is significant for these young people. Children with ADHD appear to have similar levels of intense worries compared to children with anxiety disorders (Perrin & Last, 1992). If we compare children with ADHD and ASC who are anxious we see an interesting pattern; the children with ADHD and anxiety have more severe worries compared to the children with ASC and anxiety. However, they also report less avoidance than these peers (Jang et al., 2013). It has been proposed that worry might be a significant problem for children with ADHD due to problems with inhibition. Children with ADHD also have difficulties with EF (Brown, Reichel, & Quinlan, 2009), particularly self-regulation (Shiels & Hawk, 2010; Wåhlstedt, Thorell, & Bohlin, 2008). These difficulties in self-regulation can be seen across cognitive and emotional domains (Biederman et al., 2012). There may be interesting relationships between EF, ADHD symptoms, and worry. We know that worry impairs working memory (Hirsch & Mathews, 2012), an important component of EF. We also know that young people with ADHD have impaired EF. It is therefore unsurprising that children with difficulties in both domains (attentional difficulties and anxiety) have poorer outcomes and perhaps it is more concerning that they respond worse to both medication and talking therapy. However, it appears that there are adaptations we can make to psychological therapies that improve outcomes for these children (Houghton et al., 2017), including involving parents (Maric, van Steensel, & Bögels, 2018).

Understanding worry in the context of ADHD may lead to better understanding of the role of cognitive development, especially the development of EF over time, in putting young people at risk of developing problems with worry, or exploring new avenues for intervention and prevention of the negative outcomes of worry in children with and without ADHD.

TREATMENT OF WORRY

Most interventions for worry have focused on the treatment of GAD in childhood or have incorporated work on worry into general CBT interventions for children with anxiety disorders. Understanding what works for worry in the context of childhood anxiety disorders may be important in determining whether these kinds of interventions could be helpful for other psychological disorders.

TREATMENT OF CHILDREN WITH GAD

Typically children's anxiety disorders have been treated with generic interventions that have been shown to be successful across a number of single cases, open trials, randomised trials, and meta-analyses. In the earliest randomised controlled trial of a psychological intervention for children with anxiety disorders, Kendall (1994) randomised 47 children into an intervention group and a control group. Sixty-four per cent of the 9–13 year olds had a primary diagnosis of OAD (see earlier discussion of the relationship between OAD and GAD), with the rest having separation anxiety disorder or avoidant disorder. The 16 session CBT intervention was successful with 64% of those receiving the intervention not meeting diagnostic criteria post treatment, compared with 5% of the wait list control group. This has been replicated several times, with a meta-analysis finding that for children without a diagnosis of ASC CBT impacts both on the primary anxiety disorder and on co-morbid anxiety disorders (Warwick et al., 2017). Single case designs have shown generic CBT for anxiety to be effective for children with GAD (Kolomeyer & Renk, 2016; Michael, Payne, & Albright, 2012; Whitton, Luiselli, & Donaldson, 2006), as have open trials (Eisen & Silverman, 1998; Waters, Donaldson, & Zimmer-Gembeck, 2008); however, there have been no randomised trials of generic CBT that recruit solely children with GAD (Oldham-Cooper & Loades, 2017). However, as the number of well conducted trials of CBT for children with anxiety disorders has increased it has been possible to explore whether children with specific diagnoses respond better or worse to therapy by combining data. Hudson et al. (2015a, 2015b) found that children with GAD responded better to a broad-based family CBT than children with social anxiety disorder, whereas Waters et al. (2017) found that, post-therapy, children with GAD and social anxiety disorder were doing worse than children with other anxiety disorders in a group CBT programme. However, by follow up only children with social anxiety disorder were doing worse. It could therefore be that children with GAD respond better to family interventions than to group interventions; however, this wasn't found by McKinnon et al. (2018). In this analysis of many sets of trial data they found that children with GAD responded equally well to individual, group, and parent-directed CBT.

Despite this evidence that many children with GAD do respond well to generic CBT, a number do not and there are also a number of children who drop out of therapy or do not find it acceptable. It has been questioned whether GAD-specific interventions may be necessary to meet the needs of children with GAD (Walczak et al., 2019). To date four open trials and two randomised trials and a case series have tested whether GAD-specific interventions are effective. Four of these have focused on Dugas' model of GAD and have incorporated work on uncertainty into the intervention. Payne, Bolton, and Perrin (2011) treated 16 children aged 7–17 years with an individual cognitive behavioural intervention focused on changing intolerance of uncertainty, based strongly on the adult intervention developed by Dugas and colleagues (Dugas & Robichaud, 2007). The intervention was highly successful with 81% children losing GAD diagnosis. In addition, 80% of the children with co-morbid disorders lost these as well. In a follow up randomised controlled trial of this, similar results were found, with none of the waiting list losing their GAD diagnosis during the treatment period, but 80% of those undertaking the intervention losing their GAD diagnosis (Perrin et al., 2019). A group version of this therapy was not quite so successful immediately after therapy, but the benefits continued to accrue in the follow up period (Holmes et al., 2014); 53% of children in the treatment condition did not meet diagnostic criteria post therapy, but this rose to 100% not meeting criteria at follow up. Again none of the children in the wait list control condition lost their diagnosis. In addition, 18% of children lost all their anxiety disorder diagnoses, with 50% losing them by follow up. Worry and quality of life improved more for the treatment group compared to the control group. Wahlund et al. (2019) extended these findings by offering an IU-based cognitive behavioural therapy to 12 children aged 13–17 years who presented with excessive worry either in the context of GAD or in the context of social anxiety disorder. The intervention was successful in reducing worry, anxiety, depression, and IU, and approximately 60% of the young people were rated as much or very much improved. However, the intervention did appear to impact more positively on young people with GAD than it did on young people with SAD.

It therefore appears that incorporating tolerance of uncertainty into therapy does lead to positive outcomes for children with GAD. Trials are clearly needed to determine whether this specific approach is more effective than generic CBT for anxiety, or whether it works better for some children, or whether it is more acceptable for some.

As seen earlier there are other models of adult GAD that have led to improvements in treatments for adults that may be applicable to working with children. Esbjørn and colleagues (Esbjørn et al., 2018; Esbjørn, Normann, & Reinholdt-Dunne, 2015) adapted Wells' meta-cognitive therapy (Wells, 2011) for 44 children aged 7–14 years. In this eight session group therapy children attended two-hour sessions for the eight weeks while the parents attended two workshops. Within the intervention there was attention training, detached mindfulness, and challenging of meta-cognitive beliefs. This approach also proved to be as effective as CBT (Walczak et al., 2019) with 86.4% children free of their GAD and 73% free of all anxiety disorders post-therapy, reducing slightly at follow up to 75% and 66%, respectively, in an open trial (Esbjørn et al., 2018). Meagher, Chessor, and Fogliati (2018) had slightly less success adapting the treatment based on the acceptance model of GAD for excessive worriers, with only small changes in worry and anxiety for the 11 children who took part in this eight week group therapy. However, these children were not diagnosed with anxiety disorders, and for half of the children the intervention incorporated a device to help with psychoeducation, making the interpretation of the overall results more complicated.

In a small, but promising, case series, Clementi and Alfano (2014) focused more on the behavioural aspects of therapy and included a sleep intervention given the overlap between anxiety and sleep problems (see earlier discussion). Of the four 7–12 year olds with GAD they treated two no longer met criteria for the diagnosis post-therapy, with the others not meeting diagnostic criteria at follow up.

These trials suggest that a targeted intervention can be highly effective for children with GAD and may work via a variety of mechanisms. All of these interventions, similarly to generic CBT, involve significant exposure to feared outcomes and children taking an active role in overcoming their fears and worries. They all involve working with a sympathetic and hopeful therapist, and they all involve parents being on board with the therapy. Further research is needed to determine which of these factors are important facilitators of change, and therefore how we can continue to develop our interventions to help more and more children.

TREATMENT OF WORRY

Only one intervention to date has focused on worry in young people and this intervention was targeted as a prevention programme, rather than an intervention for young people with pathological worry.

Topper et al. (2017a, 2017b) targeted young people aged 15–22 with high levels of repetitive negative thinking (RNT). They targeted worry in the intervention and looked at symptom self-report of repetitive negative thinking, anxiety, and depression following the intervention, as well as incidence of depression and GAD one year later. This worry-based intervention both decreased immediate levels of RNT, anxiety, and depression but also decreased the rates of depression and anxiety disorders one year later. This suggests that targeting worry may be effective for preventing certain kinds of psychological disorders from developing. It remains to be seen whether this could be valuable for younger children, but it is a very promising intervention.

CONCLUSIONS ABOUT WORRY ACROSS DIFFERENT PSYCHOLOGICAL DISORDERS

Worry does seem to be part of the experience in lots of psychological disorders, not just the anxiety disorders. This is true for both adults and children; however, as worry is something that starts early, it often seems to precede other symptoms. The entire literature is marked by a lack of longitudinal studies and therefore only a few studies have been able to show that worry precedes other psychological difficulties. It is likely that the temporal relationships between worry and other symptoms may be more complicated: worry could be one of the factors that accounts for distress about other symptoms of psychological problems; worry could increase arousal, exacerbating other symptoms such as bodily discomfort, pain, and hallucinations; worry could maintain attention on other symptoms; or worry may be a proxy for a general vulnerability for later difficulties, perhaps representing some temperamental factor. Further research is needed to understand better what role worry plays in preceding and maintaining distress in other psychological disorders. We also need to understand what is going on for those children high in worry who do and do not go on to show additional psychological difficulties.

Understanding these children may help us build resilience in those children who do go on to develop additional difficulties. Finally, we need to consider whether these relationships hold across diverse populations of children.

There is still a lot we don't know about how worry presents across different kinds of difficulties, but we would hypothesise that the content of worry would differ across different kinds of difficulties and disorders – worry about pain, worry about body image, worry about social evaluation, and so on – but that the processes involved may be similar. There are likely to be some distinctive features; IU could be important across anxiety and pain, uncontrollability or beliefs about uncontrollability plus positive beliefs for anxiety and depression, and catastrophising in insomnia. Understanding commonalities across these processes will help us determine how best to help highly worried children in different contexts. Given what we know about special features of group work (Yalom, 1985), if there are commonalities group work incorporating children with different kinds of difficulties and disorders may be particularly effective.

There are therefore significant implications for treatment; given that worry appears to negatively impact longer term outcomes in other kinds of psychological difficulties, if we are assessing these difficulties we might need to assess for worry and determine whether an intervention focusing on worry is acceptable, desirable, and effective (as it is for psychosis). Furthermore, better understanding the cognitive processes – such as attention, biases, and memory involved in childhood worry – would be important in working out whether there are ways we can target worry within prevention programmes/interventions.

In general, we probably need a lot more strategies for targeting worry specifically rather than anxiety generally, and avoidance in particular. Most interventions don't have a lot of strategies that help directly with worry; they target other aspects of the problem. We need to develop these or test strategies that should help with worry to see if they really do (Figure 5.1).

CHAPTER FIVE: WORRY AND PSYCHOLOGICAL DISORDERS

Figure 5.1 Children's worry in their own words.

CHAPTER SIX
A new developmental understanding of worry

CHAPTER SIX: DEVELOPMENTAL UNDERSTANDING OF WORRY

From the previous chapters there are a number of unresolved issues in our understanding of children's worry. Many of these will require further research before our understanding of them can progress, but others may progress by hypothesising a new understanding of worry in children that focuses on developmental processes. This chapter aims to bring together some of the key observations about the differences and similarities in worry across childhood, adolescence, and adulthood and to propose a new developmental understanding of children's worry that draws on developmental, clinical, and neuropsychological research.

KEY ISSUES

Chapter 1 reviews definitions of worry. Despite a wish that a developmentally appropriate understanding of worry would arise, this does not appear to have happened. Exploring key aspects that are core to our understanding of adult worry we do immediately see that worry in children is likely to be considerably different. In Chapter 1 we saw that the emotional experience of worry changes from childhood to adolescence, and in childhood, worry is associated with a range of emotional experience. Furthermore, worry is not experienced as primarily verbal, but is experienced as images and verbal thoughts, is experienced with significant affective response, and is intense and leads to avoidance, as would be expected from a fear response. This is not because children cannot distinguish between fear and worry, but rather because their experience of worry does not map onto the verbal process described in the adult literature. The content and function of worry also change developmentally over time to reflect the maturity of the cognitive and self-reflective processes, with the content of worries being related to everyday experiences and to the capacity for abstract thinking, and the function of worries being pretty stable from adolescence onwards, with perhaps a reduction in the social functions of worry as adults age.

In Chapter 2 we saw that the individual processes that are involved in our current understanding of worry, such as future thinking, iterative thought, and attentional control, are all present from early in life but that these continue to develop across childhood and adolescence into adulthood. However, their relationship with worry may change over time. As cognitive and language processes develop, the impact they have on worry and the impact worry has on them may reduce. When the connections between different brain areas are less developed, as we find in early childhood, the ability to worry at the same time as doing other things isn't strong, and cognition and attention will be affected by worry. Similarly, children who struggle with language and cognition may not develop verbal worry so early. As executive functions improve children may find it easier to both control worries and worry at the same time as performing other tasks. Worries may start to be over-rehearsed, taking less cognitive load than they do earlier in life. By tracking the trajectory of worry's development across childhood, we see that it appears to be an inevitable aspect of human cognition, with developmental jumps in both content and process of worry at ages that we see similar jumps in cognitive and language development.

Chapter 3 outlined the limited role of parents in the development of children's worry. It appears that although parents do play some role, this is limited and is likely to be part of more complex systems and processes. Parenting might play an indirect role in the development and maintenance of children's worry by impacting emotional regulation, and it might be different for mothers and fathers. As children become adolescents their need for autonomy might make them actively seek out differences to their parents and thus the relationships between the processes involved in worry might become less like their parents'. It might be that parents have a more subtle role in the development of worry, however, with the possibility of sensitive periods for parenting influencing children's worry, or for a role in the treatment of worry over time. It is also worth noting that many of the relationships between parent and child processes in worry are likely to be bi-directional, with worried children influencing their parents' parenting behaviours and cognitions, and parents influencing their children's worry.

Following on from the finding that parenting has a limited role in the development of children's worry, Chapter 4 outlined some key findings about processes going on within the children themselves. It appears that our models of problematic worry are quite appropriate from later adolescence into adulthood, but quite different things might be going on for children. Children are able to generate beliefs about worry, but these beliefs may be post-hoc reflections on worrying, rather than causal in the maintenance of worry. Intolerance of uncertainty, on the other hand, might be a primary temperamental factor that is a risk factor for later worry. Worry itself might be the primary process in anxiety disorders, especially GAD, with other cognitive biases and beliefs that we see in anxiety, a result of worry. Certain individual differences, such as cognitive and verbal ability, might differentiate those children who develop problems with worry and those who don't, but it may also be family or wider social contextual factors. Indeed, it is likely that problematic worry is multi-factorial in its causes, and that the factors involved interact with each other.

The idea that worry might be a primary process also arises from Chapter 5, where it is clear that for all kinds of psychological difficulties, worry is a precursor. Once other psychological difficulties have emerged, then there are likely bi-directional influences between worry and these other difficulties, but due to worry starting early, it can be seen as an important precursor. It may be a generic risk factor indicating other aspects of distress or vulnerability, or it may play specific roles due to its sticky cognitive nature.

THE DEVELOPMENTAL PROGRESSION OF WORRY FROM INFANCY TO ADOLESCENCE

Traditionally, worry has been seen to emerge at about the same time language does, primarily because of its definition as a verbal process. However, it may be that we can see the precursors of worry even earlier than this. Early worry is not separate from anxious affect; it may be that by later childhood this affect is less intense than a fear experience, but for younger children I propose that worry is experienced as intensely as fear. Indeed, the proposal is that it is extremely difficult to differentiate fear and worry as separable experiences in infants and very young children. However, different components of an anxious experience could usefully be called worry and fear. The fear component could map well onto the affective experience of fast heart beating, feeling hot, feeling tearful, and agitation. The worry component could map well onto the cognitive and anticipatory experience. We propose that for very young infants it is this anticipatory component that is the core of worry. Even with the startle response very early in life, we see individual differences. There is a behavioural and physiological response to a loud noise or unusual event, but there are also motor movements and orientation towards or away from the threat stimulus. If threat is not resolved, either through identification and neutralisation of the threat or through soothing by a caregiver, there is increasingly frantic searching for both the threat and something that can help. This iterative searching for the threat and for something that can help may be the very earliest manifestation of the verbal worry we see later in life. The search for something to help maps well onto the problem-solving function of worry that emerges in childhood and develops then across adolescence and adulthood. However, it has not been previously considered that one of the functions of worry is to identify the source of threat. If you explore the content of worry, however, it is possible to see examples of this. It overlaps with problem-solving attempts as it represents a problem to be solved, namely what am I worried for? However, it might be associated with different psychological processes in a different way to problem solving. For example, with intolerance of uncertainty problem solving is a way of thinking through what you might do in the face of threat, whereas in the context of intolerance of uncertainty, an uneasy feeling leads to worry as the child (or adult) attempts to resolve and remove the unwanted feeling by making sense of it. One way of doing this is to identify the source of the uneasy feeling and to judge whether or not it is a threat. Once someone has a history of worry, then the sense making in the presence of worry is more elaborate and more influenced by core beliefs set down in childhood, but in these very early years, this sense making may be simpler and may be about identifying a source for uncertain threat.

This proposed function of worry may be specific to children as it may represent a developmental period where children are not confident in their ability to judge situations and stimuli as threatening, and they are more scared and worried by things in their environment. The primacy of feeling in prompting worry may also help us understand uncontrollability of worry better by exploring the interplay between unconscious and conscious processes in a worry bout. This is explored further below.

This need to identify the source of the threat, as well as to problem solve what to do about it, may differentiate a phobic response from a worry response. In phobias there is an obvious stimulus that is responded to, but in worry-based disorders there often isn't such a stimulus. This can lead to particular frustrations for parents and clinicians as working with children's individual worries can feel very much like playing whack-a-mole; as soon as one worry is dealt with another pops its head up. Given that there does appear to be different neural pathways for phobic and worry-based disorders, this differentiation is warranted.

If we see this iterative searching for a threat in even young infants, how does this aspect of worry manifest in slightly older, preschool, children? Certain children, such as young children and those who struggle with language (autistic children, or those with language disorders or delays), may not be able to verbalise their worries. This may lead to increasing frustration and distress, but in the absence of an obvious stressor or threat this may look like a fear response, with proximity seeking, tears, and agitation. What may differentiate the two at this age is that this response may not be attached to a specific stimulus. How parents deal with this behaviour might impact on whether young children learn that threats are manageable and they can deal with them or whether they learn that threats are unpredictable and that they can't deal with them. Sensitive, attuned parents may help children with a predisposition to worry or attention to threat to down regulate this reaction over time, whereas parents who cannot do this may have children who go on to develop ongoing worry.

However, this is not to over-emphasise the role of parents in this process. We know that children react very differently to threat from birth; the startle response shows significant individual differences and predicts later outcomes. It could be that some children have a predisposition for searching for the source of threat and that other children have a predisposition for searching for comfort. This may map onto the different types of attachment, with children who search for comfort looking like securely attached infants and those who search for the source of threat looking like insecurely avoidant infants.

As children's language develops, perhaps into the early school years, then worry might start to look more like our adult definitions of worry. However, this may take some time. As language develops worry will emerge, but at this stage it is likely to be not exclusively verbal and may be accompanied by intense emotion. It may be undifferentiable in experience from the emotional experience and from the urge to escape or avoid. What differentiates this from fear is whether or not the stimulus is evident.

The changes now will probably be slow and map onto developments in the relevant areas of the brain. As the pre-frontal cortex develops across childhood and adolescence, the ability to reflect on one's own perceptual experiences and thought processes will develop. From this, beliefs about worry will start to form. Similarly, as networks of brain areas form and there are developing connections between fear areas, such as the amygdala, and thinking areas, such as the pre-frontal cortex, the experience of worry will become more differentiated as a thinking process, divorced from intense emotion.

By adolescence many of the key processes involved in adult worry will be present; however, there may still be some developmental differences. The content of worry at this stage can take on more abstract forms, and with this the capacity to think more vaguely about the future will emerge. This may lead to early forms of perseverative worry. The lack of concrete content for worry brings back the idea of searching for the source of threat, combined with the iterative problem solving we see in adults. Certain aspects of adolescence, such as the emotional volatility, and the sensitivity to social stimuli can lead to certain worry-prone individuals having a significant increase in worry. There are more experiences of emotion, and for those individuals who are intolerant of uncertainty or intolerant of their physical sensations, there will be mental efforts to resolve the feeling. If these are not successful, perhaps because there is no threat to be detected, or perhaps because efforts to problem solve are not considered to be good enough, then there will be increased worry. It is likely that it is at this developmental stage that this sense-making process will involve general sense making, rather than the specific searching for threat. Furthermore, worry will become almost exclusively social. By this stage the social brain is well developed, and perhaps hyper-responsive, and processes such as social comparison and identification can lead to the negative emotion that prompts worry.

One process that is likely to start in later childhood, and continue through adolescence, is children learning to attribute their unease to certain stimuli, rather than others. This could be because certain stimuli prompt the feeling to begin with; perhaps the child always feels bad when mum isn't around as she provides the comfort needed to resolve the feeling, or perhaps the child always feels bad when they have to perform in front of classmates. For some children it will not be the stimuli itself that determines the attribution but the child's prior learning. Once the child starts to identify a source for their unease and is able to resolve the feeling, then they are more likely to continue to identify that source for their unease; their main attribution is reinforced and therefore is more likely to be available in future instances. For the worry disorders, this kind of differentiation might determine which kinds of anxiety disorders they meet diagnostic criteria for.

THE DEVELOPMENT OF PROBLEMATIC FEATURES OF WORRY

Seeing worry as a primary, inevitable, response to a negative emotional feeling in the absence of an obvious threat also leads to hypotheses about different aspects of problematic worry. Worry in children appears to be problematic when it is intense and uncontrollable, features that are also seen in problematic worry in adults. Above we hypothesised that intensity was due to a combination of the emotional reaction and beliefs about worry, making the worry feel really 'bad'. In this new model of children's worry it is the children who have more frequent and more negative emotional experiences in the absence of an obvious threat that have more worry. Therefore, it makes some sense that for these children the worry also feels more intense. Not being able to resolve the threat, either by making sense of it or by being comforted, means it goes on for longer and that the negative emotion is likely to increase the longer the threat goes unresolved. Intensity might well be different for different children, but this process of being more uncomfortable with negative feelings, having them more often, and having them persist for longer may be important components of it.

The other aspect of worry that is a feature of problematic worry is uncontrollability. Several clinical models of worry suggest that worry *is* controllable and propose instead that people simply *perceive* it to be uncontrollable. By putting the emotional reaction at the centre of worry one may find an alternative explanation. Bringing the emotional state into consciousness is one way the body draws attention to the need for conscious processing of the situation. Conscious processing is very resource heavy, and so many decisions and processes go on in the background, without us ever becoming conscious of them. However, in a threat situation we may need to consciously process our environment. This is in contrast to an obvious threat, where the adrenaline reaction takes over and does not require conscious thought; quite the opposite, it requires an immediate fight or flight reaction. In the presence of a non-obvious threat, or with a smaller emotional reaction, conscious processing may need to come on line to resolve the situation. Thus, trying to resolve the emotion is a primary human need. However, as we have seen earlier, there may be several barriers to resolving the emotion and these may serve to paradoxically prolong the emotional response. One of the problems with worry, however, is that it becomes over-rehearsed. Through several processes – including it becoming vague and abstract, it becoming word rather than image-focused, and through it becoming over-rehearsed – the emotional response is dampened. The proposal here is that worry feels uncontrollable because the resolving of the threat switches between conscious and unconscious processing. The emotion forces us to process the situation consciously, but worry processes dampen the emotion without resolving the threat, allowing the process to go back into a non-conscious domain. However, the threat remains unresolved, and therefore the emotion brings it back into the conscious domain. This popping back into consciousness after a sensation of resolving the threat, due to reducing the emotional response, is experienced as uncontrollability, as indeed it is. Strategies that have traditionally been used to demonstrate the controllability of worry bypass this system to bring the attentional system on-line in a conscious way, thus actually resolving the threat, rather than the usual worry process, where the threat isn't resolved.

Given that this flip flopping of worry between conscious and unconscious processing requires worry to be either over-rehearsed or verbal in nature, or for it to become abstract, we would expect that the uncontrollability of worry may only become an issue for older children and adolescents. For younger children how 'bad' the worry feels is likely to be a better indicator of problematic worry, and indeed this maps onto differences between diagnoses of GAD and OAD.

SUMMARY OF A NEW DEVELOPMENTAL UNDERSTANDING OF WORRY

In summary, by examining worry in its earliest forms, we propose that it is prompted by a sense of unease or low-level anxiety, which is not associated with an obvious negative stimulus. This feeling prompts the need for resolving it, or making sense of it, and worry is the outcome of this process when it is not easily resolved or made sense of. Across development, the increase in ability in introspection means that the process of resolving or making sense moves from one of comfort seeking or seeking the source of the threat, which may act at an unconscious level, through verbal sense making about possible threats, through to worry that looks like adult worry, with a focus on verbal content, abstract or vague content, and with a possibility of catastrophising.

Some people may be more prone to develop problematic worry through their temperamental style that is intolerant of uncertainty or through the strength of their natural emotional response leading to more frequent situations where an emotional response requires making sense of. Others may be more prone to develop it through their emotions being denied or rejected and their ability to resolve emotions through self-soothing being thwarted, leading to poor ability to resolve the threat. Some may experience a great deal of uncertain threat in their environment. There are likely several pathways to experiencing more worry and worry that persists. Some of the factors that maintain worry – certain beliefs about worry, attentional processes, the interaction between mood and perseveration – can be seen as a result of the worry process itself. Beliefs about worry are part of the process of making sense of threat and then of worry itself. Attentional processes can be viewed as natural responses to regular experiences of worry, with learning going wrong when paying attention to certain things dampens the emotion, and therefore is reinforced. The interaction between mood and perseveration can be seen as the brain's continued message that a threat has to be consciously processed until the emotion resolves.

Viewing worry as a natural response to an emotional stimulus in the absence of obvious threat may also help us explain the feeling of uncontrollability of worry, as there is a flip flop between the conscious processing of threat, prompted by emotion, and then the unconscious processing of threat, when the natural processes involved in problematic worry dampen the emotional response and cause the threat to go out of the conscious processing realm.

IMPLICATIONS OF THIS NEW UNDERSTANDING OF WORRY

DEVELOPMENTAL IMPLICATIONS

The main implication of this new understanding of worry is that we are likely to be able to identify the worry process, or the precursor to it, very early in life. It may not be differentiable from other aspects of anxiety in the experience of it but exploring the response to uncertain threat in infants may help us understand what factors really do pose a risk for later worry-based disorders. The second major implication of this new understanding is that worry is an inevitable part of the human condition and that its development across childhood and adolescence should map easily onto development of relevant brain areas, such as the pre-frontal cortex and the communication between this and the amygdala. Identifying children with difficulties in these areas, either through developmental conditions or through brain injury, provides unique possibilities for exploring the links between worry and brain development that may provide insights that can help us understand worry later in life. The third implication is that some of the processes that are crucial in understanding the maintenance of problematic worry that have been largely developed for work with adults may not be as relevant for younger children. These processes are likely to develop as a result of experiencing worry. However, these processes may also lead to worry becoming more entrenched over time. Therefore, while these processes are still developing other factors may be more important in determining whether worry is a significant problem to a child, and interventions may need to target these different factors (see clinical implications).

CLINICAL IMPLICATIONS

The clinical implications of this new understanding are also threefold: there are implications for identification of difficulties in childhood and the diagnoses that might go with them, there are implications for understanding worry in the context of other disorders and psychological difficulties, and there are implications for the treatment of worry.

Identification of anxiety disorders in childhood

This new understanding of worry builds on existing work that suggests that the fine-grained differences between different anxiety disorders might not be very relevant for younger children. As suggested by Weems and Egger, Angold, and Costello, it might be that useful distinctions can be made between fear-based disorders and worry-based disorders. In this new understanding of worry, the key difference is the presence of the threat; in the presence of threat we are dealing with a fear response, and in the absence of threat, or in the presence of uncertain threat, we are dealing with a worry response. The processes involved in these two kinds of difficulties are likely to be different, although overlapping – many children with fear-based disorders will become sensitive to threat and develop worry about uncertain possible futures. Tracking how children make sense of their emotional reactions to uncertain or non-present threat may also throw further light on how anxiety disorders do differentiate into adolescence and on into adulthood. It is possible that over-anxious disorder was indeed a good diagnostic category, and the lack of specificity is not a disadvantage but a true reflection of the experience of young children who have fewer ways of making sense of their emotional experience, and who are less in control of their environment, compared to older children and adults.

The role of worry in understanding other psychological difficulties

This new understanding of worry proposes that it is an inevitable result of the human condition. This need to make sense of our experiences is human, and processing information at conscious and unconscious levels means we are forced to take notice of our emotional states. Early problematic worry might indicate that the individual is particularly vulnerable to emotional states. This might be vulnerability to experiencing these emotional states frequently, or to experiencing them more intensely than other people, or experiencing them in response to more stimuli. One proposal arising from this new understanding is that the presence of worry prior to other psychological kinds of distress – such as rumination and depression, delusions, unexplained pain, or poor sleep – is simply due to the fact that threat is one of the first stimuli we respond to. Also, threat requires resolving. In contrast, sadness, also an early emotion, does not necessarily require making sense of, or resolving in the same way threat does. In all these other psychological difficulties there is a threat: whether it is a threat to the social self, a threat to the body, or an existential threat. Therefore as worry represents the sense-making process in the presence of uncertain threat, it is unsurprising that it is a key factor in these other difficulties. We see in a number of these kinds of difficulties that threat is either unresolved, for example, in unexplained pain, or that it is resolved in a complicated way that may not reflect the nature of the original threat, for example in delusions. Dealing with the core problem of experiencing a threat response in the absence of an obvious threat and feeling that it must be made sense of, or resolved in some way, may be important in the treatment of all these psychological difficulties. As suggested earlier, different processes involved in problematic worry – such as intolerance of uncertainty, experiential and cognitive avoidance, and beliefs about worry – may differentially impact on these different types of psychological difficulties, and further research is warranted to develop our understanding of the interplay of different processes and worry across childhood into adulthood.

Treatment of worry in children

We are very fortunate in that we already have a number of treatments for worry that work well for worried children across the age range. Generic CBT is likely as effective for worry-based disorders as it is for fear-based disorders. It is robust in that it appears to work when done individually with children, when done with families, and when done via parents. Targeting key processes in problematic worry such as intolerance of uncertainty also appears to show great promise in the development of alternative interventions for children with diagnoses of GAD, and thus they are likely to be useful and effective for children with problematic worry, no matter what the child's diagnosis is.

A new developmental understanding of worry may enhance the treatment of worry in a couple of ways. Given we already have effective treatments for worried children, understanding worry as a natural response to uncertain threat might help us identify the effective ingredients of these interventions. Second, this new understanding might help us develop new interventions that might be helpful for those children, and perhaps adults, who are not being helped by our current interventions.

This current understanding of worry suggests that different interventions might be effective at different times. Young children, who have not got the cognitive capacity to resolve threat themselves, may require the threat to be resolved for them. This might involve soothing the child so that the emotion that stimulated the search for threat is removed. It might involve structuring the child's exploration of threat, perhaps naming threats in a containing way, for example 'It's OK. That was just the door banging'. Some of this is similar to early parent-child interventions that have been evaluated in parents who themselves are at risk of mental health difficulties or are experiencing post-natal depression.

As the child's cognitive capacity to try and make sense of the threat increases, resolving this may involve helping them develop confidence that they both have identified a source of threat and that they have the capacity to evaluate the threat and also to develop confidence in their own abilities to deal with threat, no matter where it comes from or whether it is evident or not. It is likely that many cognitive behavioural programmes do just this.

At this stage it might also be worth considering targeted interventions/ prevention programmes for those children who appear to be developing problematic aspects of worry. These problematic aspects may include the development of strong beliefs about the utility of worry or about how dangerous and uncontrollable worry is. Developing targeted interventions may involve identifying children with poor attentional processes, whereby once the emotional response has prompted a search for meaning it is difficult to disengage from, or may involve identifying those children for whom the emotional response is so difficult to tolerate (for whatever reason) that they are developing experiential or cognitive avoidance.

Once a young person reaches adolescence, then our well-established interventions for adult GAD may be effective in the presence of problematic worry in any context, for example, in young people presenting with depression, or eating disorders, or pain, or delusions. However, in this age period, it will be crucial to consider the brain development that is occurring. It may be that in standard interventions for GAD and worry in adolescence, incorporating a greater focus on social evaluation will be useful. Interventions at this age may incorporate work on more inter-personal factors and it may be important to acknowledge that some of the processes maintaining worry may not yet be very entrenched and some of the CBT techniques that are helpful for younger children may also be valuable. In addition, emerging new adaptations to CBT that incorporate attentional processes explicitly might be particularly helpful for this age group as their attentional processes mature. Some of these interventions help people with uncontrollable worry to focus on the present moment, or the present threat, and resist trying to make sense of the threat, as this often prompts initiation of perseverative worry. It may be that during adolescence, the focus moves from resolving the threat to staying with the threat emotion without overly attending to it or interpreting it negatively. Many of the third wave behavioural therapies aim to change our relationship with our internal experiences without directly challenging them. It appears there may be potential for these to be further developed to help young people with problematic worry.

SYSTEMIC AND WIDER SYSTEM IMPLICATIONS

Although it is unlikely that parents are central to our understanding of the early development of worry, they do appear to have a role to play. For those infants who are easily startled, or who are not easily soothed, perhaps for those infants who do not like uncertainty or the uncontrollability of their environment, a parent who is sensitively attuned to the infant and who can soothe them may well help the infant to develop healthy responses to emotional experience. In the context of an infant who has a vulnerability to this kind of responding being parented by a parent who is unable for whatever reason to respond to their infant's distress in this way, it is likely that the infant will be very vulnerable to later difficulties with worry. This may be particularly the case if the infant is affected by uncertain threat more than direct threat. In some environments, there may be a combination of both certain and uncertain threat, leading to increased risk for both fear- and worry-based psychological disorders.

During childhood, a parent who can help the child make sense of their world, including their emotional world, is likely to reduce the vulnerability that child shows of developing difficulties with worry. Finally, during adolescence, a parent who can encourage their adolescent to tolerate emotion and uncertainty and can reassure them that worry is neither great nor the end of the world will also likely have an adolescent who worries less.

The interactions between the child's cognitive processes, their emotional reactions, their social and academic world, and their experience of their parents are complex, and the development of problematic worry is multi-factorial. Different factors interact with each other adding to the complexity. It is unfair to place the burden of halting the development of problematic worry on parents, but for those parents who might want pointers as to what they can do, in the context of themselves feeling helpless, these factors, and this understanding of worry, may be helpful.

WHERE NEXT? SETTING A RESEARCH AGENDA FOR CHILDREN'S WORRY

A number of researchers have suggested that the lack of a developmental understanding of worry has limited our research agenda. There is certainly interest in the topic of children's worry, with clinicians, developmental scientists, and neuroscientists all developing new understandings, but there is a need to bring these strands together. The proposed new definition of worry is that it is an attempt to make sense of an anxious emotional response that is prompted by uncertain threat. This sense making may include searching for the source of threat, problem solving possible future threats, and meaning making of both the emotional response and also the possible outcomes that are generated. The lack of resolution of the threat leads to the iterative nature of worry, and several of the maintaining factors are inevitable responses to experiencing worry. The current adult models of pathological worry are likely to be relevant from adolescence onwards and exploring the development of these in younger populations is likely to be productive. Also, because we have effective interventions for young people with pathological worry there is no need to rush to develop new interventions but exploring how our current interventions work and integrating the proposed new understanding might lead to improvements across the age range.

Therefore, in setting a research agenda there are a number of strands to be outlined. The first strand is to test this new understanding. We are in desperate need of further phenomenological studies of children's worry. These ideally will include both qualitative and quantitative phenomenological studies. These could test some of the hypotheses about the different experience of worry across childhood and adolescence. They could also shed light on the hypothesis that worry is a sense-making response and that this sense making may include searching for the source of threat. In addition, studies directly exploring responses to uncertain threat may utilise experimental designs, both to test differences in children's responses to certain and uncertain threat, and to test different kinds of response to uncertain threat.

Because of the difficulties accessing children's inner worlds, much of this research will benefit from a neuropsychological perspective. Tracking responses to uncertain threat using brain scanning methodologies will allow us to explore both conscious and unconscious processes and the relationships between the two. These methods may also throw light on the experience of uncontrollability in worry.

As well as testing the new understanding of children's worry, the synthesis of the existing literature also points to some crucial research directions. It is notable that very little of the research has focused on children with problematic worry or anxiety disorders. The assumption underlying our studies of anxiety and worry suggests that it exists on several continua, including severity, impact, frequency, and distress. However, it may be that threshold models are relevant for some anxiety disorders, whereby certain processes change at the threshold for problematic anxiety or worry to be considered a disorder. Positive beliefs about worry may be one of these processes. At normal levels of worry positive beliefs may simply act in the background to worry and are accessible if consciously asked about, but they do not impact worry, and at problematic levels of worry they may act to prompt conscious worry in the context of uncertain threat, increasing frequency and activating negative beliefs about worry.

As well as exploring worry in the context of anxiety disorders, it is clear that worry is relevant across a wide range of psychological disorders. The proposal needs testing that the focus of worry in all of these disorders is uncertain threat, but in addition, further exploration of worry in the context of other disorders is warranted. In particular, examination of what aspects of worry and the worry process are important in other psychological disorders may help us target specific worry interventions at relevant young people.

CONCLUSIONS

Worry is both a normal phenomenon and the focus of several psychological disorders. In children it is influenced by cognitive, emotional, language, and social development, which can also be seen in development of the structure and connectedness of a variety of brain areas. Children are embedded in a number of systems that influence their worry, and, in turn, these systems are influenced by their worry. By viewing worry as a response to uncertain threat we may be able to reconsider the earliest developmental manifestations of worry and understand better how the mechanisms that lead to the maintenance of problematic worry develop over time. Worry may be an inevitable part of life for conscious thinking beings, but problematic worry that interferes with living does not need to be. Our interventions work well for many worried children and it is hoped that by taking a clinical-developmental approach we can improve these even further.

BIBLIOGRAPHY

Abramovitch, A., & Schweiger, A. (2009). Unwanted intrusive and worrisome thoughts in adults with attention deficit\hyperactivity disorder. *Psychiatry Research, 168*(3), 230–233. https://doi.org/10.1016/j.psychres.2008.06.004

Affrunti, N. W., & Woodruff-Borden, J. (2016). Negative affect and child internalizing symptoms: The mediating role of perfectionism. *Child Psychiatry & Human Development, 47*(3), 358–368. https://doi.org/10.1007/s10578-015-0571-x

Alfano, C. A., Zakem, A. H., Costa, N. M., Taylor, L. K., & Weems, C. F. (2009). Sleep problems and their relation to cognitive factors, anxiety, and depressive symptoms in children and adolescents. *Depression and Anxiety, 26*(6), 503–512. https://doi.org/10.1002/da.20443

Allmann, A. E. (2018). *The bidirectional relationship between parenting practices and child symptoms of ADHD, ODD, depression, and anxiety.* (Unpublished dissertation). State University of New York; Stony Brook, New York.

Alvaro, P. K., Roberts, R. M., & Harris, J. K. (2014). The independent relationships between insomnia, depression, subtypes of anxiety, and chronotype during adolescence. *Sleep Medicine, 15*(8), 934–941. https://doi.org/10.1016/j.sleep.2014.03.019

American Psychiatric Association. (2013). *Diagnostic and statistical manual of mental disorders—DSM-5* (5th ed.). Arlington, VA: American Psychiatric Association Publishing.

Angelino, H., & Shedd, C. L. (1953). Shifts in the content of fears and worries relative to chronological age. *Proceedings of the Oklahoma Academy of Science, 34*, 180–186.

Astington, J., & Hughes, C. (2013). Theory of mind: Self-reflection and social understanding. In P. D. Zelazo (Ed.), *The Oxford handbook of developmental psychology, Vol. 2: Self and other* (pp. 398–423). Oxford, UK: Oxford University Press.

Atance, C. M., & Meltzoff, A. N. (2005). My future self: Young children's ability to anticipate and explain future states. *Cognitive Development, 20*(3), 341–361. https://doi.org/10.1016/j.cogdev.2005.05.001

Atance, C. M., & Meltzoff, A. N. (2006). Preschoolers' current desires warp their choices for the future. *Psychological Science, 17*(7), 583–587. https://doi.org/10.1111/j.1467-9280.2006.01748.x

Atance, C. M., & O'Neill, D. K. (2005a). Preschoolers' talk about future situations. *First Language, 25*(1), 5–18. https://doi.org/10.1177/0142723705045678

Atance, C. M., & O'Neill, D. K. (2005b). The emergence of episodic future thinking in humans. *Learning and Motivation, 36*(2), 126–144. https://doi.org/10.1016/j.lmot.2005.02.003

Bacow, T. L., Pincus, D. B., Ehrenreich, J. T., & Brody, L. R. (2009). The metacognitions questionnaire for children: Development and validation in a clinical sample of children and adolescents with anxiety disorders. *Journal of Anxiety Disorders, 23*(6), 727–736. https://doi.org/10.1016/j.janxdis.2009.02.013

Bandura, A. (1969). Social-learning theory of identificatory processes. In D. A. Goslin (Ed.), *Handbook of socialization theory and research* (pp. 213–262). Chicago: Rand McNally.

Bandura, A. (2001). Social cognitive theory: An agentic perspective. *Annual Review of Psychology, 52*, 1–26. https://doi.org/10.1146/annurev.psych.52.1.1

Barahmand, U. (2008). Age and gender differences in adolescent worry. *Personality and Individual Differences, 45*(8), 778–783. https://doi.org/10.1016/j.paid.2008.08.006

Bar-Haim, Y., Lamy, D., Pergamin, L., Bakermans-Kranenburg, M. J., & van IJzendoorn, M. H. (2007). Threat-related attentional bias in anxious and nonanxious individuals: A meta-analytic study. *Psychological Bulletin, 133*(1), 1–24. https://doi.org/10.1037/0033-2909.133.1.1

Barker, T. V., Reeb-Sutherland, B. C., & Fox, N. A. (2014). Individual differences in fear potentiated startle in behaviorally inhibited children: Individual differences in potentiated startle. *Developmental Psychobiology, 56*(1), 133–141. https://doi.org/10.1002/dev.21096

Barrett, H., & Wilson, C. (2019). *The development of episodic foresight in 4–6 year olds: Methodological issues and the role of verbal and cognitive ability*. Psychological Society of Ireland Annual Conference, Kilkenny.

Barrett, P. M. (1998). Evaluation of cognitive-behavioral group treatments for childhood anxiety disorders. *Journal of Clinical Child Psychology, 27*(4), 459–468. https://doi.org/10.1207/s15374424jccp2704_10

Barrett, P. M., Dadds, M. R., & Rapee, R. M. (1996). Family treatment of childhood anxiety: A controlled trial. *Journal of Consulting and Clinical Psychology, 64*(2), 333–342. https://doi.org/10.1037/0022-006X.64.2.333

Barrett, P. M., Duffy, A. L., Dadds, M. R., & Rapee, R. M. (2001). Cognitive-behavioral treatment of anxiety disorders in children: Long-term (6-year) follow-up. *Journal of Consulting and Clinical Psychology, 69*(1), 135–141. https://doi.org/10.1037/0022-006X.69.1.135

Barrett, P. M., Rapee, R. M., Dadds, M. M., & Ryan, S. M. (1996). Family enhancement of cognitive style in anxious and aggressive children. *Journal of Abnormal Child Psychology, 24*(2), 187–203. https://doi.org/10.1007/BF01441484

Beck, A. T., Brown, G., & Steer, R. T. A. (1988). An inventory for measuring clinical anxiety: Psychometric properties. *Journal of Consulting and Clinical Psychology, 56*, 893–897. https://doi: 10.1037//0022-006x.56.6.893

Beck, S. R., Weisberg, D. P., Burns, P., & Riggs, K. J. (2014). Conditional reasoning and emotional experience: A review of the development of counterfactual thinking. *Studia Logica, 102*(4), 673–689. https://doi.org/10.1007/s11225-013-9508-1

Bedard, A.-C., & Tannock, R. (2008). Anxiety, methylphenidate response, and working memory in children with ADHD. *Journal of Attention Disorders, 11*(5), 546–557. https://doi.org/10.1177/1087054707311213

Behar, E., DiMarco, I. D., Hekler, E. B., Mohlman, J., & Staples, A. M. (2009). Current theoretical models of generalized anxiety disorder (GAD): Conceptual review and treatment implications. *Journal of Anxiety Disorders, 23*(8), 1011–1023. https://doi.org/10.1016/j.janxdis.2009.07.006

Behar, E., Zuellig, A. R., & Borkovec, T. D. (2005). Thought and imaginal activity during worry and trauma recall. *Behavior Therapy, 36*(2), 157–168. https://doi.org/10.1016/S0005-7894(05)80064-4

Beidel, D. C., & Turner, S. M. (1997). At risk for anxiety: I. Psychopathology in the offspring of anxious parents. *Journal of the American Academy of Child & Adolescent Psychiatry, 36*(7), 918–924. https://doi.org/10.1097/00004583-199707000-00013

Belsky, J., Steinberg, L., & Draper, P. (1991). Childhood experience, interpersonal development, and reproductive strategy: An evolutionary theory of socialization. *Child Development, 62*(4), 647–670. https://doi: 10.1111/j.1467-8624.1991.tb01558.x

Bender, P. K., Reinholdt-Dunne, M. L., Esbjørn, B. H., & Pons, F. (2012). Emotion dysregulation and anxiety in children and adolescents: Gender differences. *Personality and Individual Differences, 53*(3), 284–288. https://doi.org/10.1016/j.paid.2012.03.027

Benoit Allen, K., Silk, J. S., Meller, S., Tan, P. Z., Ladouceur, C. D., Sheeber, L. B., Forbes, E. E., Dahl, R. E., Siegle, G. J., McMakin, D. L., & Ryan, N. D. (2016). Parental autonomy granting and child perceived control: Effects on the everyday emotional experience of anxious youth. *Journal of Child Psychology and Psychiatry, 57*(7), 835–842. https://doi.org/10.1111/jcpp.12482

Biederman, J., Spencer, T. J., Petty, C., Hyder, L. L., O'Connor, K. B., Surman, C. B., & Faraone, S. V. (2012). Longitudinal course of deficient emotional self-regulation CBCL profile in youth with ADHD: Prospective controlled study. *Neuropsychiatric Disease and Treatment, 8,* 267–276. https://doi.org/10.2147/NDT.S29670

Bird, J. C., Waite, F., Rowsell, E., Fergusson, E. C., & Freeman, D. (2017). Cognitive, affective, and social factors maintaining paranoia in adolescents with mental health problems: A longitudinal study. *Psychiatry Research, 257,* 34–39. https://doi.org/10.1016/j.psychres.2017.07.023

Birmaher, B., Khetarpal, S., Brent, D., Cully, M., Balach, L., Kaufman, J., & Neer, S. M. (1997). The screen for child anxiety related emotional disorders (SCARED): Scale construction and psychometric characteristics. *Journal of the American Academy of Child and Adolescent Psychiatry, 36*(4), 545–553. https://doi.org/10.1097/00004583-199704000-00018

Bishop, C., Mulraney, M., Rinehart, N., & Sciberras, E. (2019). An examination of the association between anxiety and social functioning in youth with ADHD: A systematic review. *Psychiatry Research, 273,* 402–421. https://doi.org/10.1016/j.psychres.2019.01.039

Bittner, A., Egger, H. L., Erkanli, A., Costello, J. E., Foley, D. L., & Angold, A. (2007). What do childhood anxiety disorders predict? *Journal of Child Psychology and Psychiatry, 48*(12), 1174–1183. https://doi.org/10.1111/j.1469-7610.2007.01812.x

Blake, M. J., Sheeber, L. B., Youssef, G. J., Raniti, M. B., & Allen, N. B. (2017). Systematic review and meta-analysis of adolescent cognitive–behavioral sleep interventions. *Clinical Child and Family Psychology Review, 20*(3), 227–249. https://doi.org/10.1007/s10567-017-0234-5

Blake, M. J., Trinder, J. A., & Allen, N. B. (2018). Mechanisms underlying the association between insomnia, anxiety, and depression in adolescence: Implications for behavioral sleep interventions. *Clinical Psychology Review, 63,* 25–40. https://doi.org/10.1016/j.cpr.2018.05.006

Blakemore, S.-J. (2008). The social brain in adolescence. *Nature Reviews Neuroscience, 9*(4), 267–277. https://doi: 10.1038/nrn2353

Blakemore, S.-J. (2018). *Inventing ourselves: The secret life of the teenage brain.* London: Penguin, Random House.

Bodden, D. H. M., Bögels, S. M., Nauta, M. H., De Haan, E., Ringrose, J., Appelboom, C., Brinkman, A. G., & Appelboom-Geerts, K. C. M. M. J. (2008). Child versus family cognitive-behavioral therapy in clinically anxious youth: An efficacy and partial effectiveness study. *Journal of the American Academy of Child & Adolescent Psychiatry, 47*(12), 1384–1394. https://doi.org/10.1097/CHI.0b013e318189148e

Boehnke, K., Stromberg, C., Regmi, M. P., Richmond, B. O., & Chandra, S. (1998). Reflecting the world "out there": A cross-cultural perspective on worries, values and well-being. *Journal of Social and Clinical Psychology, 17*(2), 227–247. https://doi.org/10.1521/jscp.1998.17.2.227

Bögels, S., & Phares, V. (2008). Fathers' role in the etiology, prevention and treatment of child anxiety: A review and new model. *Clinical Psychology Review, 28*(4), 539–558. https://doi.org/10.1016/j.cpr.2007.07.011

Bomyea, J., Ramsawh, H., Ball, T. M., Taylor, C. T., Paulus, M. P., Lang, A. J., & Stein, M. B. (2015). Intolerance of uncertainty as a mediator of reductions in worry in a cognitive behavioral treatment program for generalized anxiety disorder. *Journal of Anxiety Disorders, 33*, 90–94. https://doi.org/10.1016/j.janxdis.2015.05.004

Borgogna, N. C., McDermott, R. C., Berry, A., Lathan, E. C., & Gonzales, J. (2020). A multicultural examination of experiential avoidance: AAQ – II measurement comparisons across Asian American, Black, Latinx, Middle Eastern, and White college students. *Journal of Contextual Behavioral Science, 16*, 1–8. https://doi.org/10.1016/j.jcbs.2020.01.011

Borkovec, T. D. (1994). The nature, functions, and origins of worry. In G. C. L. Davey, & F. Tallis (Eds.), *Worrying: Perspectives on theory, assessment and treatment* (pp. 5–33). New York: John Wiley & Sons.

Borkovec, T. D., Hazlett-Stevens, H., & Diaz, M. L. (1999). The role of positive beliefs about worry in generalized anxiety disorder and its treatment. *Clinical Psychology & Psychotherapy: An International Journal of Theory & Practice, 6*(2), 126–138.

Borkovec, T. D., & Inz, J. (1990). The nature of worry in generalized anxiety disorder: A predominance of thought activity. *Behaviour Research and Therapy, 28*(2), 153–158. https://doi.org/10.1016/0005-7967(90)90027-G

Borkovec, T. D., Robinson, E., Pruzinsky, T., & DePree, J. A. (1983). Preliminary exploration of worry: Some characteristics and processes. *Behaviour Research and Therapy*, *21*(1), 9–16. https://doi.org/10.1016/0005-7967(83)90121-3

Borkovec, T. D., & Roemer, L. (1995). Perceived functions of worry among generalized anxiety disorder subjects: Distraction from more emotionally distressing topics? *Journal of Behavior Therapy and Experimental Psychiatry*, *26*(1), 25–30. https://doi.org/10.1016/0005-7916(94)00064-S

Bosquet, M., & Egeland, B. R. (2006). The development and maintenance of anxiety symptoms from infancy through adolescence in a longitudinal sample. *Development and Psychopathology*, *18*(2), 517–550. https://doi.org/10.1017/S0954579406060275

Bottesi, G., Ghisi, M., Carraro, E., Barclay, N., Payne, R., & Freeston, M. H. (2016). Revising the intolerance of uncertainty model of generalized anxiety disorder: Evidence from UK and Italian undergraduate samples. *Frontiers in Psychology*, *7*. https://10.3389/fpsyg.2016.01723

Bowlby, J. (1969). *Attachment* (2nd ed., Vol. 1). New York: Basic Books.

Breinholst, S., Esbjørn, B. H., & Reinholdt-Dunne, M. L. (2015). Effects of attachment and rearing behavior on anxiety in normal developing youth: A mediational study. *Personality and Individual Differences*, *81*, 155–161. https://doi.org/10.1016/j.paid.2014.08.022

Breinholst, S., Esbjørn, B. H., Reinholdt-Dunne, M. L., & Stallard, P. (2012). CBT for the treatment of child anxiety disorders: A review of why parental involvement has not enhanced outcomes. *Journal of Anxiety Disorders*, *26*(3), 416–424. https://10.1016/j.janxdis.2011.12.014

Breinholst, S., Tolstrup, M., & Esbjørn, B. H. (2019). The direct and indirect effect of attachment insecurity and negative parental behavior on anxiety in clinically anxious children: It's down to dad. *Child and Adolescent Mental Health*, *24*(1), 44–50. https://doi.org/10.1111/camh.12269

Broeren, S., Muris, P., Bouwmeester, S., van der Heijden, K. B., & Abee, A. (2011). The role of repetitive negative thoughts in the vulnerability for emotional problems in non-clinical children. *Journal of Child and Family Studies*, *20*(2), 135–148. https://doi.org/10.1007/s10826-010-9380-9

Brown, A. M., & Whiteside, S. P. (2008). Relations among perceived parental rearing behaviors, attachment style, and worry in anxious children. *Journal of Anxiety Disorders*, *22*(2), 263–272. https://doi.org/10.1016/j.janxdis.2007.02.002

Brown, S. L., Teufel, J. A., Birch, D. A., & Kancherla, V. (2006). Gender, age, and behavior differences in early adolescent worry. *Journal of School Health, 76*(8), 430–437. https://doi.org/10.1111/j.1746-1561.2006.00137.x

Brown, T. E., Reichel, P. C., & Quinlan, D. M. (2009). Executive function impairments in high IQ adults with ADHD. *Journal of Attention Disorders, 13*(2), 161–167. https://doi.org/10.1177/1087054708326113

Brzezinski, S., Millar, R., & Tracey, A. (2018). What do tertiary level students in the U.S.A. and Northern Ireland (UK) worry about? An exploratory study. *British Journal of Guidance & Counselling, 46*(4), 402–417. https://doi.org/10.1080/03069885.2017.1286634

Buhr, K., & Dugas, M. J. (2002). The intolerance of uncertainty scale: Psychometric properties of the English version. *Behaviour Research and Therapy, 40*(8), 931–945. https://doi.org/10.1016/S0005-7967(01)00092-4

Bulik, C. M., Sullivan, P. F., Fear, J. I., & Joyce, P. R. (1997). Eating disorders and antecedent anxiety disorders: A controlled study. *Acta Psychiatrica Scandinavica, 96*(2), 101–107. https://doi.org/10.1111/j.1600-0447.1997.tb09913.x

Burns, R., & Wilson, C. (2016). *Thought suppression in children*. British Psychological Society, Developmental Psychology Section, Belfast.

Buschgens, C. J. M., Van Aken, M. A. G., Swinkels, S. H. N., Ormel, J., Verhulst, F. C., & Buitelaar, J. K. (2010). Externalizing behaviors in preadolescents: Familial risk to externalizing behaviors and perceived parenting styles. *European Child & Adolescent Psychiatry, 19*(7), 567–575. https://doi.org/10.1007/s00787-009-0086-8

Caes, L., Fisher, E., Clinch, J., Tobias, J. H., & Eccleston, C. (2016). The development of worry throughout childhood: Avon longitudinal study of parents and children data. *British Journal of Health Psychology, 21*(2), 389–406. https://doi.org/10.1111/bjhp.12174

Calmes, C. A., & Roberts, J. E. (2007). Repetitive thought and emotional distress: Rumination and worry as prospective predictors of depressive and anxious symptomatology. *Cognitive Therapy and Research, 31*(3), 343–356. https://doi.org/10.1007/s10608-006-9026-9

Campbell, M. A., Rapee, R. M., & Spence, S. H. (2001). Developmental changes in the interpretation of rating format on a questionnaire measure of worry. *Clinical Psychologist, 5*(2), 49–59. https://doi.org/10.1080/13284200108521078

Caplan, M., Weissberg, R. P., Bersoff, D., Ezekowitz, W., & Well, M. L. (1986). *The middle school alternative solutions test (AST) scoring manual*. New Haven: Unpublished manuscript, Yale University, Psychology Department.

Carleton, R. N. (2016). Into the unknown: A review and synthesis of contemporary models involving uncertainty. *Journal of Anxiety Disorders, 39*, 30–43. https://doi.org/10.1016/j.janxdis.2016.02.007

Carney, C. E., Harris, A. L., Moss, T. G., & Edinger, J. D. (2010). Distinguishing rumination from worry in clinical insomnia. *Behaviour Research and Therapy, 48*(6), 540–546. https://doi.org/10.1016/j.brat.2010.03.004

Carthy, T., Horesh, N., Apter, A., & Gross, J. J. (2010a). Patterns of emotional reactivity and regulation in children with anxiety disorders. *Journal of Psychopathology and Behavioral Assessment, 32*(1), 23–36. https://doi.org/10.1007/s10862-009-9167-8

Carthy, T., Horesh, N., Apter, A., Edge, M. D., & Gross, J. J. (2010b). Emotional reactivity and cognitive regulation in anxious children. *Behaviour Research and Therapy, 48*(5), 384–393. https://doi.org/10.1016/j.brat.2009.12.013

Cartwright-Hatton, S. (2006). Worry in childhood and adolescence. In G. C. L. Davey, & A. Wells (Eds.), *Worry and its psychological disorders: Theory, assessment and treatment* (pp. 81–97). Chichester: John Wiley & Sons Ltd. https://doi.org/10.1002/9780470713143.ch6

Cartwright-Hatton, S., Mather, A., Illingworth, V., Brocki, J., Harrington, R., & Wells, A. (2004). Development and preliminary validation of the meta-cognitions questionnaire—adolescent version. *Journal of Anxiety Disorders, 18*(3), 411–422. https://doi.org/10.1016/S0887-6185(02)00294-3

Cartwright-Hatton, S., McNally, D., Field, A. P., Rust, S., Laskey, B., Dixon, C., Gallagher, B., Harrington, R., Miller, C., Pemberton, K., Symes, W., White, C., & Woodham, A. (2011). A new parenting-based group intervention for young anxious children: Results of a randomized controlled trial. *Journal of the American Academy of Child & Adolescent Psychiatry, 50*(3), 242–251.e6. https://doi.org/10.1016/j.jaac.2010.12.015

Cartwright-Hatton, S., & Wells, A. (1997). Beliefs about worry and intrusions: The meta-cognitions questionnaire and its correlates. *Journal of Anxiety Disorders, 11* (3), 279–296. https://doi:10.1016/s0887-6185(97)00011-x.

Cassidy, J. (1995). Attachment and generalized anxiety disorder. In D. Cicchetti & S. L. Toth (Eds.), *Emotion, cognition, and representation* (pp. 343–370). Rochester: University of Rochester Press.

Cassidy, J., Lichtenstein-Phelps, J., Sibrava, N. J., Thomas Jr., C. L., & Borkovec, T. D. (2009). Generalized anxiety disorder: Connections with self-reported attachment. *Behavior Therapy, 40*(1), 23–38. https://doi: 10.1016/j.beth.2007.12.004

Castro, J., Toro, J., Van der Ende, J., & Arrindell, W. A. (1993). Exploring the feasibility of assessing perceived parental rearing styles in Spanish children with

The EMBU. *International Journal of Social Psychiatry*, *39*(1), 47–57. https://doi.org/10.1177/002076409303900105

Chorpita, B. F., Tracey, S. A., Brown, T. A., Collica, T. J., & Barlow, D. H. (1997). Assessment of worry in children and adolescents: An adaptation of the Penn State Worry Questionnaire. *Behaviour Research and Therapy*, *35*(6), 569–581. https://doi.org/10.1016/S0005-7967(96)00116-7

Clauss, J. A., & Blackford, J. U. (2012). Behavioral inhibition and risk for developing social anxiety disorder: A meta-analytic study. *Journal of the American Academy of Child & Adolescent Psychiatry*, *51*(10), 1066–1075.

Clefberg Liberman, L., & Öst, L.-G. (2016). The relation between fears and anxiety in children with specific phobia and parental fears and anxiety. *Journal of Child and Family Studies*, *25*(2), 598–606. https://doi.org/10.1007/s10826-015-0222-7

Clementi, M. A., & Alfano, C. A. (2014). Targeted behavioral therapy for childhood generalized anxiety disorder: A time-series analysis of changes in anxiety and sleep. *Journal of Anxiety Disorders*, *28*(2), 215–222. https://doi.org/10.1016/j.janxdis.2013.10.006

Cobham, V. E., Dadds, M. R., & Spence, S. H. (1998). The role of parental anxiety in the treatment of childhood anxiety. *Journal of Consulting and Clinical Psychology*, *66*(6), 893–905. https://doi.org/10.1037/0022-006X.66.6.893

Cobham, V. E., Dadds, M. R., Spence, S. H., & McDermott, B. (2010). Parental anxiety in the treatment of childhood anxiety: A different story three years later. *Journal of Clinical Child & Adolescent Psychology*, *39*(3), 410–420. https://doi.org/10.1080/15374411003691719

Cobham, V. E., Filus, A., & Sanders, M. R. (2017). Working with parents to treat anxiety-disordered children: A proof of concept RCT evaluating fear-less triple P. *Behaviour Research and Therapy*, *95*, 128–138. https://doi.org/10.1016/j.brat.2017.06.004

Cohen, L. L., Vowles, K. E., & Eccleston, C. (2010). The impact of adolescent chronic pain on functioning: Disentangling the complex role of anxiety. *The Journal of Pain*, *11*(11), 1039–1046. https://doi.org/10.1016/j.jpain.2009.09.009

Coll, C. G., Kagan, J., & Reznick, J. S. (1984). Behavioral inhibition in young children. *Child Development*, *55*(3), 1005–1019. https://doi.org/10.2307/1130152

Colonnesi, C., Draijer, E. M., Jan J. M. Stams, G., Van der Bruggen, C. O., Bögels, S. M., & Noom, M. J. (2011). The relation between insecure attachment and child anxiety: A meta-analytic review. *Journal of Clinical Child & Adolescent Psychology*, *40*(4), 630–645. https://doi.org/10.1080/15374416.2011.581623

Cooper, P. J., Gallop, C., Willetts, L., & Creswell, C. (2008). Treatment response in child anxiety is differentially related to the form of maternal anxiety disorder. *Behavioural and Cognitive Psychotherapy, 36*(1), 41–48. https://doi.org/10.1017/S1352465807003943

Cooper, S. E., Miranda, R., & Mennin, D. S. (2013). Behavioral indicators of emotional avoidance and subsequent worry in generalized anxiety disorder and depression. *Journal of Experimental Psychopathology, 4*(5), 566–583. https://doi.org/10.5127/jep.033512

Costello, E. J., Egger, H. L., & Angold, A. (2004). Epidemiology of anxiety disorders. In T. H. Ollendick, & J. S. March (Eds.) *Phobic and anxiety disorders in children and adolescents: A clinician's guide to effective psychosocial and pharmacological interventions* (pp. 61–91). Oxford: Oxford University Press. https://doi.org/10.1093/med:psych/9780195135947.003.0003

Cox, R. C., Cole, D. A., Kramer, E. L., & Olatunji, B. O. (2018). Prospective associations between sleep disturbance and repetitive negative thinking: The mediating roles of focusing and shifting attentional control. *Behavior Therapy, 49*(1), 21–31. https://doi.org/10.1016/j.beth.2017.08.007

Creswell, C., Apetroaia, A., Murray, L., & Cooper, P. (2013). Cognitive, affective, and behavioral characteristics of mothers with anxiety disorders in the context of child anxiety disorder. *Journal of Abnormal Psychology, 122* (1), 26–38. https://doi.org/10.1037/a0029516

Creswell, C., & Cartwright-Hatton, S. (2007). Family treatment of child anxiety: Outcomes, limitations and future directions. *Clinical Child and Family Psychology Review, 10*(3), 232–252. https://doi.org/10.1007/s10567-007-0019-3

Creswell, C., & O'Connor, T. G. (2006). "Anxious cognitions" in children: An exploration of associations and mediators. *British Journal of Developmental Psychology, 24*(4), 761–766. https://doi.org/10.1348/026151005X70418

Crick, N. R., & Dodge, K. A. (1994). A review and reformulation of social information-processing mechanisms in children's social adjustment. *Psychological Bulletin, 115*(1), 74–101. https://doi.org/10.1037/0033-2909.115.1.74

Crick, N. R., & Dodge, K. A. (1996). Social information-processing mechanisms in reactive and proactive aggression. *Child Development, 67*(3), 993–1002. https://doi.org/10.2307/1131875

Crombez, G., Bijttebier, P., Eccleston, C., Mascagni, T., Mertens, G., Goubert, L., & Verstraeten, K. (2003). The child version of the pain catastrophizing scale (PCS-C): A preliminary validation. *Pain, 104*(3), 639–646. https://doi.org/10.1016/s0304-3959(03)00121-0

Crosby Budinger, M., Drazdowski, T. K., & Ginsburg, G. S. (2013). Anxiety-promoting parenting behaviors: A comparison of anxious parents with and without social anxiety disorder. *Child Psychiatry & Human Development*, 44(3), 412–418. https://doi.org/10.1007/s10578-012-0335-9

Cuffe, S. P., Visser, S. N., Holbrook, J. R., Danielson, M. L., Geryk, L. L., Wolraich, M. L., & McKeown, R. E. (2015). ADHD and psychiatric comorbidity: Functional outcomes in a school-based sample of children. *Journal of Attention Disorders*, 1087054715613437. https://doi.org/10.1177/1087054715613437

D'Zurilla, T. J., & Goldfried, M. R. (1971). Problem solving and behavior modification. *Behavior Therapy*, 78(1), 107–126. https://doi.org/10.1037/h0031360

Dai, L., Zhou, Y., Yin, M., Wang, X., & Deng, Y. (2019). Preliminary examination of the measurement invariance of the metacognition about health questionnaire: A study on Chinese and British nursing students. *Current Psychology*. https://doi.org/10.1007/s12144-019-00517-1

Daleiden, E. L., & Vasey, M. W. (1997). An information-processing perspective on childhood anxiety. *Clinical Psychology Review*, 17(4), 407–429. https://doi.org/10.1016/s0272-7358(97)00010-x

Danielsson, N. S., Harvey, A. G., MacDonald, S., Jansson-Fröjmark, M., & Linton, S. J. (2013). Sleep disturbance and depressive symptoms in adolescence: The role of catastrophic worry. *Journal of Youth and Adolescence*, 42(8), 1223–1233. https://doi.org/10.1007/s10964-012-9811-6

Davey, G. C. L. (1994a). Pathological worrying as exacerbated problem-solving. In G. C. L. Davey, & F. Tallis (Eds.), *Worrying: Perspectives on theory, assessment and treatment* (pp. 35–59). New York: John Wiley & Sons.

Davey, G. C. L. (1994b). Worrying, social problem-solving abilities, and social problem-solving confidence. *Behaviour Research and Therapy*, 32(3), 327–330. https://doi.org/10.1016/0005-7967(94)90130-9

Davey, G. C. L. (2006). The catastrophising interview procedure. In G. C. L. Davey, & A. Wells (Eds.), *Worry and its psychological disorders: Theory, assessment and treatment* (pp. 157–176). Chichester: John Wiley & Sons Ltd. https://doi.org/10.1002/9780470713143.ch10

de Rosnay, M., Cooper, P. J., Tsigaras, N., & Murray, L. (2006). Transmission of social anxiety from mother to infant: An experimental study using a social referencing paradigm. *Behaviour Research and Therapy*, 44(8), 1165–1175. https://doi.org/10.1016/j.brat.2005.09.003

Derakshan, N., & Eysenck, M. W. (2009). Anxiety, processing efficiency, and cognitive performance: New developments from attentional control theory.

European Psychologist, *14*(2), 168–176. https://doi.org/10.1027/1016-9040.14.2.168

Diamond, A. (2013). Executive functions. *Annual Review of Psychology*, *64*(1), 135–168. https://doi.org/10.1146/annurev-psych-113011-143750

DiBonaventura, M., Toghanian, S., Järbrink, K., & Locklear, J. (2014). Economic and humanistic burden of illness in generalized anxiety disorder: An analysis of patient survey data in Europe. *ClinicoEconomics and Outcomes Research*, 151. https://doi.org/10.2147/CEOR.S55429

Dodge, K. A., & Crick, N. (1990). Social information-processing bases of aggressive behavior in children. *Personality and Social Psychology Bulletin*, *16*(1), 8–22. https://doi.org/10.1177/0146167290161002

Donovan, C. L., Holmes, M. C., & Farrell, L. J. (2016). Investigation of the cognitive variables associated with worry in children with generalised anxiety disorder and their parents. *Journal of Affective Disorders*, *192*, 1–7. https://doi.org/10.1016/j.jad.2015.12.003

Donovan, C. L., Holmes, M. C., Farrell, L. J., & Hearn, C. S. (2017). Thinking about worry: Investigation of the cognitive components of worry in children. *Journal of Affective Disorders*, *208*, 230–237. https://doi.10.1016/j.jad.2016.09.061

Drake, K. L., & Ginsburg, G. S. (2011). Parenting practices of anxious and nonanxious mothers: A multi-method, multi-informant approach. *Child & Family Behavior Therapy*, *33*(4), 299–321. https://doi.org/10.1080/07317107.2011.623101

Dudeney, J., Sharpe, L., & Hunt, C. (2015). Attentional bias towards threatening stimuli in children with anxiety: A meta-analysis. *Clinical Psychology Review*, *40*, 66–75. https://doi.org/10.1016/j.cpr.2015.05.007

Dugas, M. J., & Ladouceur, R. (2000). Targeting intolerance of uncertainty in two types of worry. *Behavioral Modification, 24* (5), 635–657.

Dugas, M. J., Ladouceur, R., Léger, E., Freeston, M. H., Langolis, F., Provencher, M. D., & Boisvert, J.-M. (2003). Group cognitive-behavioral therapy for generalized anxiety disorder: Treatment outcome and long-term follow-up. *Journal of Consulting and Clinical Psychology*, *71*(4), 821–825. https://doi.org/10.1037/0022-006X.71.4.821

Dugas, M. J., Laugesen, N., & Bukowski, W. M. (2012). Intolerance of uncertainty, fear of anxiety, and adolescent worry. *Journal of Abnormal Child Psychology*, *40*(6), 863–870. https://doi.org/10.1007/s10802-012-9611-1

Dugas, M. J., Marchand, A., & Ladouceur, R. (2005). Further validation of a cognitive-behavioral model of generalized anxiety disorder: Diagnostic and symptom specificity. *Journal of Anxiety Disorders*, *19*(3), 329–343. https://doi.org/10.1016/j.janxdis.2004.02.002

Dugas, M. J., & Robichaud, M. (2007). *Cognitive behavioral therapy for generalized anxiety disorder: From science to practice.* New York: Routledge.

Dugas, M. J., Savard, P., Gaudet, A., Turcotte, J., Laugesen, N., Robichaud, M., Francis, K., & Koerner, N. (2007). Can the components of a cognitive model predict the severity of generalized anxiety disorder? *Behavior Therapy, 38*(2), 169–178. https://doi.org/10.1016/j.beth.2006.07.002

Dumontheil, I. (2014). Development of abstract thinking during childhood and adolescence: The role of rostrolateral prefrontal cortex. *Developmental Cognitive Neuroscience, 10,* 57–76. https://doi.org/10.1016/j.dcn.2014.07.009

Dunn, J. (1988). *The beginnings of social understanding.* Cambridge, MA: Harvard University Press.

Dunn, L. M., & Dunn, D. M. (2009). *The British picture vocabulary scale.* London: GL Assessment Limited

Eccleston, C., Crombez, G., Scotford, A., Clinch, J., & Connell, H. (2004). Adolescent chronic pain: Patterns and predictors of emotional distress in adolescents with chronic pain and their parents. *PAIN, 108*(3), 221. https://doi.org/10.1016/j.pain.2003.11.008

Eccleston, C., Fisher, E. A., Vervoort, T., & Crombez, G. (2012). Worry and catastrophizing about pain in youth: A reappraisal. *Pain, 153*(8), 1560–1562. https://doi.org/10.1016/j.pain.2012.02.039

Eisen, A. R., & Silverman, W. K. (1998). Prescriptive treatment for generalized anxiety disorder in children. *Behavior Therapy, 29*(1), 105–121. https://doi.org/10.1016/S0005-7894(98)80034-8

Eley, T. C., McAdams, T. A., Rijsdijk, F. V., Lichtenstein, P., Narusyte, J., Reiss, D., Spotts, E. L., Ganiban, J. M., & Neiderhiser, J. M. (2015). The intergenerational transmission of anxiety: A children-of-twins study. *American Journal of Psychiatry, 172*(7), 630–637. https://doi.org/10.1176/appi.ajp.2015.14070818

Ellis, D. M., & Hudson, J. L. (2010). The metacognitive model of generalized anxiety disorder in children and adolescents. *Clinical Child and Family Psychology Review, 13*(2), 151–163. https:// https://doi.org/10.1007/s10567-010-0065-0

Emde, R. N. (1992). Social referencing research. In S. Feinman (Ed.), *Social referencing and the social construction of reality in infancy* (pp. 79–94). New York: Springer US. https://doi.org/10.1007/978-1-4899-2462-9_4

Eng, W., & Heimberg, R. G. (2006). Interpersonal correlates of generalized anxiety disorder: Self versus other perception. *Journal of Anxiety Disorders, 20*(3), 380–387. https://doi.org/10.1016/j.janxdis.2005.02.005

Esbjørn, B. H., Bender, P. K., Reinholdt-Dunne, M. L., Munck, L. A., & Ollendick, T. H. (2012). The development of anxiety disorders: Considering the contributions of attachment and emotion regulation. *Clinical Child and Family Psychology Review, 15*(2), 129–143. https://doi.org/10.1007/s10567-011-0105-4

Esbjørn, B. H., Breinholst, S., Christiansen, B. M., Bukh, L., & Walczak, M. (2019). Increasing access to low-intensity interventions for childhood anxiety: A pilot study of a guided self-help program for Scandinavian parents. *Scandinavian Journal of Psychology, 60*(4), 323–328. https://doi.org/10.1111/sjop.12544

Esbjørn, B. H., Lønfeldt, N. N., Nielsen, S., Reinholdt-Dunne, M. L., Sømhovd, M. J., & Cartwright-Hatton, S. (2015). Meta-worry, worry, and anxiety in children and adolescents: Relationships and interactions. *Journal of Clinical Child & Adolescent Psychology, 44*(1), 145–156.

Esbjørn, B. H., Normann, N., Christiansen, B. M., & Reinholdt-Dunne, M. L. (2018). The efficacy of group metacognitive therapy for children (MCT-c) with generalized anxiety disorder: An open trial. *Journal of Anxiety Disorders, 53*, 16–21. https://doi.org/10.1016/j.janxdis.2017.11.002

Esbjørn, B. H., Normann, N., Lonfeldt, N. N., Tolstrup, M., & Reinholdt-Dunne, M. L. (2016). Exploring the relationships between maternal and child metacognitions and child anxiety. *Scandinavian Journal of Psychology, 57*(3), 201–206. https://doi.org/10.1111/sjop.12286

Esbjørn, B. H., Normann, N., & Reinholdt-Dunne, M. L. (2015). Adapting metacognitive therapy to children with generalised anxiety disorder: Suggestions for a manual. *Journal of Contemporary Psychotherapy, 45*(3), 159–166. https://doi.org/10.1007/s10879-015-9294-3

Esbjørn, B. H., Sømhovd, M. J., Holm, J. M., Lonfeldt, N. N., Bender, P. K., Nielsen, S. K., & Reinholdt-Dunne, M. L. (2013). A structural assessment of the 30-item metacognitions questionnaire for children and its relations to anxiety symptoms. *Psychological Assessment, 25*(4), 1211–1219. https://doi.org/10.1037/a0033793

Esbjørn, B. H., Sømhovd, M. J., Nielsen, S. K., Normann, N., Leth, I., & Reinholdt-Dunne, M. L. (2014). Parental changes after involvement in their anxious child's cognitive behavior therapy. *Journal of Anxiety Disorders, 28*(7), 664–670. https://doi.org/10.1016/j.janxdis.2014.07.008

Essau, C. A., Sakano, Y., Ishikawa, S., & Sasagawa, S. (2004). Anxiety symptoms in Japanese and in German children. *Behaviour Research and Therapy, 42*(5), 601–612. https://doi.org/10.1016/S0005-7967(03)00164-5

Esters, I. G. (2003). Salient Worries of at-risk youth: Needs assessment using the things I worry about scale. *Adolescence, 38*(150), 279–285.

Evans, R., Hill, C., O'Brien, D., & Creswell, C. (2019). Evaluation of a group format of clinician-guided, parent-delivered cognitive behavioural therapy for child anxiety in routine clinical practice: A pilot-implementation study. *Child and Adolescent Mental Health*, 24(1), 36–43. https://doi.org/10.1111/camh.12274

Eysenck, M. W., Derakshan, N., Santos, R., & Calvo, M. G. (2007). Anxiety and cognitive performance: Attentional control theory. *Emotion*, 7(2), 336–353. https://doi.org/10.1037/1528-3542.7.2.336

Feng, Y.-C., Krahé, C., Sumich, A., Meeten, F., Lau, J. Y. F., & Hirsch, C. R. (2019). Using event-related potential and behavioural evidence to understand interpretation bias in relation to worry. *Biological Psychology*, 148, 107746. https://doi.org/10.1016/j.biopsycho.2019.107746

Ferdinand, R. F., Dieleman, G., Ormel, J., & Verhulst, F. C. (2007). Homotypic versus heterotypic continuity of anxiety symptoms in young adolescents: Evidence for Distinctions between DSM-IV subtypes. *Journal of Abnormal Child Psychology*, 35(3), 325–333. https://doi.org/10.1007/s10802-006-9093-0

Fialko, L., Bolton, D., & Perrin, S. (2012). Applicability of a cognitive model of worry to children and adolescents. *Behaviour Research and Therapy*, 50(5), 341–349. https://doi.org/10.1016/j.brat.2012.02.003

Field, A. P., & Lawson, J. (2003). Fear information and the development of fears during childhood: Effects on implicit fear responses and behavioural avoidance. *Behaviour Research and Therapy*, 41(11), 1277–1293. https://doi.org/10.1016/S0005-7967(03)00034-2

Fisak, B., Holderfield, K. G., Douglas-Osborn, E., & Cartwright-Hatton, S. (2012). What do parents worry about? Examination of the construct of parent worry and the relation to parent and child anxiety. *Behavioural and Cognitive Psychotherapy*, 40(05), 542–557. https://doi.org/10.1017/S1352465812000410

Fisak, B., Mentuccia, M., & Przeworski, A. (2014). Meta-worry in adolescents: examination of the psychometric properties of the meta-worry questionnaire in an adolescent sample. *Behavioural and Cognitive Psychotherapy*, 42(04), 491–496. https://doi.org/10.1017/S1352465813000374

Fisher, E., Keogh, E., & Eccleston, C. (2017). Everyday worry in adolescents with and without chronic pain: A diary study. *Psychology, Health & Medicine*, 22(7), 800–807. https://doi.org/10.1080/13548506.2017.1280175

Flavell, J. H. (1979). Metacognition and cognitive monitoring: A new area of cognitive–developmental inquiry. *American Psychologist*, 34(10), 906. https://doi.10.1037/0003-066X.34.10.906

Flavell, J. H. (1999). Cognitive development: Children's knowledge about the mind. *Annual Review of Psychology*, 50(1), 21–45. https://doi.org/10.1146/annurev.psych.50.1.21

Flavell, J. H., Friedrichs, A. G., & Hoyt, J. D. (1970). Developmental changes in memorization processes. *Cognitive Psychology*, *1*(4), 324–340. https://doi.org/10.1016/0010-0285(70)90019-8

Fletcher, F. E., Conduit, R., Foster-Owens, M. D., Rinehart, N. J., Rajaratnam, S. M. W., & Cornish, K. M. (2018). The association between anxiety symptoms and sleep in school-aged children: A combined insight from the children's sleep habits questionnaire and actigraphy. *Behavioral Sleep Medicine*, *16*(2), 169–184. https://doi.org/10.1080/15402002.2016.1180522

Flynn, B., & Wilson, C. (submitted). *Adolescents experience of worry, fear and stress; comparing autistic and neurotypical adolescents*.

Folk, J. B., Zeman, J. L., Poon, J. A., & Dallaire, D. H. (2014). A longitudinal examination of emotion regulation: Pathways to anxiety and depressive symptoms in urban minority youth. *Child and Adolescent Mental Health*, *19*(4), 243–250. https://doi.org/10.1111/camh.12058

Forslund, T., Brocki, K. C., Bohlin, G., Granqvist, P., & Eninger, L. (2016). The heterogeneity of attention-deficit/hyperactivity disorder symptoms and conduct problems: Cognitive inhibition, emotion regulation, emotionality, and disorganized attachment. *British Journal of Developmental Psychology*, *34*(3), 371–387. https://doi.org/10.1111/bjdp.12136

Foster, C., Startup, H., Potts, L., & Freeman, D. (2010). A randomised controlled trial of a worry intervention for individuals with persistent persecutory delusions. *Journal of Behavior Therapy and Experimental Psychiatry*, *41*(1), 45–51. https://doi.org/10.1016/j.jbtep.2009.09.001

Fowler, S., & Szabó, M. (2013). The emotional experience associated with worrying in adolescents. *Journal of Psychopathology and Behavioral Assessment*, *35*(1), 65–75. https://doi.org/10.1007/s10862-012-9316-3

Francis, K., & Dugas, M. J. (2004). Assessing positive beliefs about worry: Validation of a structured interview. *Personality and Individual Differences*, *37*(2), 405–415. https://doi.org/10.1016/j.paid.2003.09.012

Freeman, D., Dunn, G., Startup, H., Pugh, K., Cordwell, J., Mander, H., Černis, E., Wingham, G., Shirvell, K., & Kingdon, D. (2015). Effects of cognitive behaviour therapy for worry on persecutory delusions in patients with psychosis (WIT): A parallel, single-blind, randomised controlled trial with a mediation analysis. *The Lancet Psychiatry*, *2*(4), 305–313. https://doi.org/10.1016/S2215-0366(15)00039-5

Freeman, D., & Garety, P. A. (1999). Worry, worry processes and dimensions of delusions: And exploratory investigation of a role for anxiety processes in the maintenance of delusional distress. *Behavioural and Cognitive Psychotherapy, 27*, 47–52. https://doi.org/10.1017/s135246589927107x

Galbraith, N., Manktelow, K., Chen-Wilson, C.-H., Harris, R., & Nevill, A. (2014). Different combinations of perceptual, emotional, and cognitive factors predict three different types of delusional ideation during adolescence. *The Journal of Nervous and Mental Disease, 202*(9), 668–676. https://doi.org/10.1097/NMD.0000000000000179

Gauntlett-Gilbert, J., & Eccleston, C. (2007). Disability in adolescents with chronic pain: Patterns and predictors across different domains of functioning. *PAIN, 131*(1), 132. https://doi.org/10.1016/j.pain.2006.12.021

Gentes, E. L., & Ruscio, A. M. (2011). A meta-analysis of the relation of intolerance of uncertainty to symptoms of generalized anxiety disorder, major depressive disorder, and obsessive–compulsive disorder. *Clinical Psychology Review, 31*(6), 923–933. https://doi.org/10.1016/j.cpr.2011.05.001

Gerlach, A. L., Adam, S., Marschke, S., & Melfsen, S. (2008). *Development and validation of a child version of the metacognitions questionnaire*. 38th Annual Congress of the European Association for Behavioural and Cognitive Therapies.

Geronimi, E. M. C., Patterson, H. L., & Woodruff-Borden, J. (2016). Relating worry and executive functioning during childhood: The moderating role of age. *Child Psychiatry & Human Development, 47*(3), 430–439. https://doi.org/10.1007/s10578-015-0577-4

Ghafoor, H., Ahmad, R. A., Nordbeck, P., Ritter, O., Pauli, P., & Schulz, S. M. (2019). A cross-cultural comparison of the roles of emotional intelligence, metacognition, and negative coping for health-related quality of life in German versus Pakistani patients with chronic heart failure. *British Journal of Health Psychology, 24*(4), 828–846. https://doi.org/10.1111/bjhp.12381

Gifford, S., Reynolds, S., Bell, S., & Wilson, C. (2008). Threat interpretation bias in anxious children and their mothers. *Cognition & Emotion, 22*(3), 497–508. https://doi.org/10.1080/02699930801886649

Gill, A. H., Papageorgiou, C., Gaskell, S. L., & Wells, A. (2013). Development and preliminary validation of the thought control questionnaire for adolescents (TCQ-A). *Cognitive Therapy and Research, 37*(2), 242–255. https://doi.org/10.1007/s10608-012-9465-4

Ginsburg, G. S., Grover, R. L., Cord, J. J., & Ialongo, N. (2006). Observational measures of parenting in anxious and nonanxious mothers: Does type of task matter? *Journal of Clinical Child & Adolescent Psychology, 35*(2), 323–328. https://doi.org/10.1207/s15374424jccp3502_16

Ginsburg, G. S., Grover, R. L., & Ialongo, N. (2005). Parenting behaviors among anxious and non-anxious mothers: Relation with concurrent and long-term child outcomes. *Child & Family Behavior Therapy, 26*(4), 23–41. https://doi.org/10.1300/J019v26n04_02

Glod, M., Riby, D. M., & Rodgers, J. (2019). Short report: Relationships between sensory processing, repetitive behaviors, anxiety, and intolerance of uncertainty in autism spectrum disorder and Williams syndrome. *Autism Research.* https://doi.org/10.1002/aur.2096

Goodwin, H., Yiend, J., & Hirsch, C. R. (2017). Generalized anxiety disorder, worry and attention to threat: A systematic review. *Clinical Psychology Review, 54*, 107–122. https://doi.org/10.1016/j.cpr.2017.03.006

Goossen, B., van der Starre, J., & van der Heiden, C. (2019). A review of neuroimaging studies in generalized anxiety disorder: "So where do we stand?" *Journal of Neural Transmission, 126*(9), 1203–1216. https://doi.org/10.1007/s00702-019-02024-w

Gramszlo, C., Geronimi, E. M. C., Arellano, B., & Woodruff-Borden, J. (2018). Testing a cognitive pathway between temperament and childhood anxiety. *Journal of Child and Family Studies, 27*(2), 580–590. https://doi.org/10.1007/s10826-017-0914-2

Gramszlo, C., & Woodruff-Borden, J. (2015). Emotional reactivity and executive control: A pathway of risk for the development of childhood worry. *Journal of Anxiety Disorders, 35*, 35–41. https://doi.org/10.1016/j.janxdis.2015.07.005

Greenwald, A. G., McGhee, D. E., & Schwartz, J. L. K. (1998). Measuring individual differences in implicit cognition: The implicit association test. *Journal of Personality and Social Psychology, 74*(6), 1464–1480.

Gregory, A. M., & Eley, T. C. (2007). Genetic influences on anxiety in children: What we've learned and where we're heading. *Clinical Child and Family Psychology Review, 10*(3), 199–212. https://doi.org/10.1007/s10567-007-0022-8

Grüner, K., Muris, P., & Merckelbach, H. (1999). The relationship between anxious rearing behaviours and anxiety disorders symptomatology in normal children. *Journal of Behavior Therapy and Experimental Psychiatry, 30*(1), 27–35. https://doi.org/10.1016/S0005-7916(99)00004-X

Guajardo, N. R., McNally, L. F., & Wright, A. (2016). Children's spontaneous counterfactuals: The roles of valence, expectancy, and cognitive flexibility. *Journal of Experimental Child Psychology, 146*, 79–94. https://doi.org/10.1016/j.jecp.2016.01.009

Guerreiro, D. F., Cruz, D., Frasquilho, D., Santos, J. C., Figueira, M. L., & Sampaio, D. (2013). Association between deliberate self-harm and coping in adolescents:

A critical review of the last 10 years' literature. *Archives of Suicide Research*, *17*(2), 91–105. https://doi.org/10.1080/13811118.2013.776439

Hale, W. W., Engels, R., & Meeus, W. H. J. (2006). Adolescent's perceptions of parenting behaviours and its relationship to adolescent Generalized Anxiety Disorder symptoms. *Journal of Adolescence, 29*(3), 407–417. https://doi.10.1016/j.adolescence.2005.08.002

Hale, W. W., Klimstra, T. A., Branje, S. J. T., Wijsbroek, S. A. M., & Meeus, W. H. J. (2013). Is adolescent generalized anxiety disorder a magnet for negative parental interpersonal behaviors? *Depression and Anxiety, 30*(9), 849–856. https://doi.org/10.1002/da.22065

Halldorsdottir, T., Ollendick, T. H., Ginsburg, G., Sherrill, J., Kendall, P. C., Walkup, J., Sakolsky, D. J., & Piacentini, J. (2015). Treatment outcomes in anxious youth with and without comorbid ADHD in the CAMS. *Journal of Clinical Child & Adolescent Psychology, 44*(6), 985–991. https://doi.org/10.1080/15374416.2014.952008

Hare, D. J., Gracey, C., & Wood, C. (2016). Anxiety in high-functioning autism: A pilot study of experience sampling using a mobile platform. *Autism, 20*(6), 730–743. https://doi.10.1177/1362361315604817

Harris, P. L., German, T., & Mills, P. (1996). Children's use of counterfactual thinking in causal reasoning. *Cognition, 61*(3), 233–259. https://doi.org/10.1016/S0010-0277(96)00715-9

Harvey, A. G. (2002). A cognitive model of insomnia. *Behaviour Research and Therapy, 40*(8), 869–893. https://doi.org/10.1016/S0005-7967(01)00061-4

Hawton, K., Kingsbury, S., Steinhardt, K., James, A., & Fagg, J. (1999). Repetition of deliberate self-harm by adolescents: The role of psychological factors. *Journal of Adolescence, 22*(3), 369–378. https://doi.org/10.1006/jado.1999.0228

Hearn, C. S., Donovan, C. L., Spence, S. H., March, S., & Holmes, M. C. (2017). What's the worry with social anxiety? Comparing cognitive processes in children with generalized anxiety disorder and social anxiety disorder. *Child Psychiatry and Human Development, 48*(5), 786–795. https://doi.org/10.1007/s10578-016-0703-y

Hebert, E. A., Dugas, M. J., Tulloch, T. G., & Holowka, D. W. (2014). Positive beliefs about worry: A psychometric evaluation of the why worry-II. *Personality and Individual Differences, 56*, 3–8. https://doi.org/10.1016/j.paid.2013.08.009

Heffernan, M., Wilson, C., Keating, K., & McCarthy, K. (2020). "Why isn't it going away?": A qualitative exploration of worry and pain experiences in adolescents with chronic pain. *Pain Medicine*.

Henker, B., Whalen, C. K., & O'Neil, R. (1995). Worldly and workaday worries: Contemporary concerns of children and young adolescents. *Journal of Abnormal Child Psychology*, *23*(6), 685–702. https://doi.org/10.1007/BF01447472

Heppner, P. P., & Petersen, C. H. (1982). The development and implications of a personal problem-solving inventory. *Journal of Counseling Psychology*, *29*(1), 66. https://doi.org/10.1037/0022-0167.29.1.66

Heyne, D., King, N. J., Tonge, B. J., Rollings, S., Young, D., Pritchard, M., & Ollendick, T. H. (2002). Evaluation of child therapy and caregiver training in the treatment of school refusal. *Journal of the American Academy of Child & Adolescent Psychiatry*, *41*(6), 687–695. https://doi.org/10.1097/00004583-200206000-00008

Hiller, R. M., Lovato, N., Gradisar, M., Oliver, M., & Slater, A. (2014). Trying to fall asleep while catastrophising: What sleep-disordered adolescents think and feel. *Sleep Medicine*, *15*(1), 96–103. https://doi.org/10.1016/j.sleep.2013.09.014

Hirsch, C., Hayes, S., & Mathews, A. (2009). Looking on the bright side: Accessing benign meanings reduces worry. *Journal of Abnormal Psychology*, *118*(1), 44–54. https://doi.org/10.1037/a0013473

Hirsch, C. R., & Mathews, A. (2012). A cognitive model of pathological worry. *Behaviour Research and Therapy*, *50*(10), 636–646. https://doi.org/10.1016/j.brat.2012.06.007

Hirshfeld, D. R., Biederman, J., Brody, L., Faraone, S. V., & Rosenbaum, J. F. (1997). Expressed emotion toward children with behavioral inhibition: Associations with maternal anxiety disorder. *Journal of the American Academy of Child & Adolescent Psychiatry*, *36*(7), 910–917. https://doi.org/10.1097/00004583-199707000-00012

Hirshfeld-Becker, D. R., Micco, J., Henin, A., Bloomfield, A., Biederman, J., & Rosenbaum, J. (2008). Behavioral inhibition. *Depression and Anxiety*, *25*(4), 357–367. https://doi.org/10.1002/da.20490

Hodgson, A. R., Freeston, M. H., Honey, E., & Rodgers, J. (2017). Facing the unknown: Intolerance of uncertainty in children with autism spectrum disorder. *Journal of Applied Research in Intellectual Disabilities*, *30*(2), 336–344. https://doi.org/10.1111/jar.12245

Hoffman, D. L., Dukes, E. M., & Wittchen, H.-U. (2008). Human and economic burden of generalized anxiety disorder. *Depression and Anxiety*, *25*(1), 72–90. https://doi.org/10.1002/da.20257

Hollocks, M. J., Jones, C. R. G., Pickles, A., Baird, G., Happé, F., Charman, T., & Simonoff, E. (2014). The association between social cognition and executive functioning and symptoms of anxiety and depression in adolescents with autism spectrum disorders: Neurocognitive ability, anxiety, and depression. *Autism Research, 7*(2), 216–228. https://doi.org/10.1002/aur.1361

Hollocks, M. J., Lerh, J. W., Magiati, I., Meiser-Stedman, R., & Brugha, T. S. (2019). Anxiety and depression in adults with autism spectrum disorder: A systematic review and meta-analysis. *Psychological Medicine, 49*(4), 559–572. https://doi.org/10.1017/S0033291718002283

Holmes, M. C., Donovan, C. L., Farrell, L. J., & March, S. (2014). The efficacy of a group-based, disorder-specific treatment program for childhood GAD—A randomized controlled trial. *Behaviour Research and Therapy, 61*, 122–135. https://doi.org/10.1016/j.brat.2014.08.002

Hong, R. Y. (2007). Worry and rumination: Differential associations with anxious and depressive symptoms and coping behavior. *Behaviour Research and Therapy, 45*(2), 277–290. https://doi.org/10.1016/j.brat.2006.03.006

Houghton, S., Alsalmi, N., Tan, C., Taylor, M., & Durkin, K. (2017). Treating comorbid anxiety in adolescents with ADHD using a cognitive behavior therapy program approach. *Journal of Attention Disorders, 21*(13), 1094–1104. https://doi.org/10.1177/1087054712473182

Hudson, J. L., Rapee, R. M., Lyneham, H. J., McLellan, L. F., Wuthrich, V. M., & Schniering, C. A. (2015a). Comparing outcomes for children with different anxiety disorders following cognitive behavioural therapy. *Behaviour Research and Therapy, 72*, 30–37. https://doi.org/10.1016/j.brat.2015.06.007

Hudson, J. L., Rapee, R. M., Lyneham, H. J., McLellan, L. F., Wuthrich, V. M., & Schniering, C. A. (2015b). Comparing outcomes for children with different anxiety disorders following cognitive behavioural therapy. *Behaviour Research and Therapy, 72*, 30–37. https://doi.org/10.1016/j.brat.2015.06.007

Hughes, C., & Leekam, S. (2004). What are the links between theory of mind and social relations? Review, reflections and new directions for studies of typical and atypical development. *Social Development, 13*(4), 590–619. https://doi.org/10.1111/j.1467-9507.2004.00285.x

Iijima, Y., & Tanno, Y. (2013). The moderating role of positive beliefs about worry in the relationship between stressful events and worry. *Personality and Individual Differences, 55*(8), 1003–1006. https://doi.org/10.1016/j.paid.2013.08.004

Ishizu, K., Shimoda, Y., & Ohtsuki, T. (2017). The reciprocal relations between experiential avoidance, school stressor, and psychological stress response among Japanese adolescents. *PLOS ONE, 12*(11), e0188368. https://doi.org/10.1371/journal.pone.0188368

Jacob, M. L., Suveg, C., & Whitehead, M. R. (2014). Relations between emotional and social functioning in children with anxiety disorders. *Child Psychiatry & Human Development*, *45*(5), 519–532. https://doi.org/10.1007/s10578-013-0421-7

Jacobi, D. M., Calamari, J. E., & Woodard, J. L. (2006). Obsessive–compulsive disorder beliefs, metacognitive beliefs and obsessional symptoms: Relations between parent beliefs and child symptoms. *Clinical Psychology & Psychotherapy*, *13*(3), 153–162. https://doi.org/10.1002/cpp.485

Jager, J., Mahler, A., An, D., Putnick, D. L., Bornstein, M. H., Lansford, J. E., Dodge, K. A., Skinner, A. T., & Deater-Deckard, K. (2016). Early adolescents' unique perspectives of maternal and paternal rejection: Examining their across-dyad generalizability and relations with adjustment 1 year later. *Journal of Youth and Adolescence*, *45*(10), 2108–2124. https://doi.org/10.1007/s10964-016-0509-z

Jang, J., Matson, J. L., Williams, L. W., Tureck, K., Goldin, R. L., & Cervantes, P. E. (2013). Rates of comorbid symptoms in children with ASD, ADHD, and comorbid ASD and ADHD. *Research in Developmental Disabilities*, *34*(8), 2369–2378. https://doi.org/10.1016/j.ridd.2013.04.021

Jensen, P., Martin, D., & Cantwell, D. (1997). Comorbidity in ADHD implications for research, practice and DSM-V. *Journal of the American Academy of Child & Adolescent Psychiatry*, *36*(8), 1065–1079. https://doi.org./10.1097/00004583-199708000-00014

Kagan, J., Reznick, J. S., Clarke, C., & Snidman, N. (1984). Behavioral inhibition to the unfamiliar. *Child Development*, *55*, 2212–2225. https://doi.org/10.2307/1129793

Kagan, J., Reznick, J. S., & Snidman, N. (1987). The physiology and psychology of behavioral inhibition in children. *Child Development*, *58*, 1459–1473. https://doi.org/10.2307/1130685

Kaitz, M., Maytal, H. R., Devor, N., Bergman, L., & Mankuta, D. (2010). Maternal anxiety, mother–infant interactions, and infants' response to challenge. *Infant Behavior and Development*, *33*(2), 136–148. https://doi.org/10.1016/j.infbeh.2009.12.003

Keen, R. (2011). The development of problem solving in young children: A critical cognitive skill. *Annual Review of Psychology*, *62*(1), 1–21. https://doi.org/10.1146/annurev.psych.031809.130730

Keltikangas-Jarvinen, L. (2002). Aggressive problem-solving strategies, aggressive behavior, and social acceptance in early and late adolescence. *Journal of Youth and Adolescence*, *31*(4), 279–287. https://doi.org/10.1023/A:1015445500935

Kendall, P. C. (1994). Treating anxiety disorders in children: Results of a randomized clinical trial. *Journal of Consulting and Clinical Psychology, 62*(1), 100–110. https://doi.org/10.1037/0022-006X.62.1.100

Kennedy, S. M., & Ehrenreich-May, J. (2017). Assessment of emotional avoidance in adolescents: Psychometric properties of a new multidimensional measure. *Journal of Psychopathology and Behavioral Assessment, 39*(2), 279–290. https://doi.org/10.1007/s10862-016-9581-7

Kerns, C. E., Mennin, D. S., Farach, F. J., & Nocera, C. C. (2014). Utilizing an ability-based measure to detect emotion regulation deficits in generalized anxiety disorder. *Journal of Psychopathology and Behavioral Assessment, 36*(1), 115–123. https://doi.org/10.1007/s10862-013-9372-3

Kertz, S. J., Belden, A. C., Tillman, R., & Luby, J. (2016). Cognitive control deficits in shifting and inhibition in preschool age children are associated with increased depression and anxiety over 7.5 years of development. *Journal of Abnormal Child Psychology, 44*(6), 1185–1196. https://doi.org/10.1007/s10802-015-0101-0

Kertz, S., & Woodruff-Borden, J. (2013). The role of metacognition, intolerance of uncertainty, and negative problem orientation in children's worry. *Behavioural and Cognitive Psychotherapy, 41*(02), 243–248.

Klemanski, D. H., Curtiss, J., McLaughlin, K. A., & Nolen-Hoeksema, S. (2017). Emotion regulation and the transdiagnostic role of repetitive negative thinking in adolescents with social anxiety and depression. *Cognitive Therapy and Research, 41*(2), 206–219. https://doi.org/10.1007/s10608-016-9817-6

Koerner, N., & Dugas, M. J. (2006). A cognitive model of generalized anxiety disorder: The role of intolerance of uncertainty. In G. C. L. Davey, & A. Wells (Eds.), *Worry and its psychological disorders: Theory, assessment and treatment.* (pp. 201–216). Chichester: John Wiley & Sons Ltd. https://doi.org/10.1002/9780470713143.ch12

Koffel, E., Bramoweth, A. D., & Ulmer, C. S. (2018). Increasing access to and utilization of cognitive behavioral therapy for insomnia (CBT-I): A narrative review. *Journal of General Internal Medicine, 33*(6), 955–962. https://doi.org/10.1007/s11606-018-4390-1

Kolomeyer, E., & Renk, K. (2016). Family-based cognitive–behavioral therapy for an intelligent, elementary school-aged child with generalized anxiety disorder. *Clinical Case Studies, 15*(6), 443–458. https://doi.org/10.1177/1534650116668046

Kramer, H. J., Goldfarb, D., Tashjian, S. M., & Lagattuta, K. H. (2017). "These pretzels are making me thirsty": Older children and adults struggle with induced-state episodic foresight. *Child Development, 88*(5), 1554–1562. https://doi.org/10.1111/cdev.12700

Kroska, E. B., Miller, M. L., Roche, A. I., Kroska, S. K., & O'Hara, M. W. (2018). Effects of traumatic experiences on obsessive-compulsive and internalizing symptoms: The role of avoidance and mindfulness. *Journal of Affective Disorders, 225*, 326–336. https://doi.org/10.1016/j.jad.2017.08.039

Kwon, S. J., Kim, Y., & Kwak, Y. (2018). Difficulties faced by university students with self-reported symptoms of attention-deficit hyperactivity disorder: A qualitative study. *Child and Adolescent Psychiatry and Mental Health, 12*, 12. https://doi.org/10.1186/s13034-018-0218-3

Ladouceur, R., Blais, F., Freeston, M. H., & Dugas, M. J. (1998). Problem solving and problem orientation in generalized anxiety disorder. *Journal of Anxiety Disorders, 12*(2), 139–152. https://doi.org/10.1016/S0887-6185(98)00002-4

Lagattuta, K. H. (2007). Thinking about the future because of the past: Young children's knowledge about the causes of worry and preventative decisions. *Child Development, 78*(5), 1492–1509. https://doi.org/10.1111/j.1467-8624.2007.01079.x

Lagattuta, K. H., & Sayfan, L. (2011). Developmental changes in children's understanding of future likelihood and uncertainty. *Cognitive Development, 26*(4), 315–330. https://doi.org/10.1016/j.cogdev.2011.09.004

Lagattuta, K. H., & Sayfan, L. (2013). Not all past events are equal: Biased attention and emerging heuristics in children's past-to-future forecasting. *Child Development, 84*(6), 2094–2111. https://doi.org/10.1111/cdev.12082

Lagattuta, K. H., Sayfan, L., & Bamford, C. (2012). Do you know how I feel? Parents underestimate worry and overestimate optimism compared to child self-report. *Journal of Experimental Child Psychology, 113*(2), 211–232.

Lagattuta, K. H., Sayfan, L., & Harvey, C. (2014). Beliefs about thought probability: Evidence for persistent errors in mindreading and links to executive control. *Child Development, 85*(2), 659–674. https://doi.org/10.1111/cdev.12154

Lagattuta, K. H., Tashjian, S. M., & Kramer, H. J. (2018). Does the past shape anticipation for the future? Contributions of age and executive function to advanced theory of mind. *Zeitschrift Für Psychologie, 226*(2), 122–133. https://doi.org/10.1027/2151-2604/a000328

Lagattuta, K. H., & Wellman, H. M. (2001). Thinking about the past: Early knowledge about links between prior experience, thinking, and emotion. *Child Development, 72*(1), 82–102. https://doi.org/10.1111/1467-8624.00267

Lagattuta, K. H., Wellman, H. M., & Flavell, J. H. (1997). Preschoolers' understanding of the link between thinking and feeling: Cognitive cuing and emotional change. *Child Development, 68*(6), 1081–1104. https://doi.org/10.1111/j.1467-8624.1997.tb01986.x

Lahat, A., Hong, M., & Fox, N. A. (2011). Behavioural inhibition: Is it a risk factor for anxiety? *International Review of Psychiatry, 23*(3), 248–257. https://doi.org/10.3109/09540261.2011.590468

Laing, S. V., Fernyhough, C., Turner, M., & Freeston, M. H. (2009). Fear, worry, and ritualistic behaviour in childhood: Developmental trends and interrelations. *Infant and Child Development, 18*(4), 351–366. https://doi.org/10.1002/icd.627

Lancee, J., Eisma, M. C., van Zanten, K. B., & Topper, M. (2017). When thinking impairs sleep: Trait, daytime and nighttime repetitive thinking in insomnia. *Behavioral Sleep Medicine, 15*(1), 53–69. https://doi.org/10.1080/15402002.2015.1083022

Larsen, J. T., To, Y. M., & Fireman, G. (2007). Children's understanding and experience of mixed emotions. *Psychological Science, 18*(2), 186–191. https://doi.org/10.1111/j.1467-9280.2007.01870.x

Last, C. G., Hersen, M., Kazdin, A., Orvaschel, H., & Perrin, S. (1991). Anxiety disorders in children and their families. *Archives of General Psychiatry, 48*(10), 928–934. https://doi.org/10.1001/archpsyc.1991.01810340060008

Last, C. G., Phillips, J. E., & Statfeld, A. (1987). Childhood anxiety disorders in mothers and their children. *Child Psychiatry & Human Development, 18*(2), 103–112. https://doi.org/10.1007/BF00709955

Laugesen, N., Dugas, M. J., & Bukowski, W. M. (2003). Understanding adolescent worry: The application of a cognitive model. *Journal of Abnormal Child Psychology, 31*(1), 55–64. https://doi.10.1023/a:1021721332181

Lebowitz, E. R., Marin, C., Martino, A., Shimshoni, Y., & Silverman, W. K. (2019). Parent-based treatment as efficacious as cognitive-behavioral therapy for childhood anxiety: A randomized noninferiority study of supportive parenting for anxious childhood emotions. *Journal of the American Academy of Child & Adolescent Psychiatry, 59*, 362–372 S089085671930173X. https://doi.org/10.1016/j.jaac.2019.02.014

Lebowitz, E. R., Omer, H., Hermes, H., & Scahill, L. (2014). Parent training for childhood anxiety disorders: The SPACE program. *Cognitive and Behavioral Practice, 21*(4), 456–469. https://doi.org/10.1016/j.cbpra.2013.10.004

Lee, J., Kim, M., & Park, M. (2014). The impact of internalized shame on social anxiety in adolescence: The mediating role of experiential avoidance. *Journal of Asia Pacific Counseling, 4*(1), 65–81. https://doi.org/10.18401/2014.4.1.5

Lee, J. K., Orsillo, S. M., Roemer, L., & Allen, L. B. (2010). Distress and avoidance in generalized anxiety disorder: Exploring the relationships with intolerance of uncertainty and worry. *Cognitive Behaviour Therapy, 39*(2), 126–136. https://doi.org/10.1080/16506070902966918

Leslie, A. M. (1994). ToMM, ToBy, and agency: Core architecture and domain specificity. In L.A. Hirschfeld, & S. A. Gelman (Eds). *Mapping the mind: Domain specificity in cognition and culture* (pp. 119–148). Cambridge: Cambridge University Press. https://doi.org/10.1017/CBO9780511752902.006

Lester, K. J., Field, A. P., & Cartwright-Hatton, S. (2012). Maternal anxiety and cognitive biases towards threat in their own and their child's environment. *Journal of Family Psychology, 26*(5), 756–766. https://doi.org/10.1037/a0029711

Lester, K. J., Field, A. P., Oliver, S., & Cartwright-Hatton, S. (2009). Do anxious parents' interpretive biases towards threat extend into their child's environment? *Behaviour Research and Therapy, 47*(2), 170–174. https://doi.org/10.1016/j.brat.2008.11.005

Levy, S., & Guttman, L. (1976). Worry, fear, and concern differentiated. *Israel Annals of Psychiatry & Related Disciplines, 14*(3), 211–228.

Lewandowski, L., Gathje, R. A., Lovett, B. J., & Gordon, M. (2013). Test-taking skills in college students with and without ADHD. *Journal of Psychoeducational Assessment, 31*(1), 41–52. https://doi.org/10.1177/0734282912446304

Lewinsohn, P. M., Clarke, G. N., Seeley, J. R., & Rohde, P. (1994). Major depression in community adolescents: Age at onset, episode duration, and time to recurrence. *Journal of the American Academy of Child & Adolescent Psychiatry, 33*(6), 809–818. https://doi.org/10.1097/00004583-199407000-00006

Lewinsohn, P. M., Duncan, E. M., Stanton, A. K., & Hautzinger, M. (1986). Age at first onset for nonbipolar depression. *Journal of Abnormal Psychology, 95*(4), 378–383. https://doi.org/10.1037/0021-843X.95.4.378

Liber, J. M., van Widenfelt, B. M., Goedhart, A. W., Utens, E. M. W. J., van der Leeden, A. J. M., Markus, M. T., & Treffers, P. D. A. (2008). Parenting and parental anxiety and depression as predictors of treatment outcome for childhood anxiety disorders: Has the role of fathers been underestimated? *Journal of Clinical Child & Adolescent Psychology, 37*(4), 747–758. https://doi.org/10.1080/15374410802359692

Liew, S. M., Thevaraja, N., Hong, R. Y., & Magiati, I. (2015). The relationship between autistic traits and social anxiety, worry, obsessive–compulsive, and depressive symptoms: Specific and non-specific mediators in a student sample. *Journal of Autism and Developmental Disorders, 45*(3), 858–872. https://doi.org/10.1007/s10803-014-2238-z

Lin, R.-M., Xie, S.-S., Yan, Y.-W., & Yan, W.-J. (2017). Intolerance of uncertainty and adolescent sleep quality: The mediating role of worry. *Personality and Individual Differences, 108*, 168–173. https://doi.org/10.1016/j.paid.2016.12.025

Lockman, J. J. (2000). A perception-action perspective on tool use development. *Child Development, 71*(1), 137–144. https://doi.org/10.1111/1467-8624.00127

Lønfeldt, N. N., Esbjørn, B. H., Normann, N., Breinholst, S., & Francis, S. E. (2017). Do mother's metacognitions, beliefs, and behaviors predict child anxiety-related metacognitions? *Child & Youth Care Forum, 46*(4), 577–599. https://doi.org/10.1007/s10566-017-9396-z

Lovibond, P. F., & Lovibond, S. H. (1995). The structure of negative emotional states: comparison of the depression anxiety stress scales (DASS) with the beck depression and anxiety inventories. *Behaviour Research and Therapy, 33*(3), 335–343. https://doi.org/10.1016/0005-7967(94)00075-U

Luis, T. M., Varela, R. E., & Moore, K. W. (2008). Parenting practices and childhood anxiety reporting in Mexican, Mexican American, and European American families. *Journal of Anxiety Disorders, 22*(6), 1011–1020. https://doi.org/10.1016/j.janxdis.2007.11.001

MacNeil, S., Deschênes, S. S., Caldwell, W., Brouillard, M., Dang-Vu, T.-T., & Gouin, J.-P. (2017). High-frequency heart rate variability reactivity and trait worry interact to predict the development of sleep disturbances in response to a naturalistic stressor. *Annals of Behavioral Medicine, 51*(6), 912–924. https://doi.org/10.1007/s12160-017-9915-z

Madhavakkannan, H., Jordan, A., Fisher, E., Wilson, C., Mullen, D., & Wainwright, E. (in preparation). *Worries, beliefs about worry and pain in adolescents with and without chronic pain.*

Mahy, C. E. V., Grass, J., Wagner, S., & Kliegel, M. (2014). These pretzels are going to make me thirsty tomorrow: Differential development of hot and cool episodic foresight in early childhood? *British Journal of Developmental Psychology, 32*(1), 65–77. https://doi.org/10.1111/bjdp.12023

Manassis, K., Lee, T. C., Bennett, K., Zhao, X. Y., Mendlowitz, S., Duda, S., Saini, M., Wilansky, P., Baer, S., Barrett, P., Bodden, D., Cobham, V. E., Dadds, M. R., Flannery-Schroeder, E., Ginsburg, G., Heyne, D., Hudson, J. L., Kendall, P. C., Liber, J., … Wood, J. J. (2014). Types of parental involvement in CBT with anxious youth: A preliminary meta-analysis. *Journal of Consulting and Clinical Psychology, 82*(6), 1163–1172. https://doi.org/10.1037/a0036969

March, J. S., Parker, J. D., Sullivan, K., Stallings, P., & Conners, C. K. (1997). The multidimensional anxiety scale for children (MASC): Factor structure, reliability, and validity. *Journal of the American Academy of Child and Adolescent Psychiatry*, *36*(4), 554–565. https://doi.org/10.1097/00004583-199704000-00019

Marganska, A., Gallagher, M., & Miranda, R. (2013). Adult attachment, emotion dysregulation, and symptoms of depression and generalized anxiety disorder. *American Journal of Orthopsychiatry*, *83*(1), 131–141. https://doi.org/10.1111/ajop.12001

Maric, M., van Steensel, F. J. A., & Bögels, S. M. (2018). Parental involvement in CBT for anxiety-disordered youth revisited: Family CBT outperforms child CBT in the long term for children with comorbid ADHD symptoms. *Journal of Attention Disorders*, *22*(5), 506–514. https://doi.org/10.1177/1087054715573991

McCathie, H., & Spence, S. H. (1991). What is the revised fear survey schedule for children measuring? *Behaviour Research and Therapy*, *29*(5), 495–502. https://doi.org/10.1016/0005-7967(91)90134-O

McEvoy, P. M., Erceg-Hurn, D. M., Anderson, R. A., Campbell, B. N. C., Swan, A., Saulsman, L. M., Summers, M., & Nathan, P. R. (2015). Group metacognitive therapy for repetitive negative thinking in primary and non-primary generalized anxiety disorder: An effectiveness trial. *Journal of Affective Disorders*, *175*, 124–132. https://doi.org/10.1016/j.jad.2014.12.046

McGowan, S. K., Behar, E., & Luhmann, M. (2016). Examining the relationship between worry and sleep: A daily process approach. *Behavior Therapy*, *47*(4), 460–473. https://doi.org/10.1016/j.beth.2015.12.003

McKinnon, A., Keers, R., Coleman, J. R. I., Lester, K. J., Roberts, S., Arendt, K., Bögels, S. M., Cooper, P., Creswell, C., Hartman, C. A., Fjermestad, K. W., In-Albon, T., Lavallee, K., Lyneham, H. J., Smith, P., Meiser-Stedman, R., Nauta, M. H., Rapee, R. M., Rey, Y., … Hudson, J. L. (2018). The impact of treatment delivery format on response to cognitive behaviour therapy for preadolescent children with anxiety disorders. *Journal of Child Psychology and Psychiatry*, *59*, 763–72. https://doi.org/10.1111/jcpp.12872

McLeod, B. D., Wood, J. J., & Weisz, J. R. (2007). Examining the association between parenting and childhood anxiety: A meta-analysis. *Clinical Psychology Review*, *27*(2), 155–172. https://doi.org/10.1016/j.cpr.2006.09.002

McMahon, A., Duane, Y., & Wilson, C. (in preparation). *Worry and associated processes in young people with sickle cell disease.*

McWilliams, L. A., Cox, B. J., & Enns, M. W. (2003). Mood and anxiety disorders associated with chronic pain: An examination in a nationally representative sample. *PAIN*, *106*(1), 127. https://doi.org/10.1016/S0304-3959(03)00301-4

Meagher, R., Chessor, D., & Fogliati, V. J. (2018). Treatment of pathological worry in children with acceptance-based behavioural therapy and a multisensory learning aide: A pilot study: Acceptance-based anxiety treatment for children. *Australian Psychologist, 53*(2), 134–143. https://doi.org/10.1111/ap.12288

Meeten, F., & Davey, G. C. L. (2011). Mood-as-input hypothesis and perseverative psychopathologies. *Clinical Psychology Review, 31*(8), 1259–1275. https://doi.org/10.1016/j.cpr.2011.08.002

Mendez, F. X., Quiles, M. J., & Hidalgo, M. D. (2001). The children's surgical worries questionnaire: Reliability and validity of a new self-report measure. *Children's Health Care, 30*(4), 271–281. https://doi.org/10.1207/S15326888CHC3004_02

Mendlowitz, S. L., Manassis, K., Bradley, S., Scapillato, D., Miezitis, S., & Shaw, B. E. (1999). Cognitive-behavioral group treatments in childhood anxiety disorders: The role of parental involvement. *Journal of the American Academy of Child & Adolescent Psychiatry, 38*(10), 1223–1229. https://doi.org/10.1097/00004583-199910000-00010

Mennin, D. S., Heimberg, R. G., Turk, C. L., & Fresco, D. M. (2002). Applying an emotion regulation framework to integrative approaches to generalized anxiety disorder. *Clinical Psychology: Science and Practice, 9*(1), 85–90. https://doi.org/10.1093/clipsy/9.1.85

Mennin, D. S., Heimberg, R. G., Turk, C. L., & Fresco, D. M. (2005). Preliminary evidence for an emotion dysregulation model of generalized anxiety disorder. *Behaviour Research and Therapy, 43*(10), 1281–1310. https://doi.org/10.1016/j.brat.2004.08.008

Mennin, D. S., McLaughlin, K. A., & Flanagan, T. J. (2009). Emotion regulation deficits in generalized anxiety disorder, social anxiety disorder, and their co-occurrence. *Journal of Anxiety Disorders, 23*(7), 866–871. https://doi.org/10.1016/j.janxdis.2009.04.006

Michael, K. D., Payne, L. O., & Albright, A. E. (2012). An adaptation of the coping cat program: The successful treatment of a 6-year-old boy with generalized anxiety disorder. *Clinical Case Studies, 11*(6), 426–440. https://doi.org/10.1177/1534650112460912

Molfese, V. J., & Molfese, D. L. (Eds.). (2000). *Temperament and personality development across the life span.* London: Routledge.

Möller, E. L., Majdandžić, M., & Bögels, S. M. (2015). Parental anxiety, parenting behavior, and infant anxiety: Differential associations for fathers and mothers. *Journal of Child and Family Studies, 24*(9), 2626–2637. https://doi.org/10.1007/s10826-014-0065-7

Monestès, J.-L., Karekla, M., Jacobs, N., Michaelides, M., Hooper, N., Kleen, M., Ruiz, F. J., Miselli, G., Presti, G., Luciano, C., Villatte, M., Bond, F. W., Kishita, N., & Hayes, S. (2018). Experiential avoidance as a common psychological process in European cultures. *European Journal of Psychological Assessment*, *34*(4), 247–257. https://doi.org/10.1027/1015-5759/a000327

Mothander, P. R., & Wang, M. (2014). Parental rearing, attachment, and social anxiety in Chinese adolescents. *Youth & Society*, *46*(2), 155–175. https://doi.org/10.1177/0044118X11427573

Mousavi, S. E., Low, W. Y., & Hashim, A. H. (2016). Perceived parenting styles and cultural influences in adolescent's anxiety: A cross-cultural comparison. *Journal of Child and Family Studies*, *25*(7), 2102–2110. https://doi.org/10.1007/s10826-016-0393-x

Mullen, D., Wilson, C., Jordan, A., Fisher, E., Madhavakkannan, H., & Wainright, E. (in preparation). *Beliefs about worry and pain in young people*.

Muris, P. (2002). Parental rearing behaviors and worry of normal adolescents. *Psychological Reports*, *91*(2), 428–430. https://doi.org/10.2466/pr0.2002.91.2.428

Muris, P., Meesters, C., & Gobel, M. (2001). Reliability, validity, and normative data of the Penn State Worry Questionnaire in 8–12-yr-old children. *Journal of Behavior Therapy and Experimental Psychiatry*, *32*(2), 63–72. https://doi.org/10.1016/s0005-7916(01)00022-2

Muris, P., Meesters, C., Merckelbach, H., & Hülsenbeck, P. (2000). Worry in children is related to perceived parental rearing and attachment. *Behaviour Research and Therapy*, *38*(5), 487–497. https://doi.org/ 10.1016/s0005-7967(99)00072-8

Muris, P., Meesters, C., Merckelbach, H., Sermon, A., & Zwakhalen, S. (1998). Worry in normal children. *Journal of the American Academy of Child & Adolescent Psychiatry*, *37*(7), 703–710. https://doi.org/10.1097/00004583-199807000-00009

Muris, P., Merckelbach, H., Gadet, B., & Moulaert, V. (2000). Fears, worries, and scary dreams in 4-to 12-year-old children: Their content, developmental pattern, and origins. *Journal of Clinical Child Psychology*, *29*(1), 43–52. https://doi.org/10.1207/S15374424jccp2901_5

Muris, P., Merckelbach, H., & Luijten, M. (2002). The connection between cognitive development and specific fears and worries in normal children and children with below-average intellectual abilities: A preliminary study. *Behaviour Research and Therapy*, *40*(1), 37–56. https://doi.org/10.1016/S0005-7967(00)00115-7

Muris, P., Merckelbach, H., Meesters, C., & van den Brand, K. (2002). Cognitive development and worry in normal children. *Cognitive Therapy and Research*, *26*(6), 775–787. https://doi.org/10.1023/A:1021241517274

Muris, P., Merckelbach, H., Ollendick, T., King, N., & Bogie, N. (2002). Three traditional and three new childhood anxiety questionnaires: Their reliability and validity in a normal adolescent sample. *Behaviour Research and Therapy*, *40*(7), 753–772. https://doi.org/10.1016/S0005-7967(01)00056-0

Muris, P., Roelofs, J., Meesters, C., & Boomsma, P. (2004). Rumination and worry in nonclinical adolescents. *Cognitive Therapy and Research*, *28*(4), 539–554. https://doi.org/10.1023/B:COTR.0000045563.66060.3e

Murray, L., Cooper, P., Creswell, C., Schofield, E., & Sack, C. (2007). The effects of maternal social phobia on mother? Infant interactions and infant social responsiveness. *Journal of Child Psychology and Psychiatry*, *48*(1), 45–52. https://doi.org/10.1111/j.1469-7610.2006.01657.x

Murray, L., Lau, P. Y., Arteche, A., Creswell, C., Russ, S., Zoppa, L. D., Muggeo, M., Stein, A., & Cooper, P. (2012). Parenting by anxious mothers: Effects of disorder subtype, context and child characteristics: Specificity of anxiety disorder-subtype effects on parenting. *Journal of Child Psychology and Psychiatry*, *53*(2), 188–196. https://doi.org/10.1111/j.1469-7610.2011.02473.x

Murray, L., Rosnay, M. D., Pearson, J., Bergeron, C., Schofield, E., Royal-Lawson, M., & Cooper, P. J. (2008). Intergenerational transmission of social anxiety: The role of social referencing processes in infancy. *Child Development*, *79*(4), 1049–1064. https://doi.org/10.1111/j.1467-8624.2008.01175.x

Nauta, M. H., Scholing, A., Emmelkamp, P. M. G., & Minderaa, R. B. (2001). Cognitive-behavioural therapy for anxiety disordered children in a clinical setting: Does additional cognitive parent training enhance treatment effectiveness? *Clinical Psychology & Psychotherapy*, *8*(5), 330–340. https://doi.org/10.1002/cpp.314

Nelemans, S. A., Hale, W. W., Branje, S. J. T., Hawk, S. T., & Meeus, W. H. J. (2014). Maternal criticism and adolescent depressive and generalized anxiety disorder symptoms: A 6-year longitudinal community study. *Journal of Abnormal Child Psychology*, *42*(5), 755–766. https://doi.org/10.1007/s10802-013-9817-x

Nelson, E. E., Leibenluft, E., McClure, E. B., & Pine, D. S. (2005). The social re-orientation of adolescence: A neuroscience perspective on the process and its relation to psychopathology. *Psychological Medicine*, *35*(2), 163–174. https://doi.org/10.1017/S0033291704003915

Newman, M. G., Castonguay, L. G., Jacobson, N. C., & Moore, G. A. (2015). Adult attachment as a moderator of treatment outcome for generalized anxiety disorder: Comparison between cognitive–behavioral therapy (CBT) plus supportive listening and CBT plus interpersonal and emotional processing therapy. *Journal of Consulting and Clinical Psychology, 83*(5), 915–925. https://doi.org/10.1037/a0039359

Newman, M. G., & Llera, S. J. (2011). A novel theory of experiential avoidance in generalized anxiety disorder: A review and synthesis of research supporting a contrast avoidance model of worry. *Clinical Psychology Review, 31*(3), 371–382. https://doi.org/10.1016/j.cpr.2011.01.008

Ng-Cordell, E., Hanley, M., Kelly, A., & Riby, D. M. (2018). Anxiety in Williams syndrome: The role of social behaviour, executive functions and change over time. *Journal of Autism and Developmental Disorders, 48*(3), 796–808. https://doi.org/10.1007/s10803-017-3357-0

Normann, N., & Esbjørn, B. H. (2018). How do anxious children attempt to regulate worry? Results from a qualitative study with an experimental manipulation. *Psychology and Psychotherapy: Theory, Research and Practice.* https://doi.org/10.1111/papt.12210

Norton, P. J. (2005). A psychometric analysis of the intolerance of uncertainty scale among four racial groups. *Journal of Anxiety Disorders, 19*(6), 699–707. https://doi.org/10.1016/j.janxdis.2004.08.002

O'Kearney, R., & Pech, M. (2014). General and sleep-specific worry in insomnia: General and sleep-specific worry in insomnia. *Sleep and Biological Rhythms, 12*(3), 212–215. https://doi.org/10.1111/sbr.12054

Okado, Y., & Bierman, K. L. (2015). Differential risk for late adolescent conduct problems and mood dysregulation among children with early externalizing behavior problems. *Journal of Abnormal Child Psychology, 43*(4), 735–747. https://doi.org/10.1007/s10802-014-9931-4

Oldham-Cooper, R., & Loades, M. (2017). Disorder-specific versus generic cognitive-behavioral treatment of anxiety disorders in children and young people: A systematic narrative review of evidence for the effectiveness of disorder-specific CBT compared with the disorder-generic treatment. *Journal of Child and Adolescent Psychiatric Nursing, 30*(1), 6–17. https://doi.org/10.1111/jcap.12165

Ollendick, T. H., & Benoit, K. E. (2012). A parent–child interactional model of social anxiety disorder in youth. *Clinical Child and Family Psychology Review, 15*(1), 81–91. https://doi.org/10.1007/s10567-011-0108-1

Orton, G. L. (1982). A comparative study of children's worries. *The Journal of Psychology: Interdisciplinary and Applied, 110*(2), 153–162. https://doi.org/10.1080/00223980.1982.9915336

Osleger, C. (2012). *Can the catastrophizing interview technique be used to develop understanding of childhood worry?* Unpublished dissertation. Norwich: University of East Anglia.

Osmanağaoğlu, N., Creswell, C., & Dodd, H. F. (2018). Intolerance of Uncertainty, anxiety, and worry in children and adolescents: A meta-analysis. *Journal of Affective Disorders, 225,* 80–90. https://doi.org/10.1016/j.jad.2017.07.035

Ottaviani, C., Thayer, J. F., Verkuil, B., Lonigro, A., Medea, B., Couyoumdjian, A., & Brosschot, J. F. (2016). Physiological concomitants of perseverative cognition: A systematic review and meta-analysis. *Psychological Bulletin, 142*(3), 231–259. https://doi.org/10.1037/bul0000036

Ozsivadjian, A., Knott, F., & Magiati, I. (2012). Parent and child perspectives on the nature of anxiety in children and young people with autism spectrum disorders: A focus group study. *Autism, 16*(2), 107–121. https://doi.org/10.1177/1362361311431703

Papachristou, H., Theodorou, M., Neophytou, K., & Panayiotou, G. (2018). Community sample evidence on the relations among behavioural inhibition system, anxiety sensitivity, experiential avoidance, and social anxiety in adolescents. *Journal of Contextual Behavioral Science, 8,* 36–43. https://doi.org/10.1016/j.jcbs.2018.03.001

Parkinson, M., & Creswell, C. (2011). Worry and problem-solving skills and beliefs in primary school children: Worry and problem-solving skills. *British Journal of Clinical Psychology, 50*(1), 106–112. https://doi.org/10.1348/014466510X523887

Pasarelu, C. R., Dobrean, A., Balazsi, R., Podina, I. R., & Mogoase, C. (2017). Interpretation biases in the intergenerational transmission of worry: A path analysis. *Journal of Evidence-Based Psychotherapies, 17*(1), 31–49.

Payne, S., Bolton, D., & Perrin, S. (2011). A pilot investigation of cognitive therapy for generalized anxiety disorder in children aged 7–17 years. *Cognitive Therapy and Research, 35*(2), 171–178. https://doi.org/10.1007/s10608-010-9341-z

Penney, A. M., Mazmanian, D., & Rudanycz, C. (2013). Comparing positive and negative beliefs about worry in predicting generalized anxiety disorder symptoms. *Canadian Journal of Behavioural Science/Revue canadienne des sciences du comportement, 45*(1), 34–41. https://doi.org/10.1037/a0027623

Perquin, C. W., Hazebroek-Kampschreur, A. A. J. M., Hunfeld, J. A. M., Bohnen, A. M., van Suijlekom-Smit, L. W. A., Passchier, J., & van der Wouden, J. C. (2000). Pain in children and adolescents: A common experience. *PAIN, 87*(1), 51. https://doi.org/10.1016/S0304-3959(00)00269-4

Perrin, S., Bevan, D., Payne, S., & Bolton, D. (2019). GAD-specific cognitive behavioral treatment for children and adolescents: A pilot randomized controlled trial. *Cognitive Therapy and Research, 43*(6), 1051–1064. https://doi.org/10.1007/s10608-019-10020-3

Perrin, S., & Last, C. G. (1992). Do childhood anxiety measures measure anxiety? *Journal of Abnormal Child Psychology, 20*(6), 567–578. https://doi.org/10.1007/BF00911241

Pestle, S. L., Chorpita, B. F., & Schiffman, J. (2008). Psychometric properties of the Penn State Worry Questionnaire for children in a large clinical sample. *Journal of Clinical Child & Adolescent Psychology, 37*(2), 465–471. https://doi.org/10.1080/15374410801955896

Pinquart, M. (2017). Associations of parenting dimensions and styles with internalizing symptoms in children and adolescents: A meta-analysis. *Marriage & Family Review, 53*(7), 613–640. https://doi.org/10.1080/01494929.2016.1247761

Pintner, R., & Lev, J. (1940). Worries of school children. *The Pedagogical Seminary and Journal of Genetic Psychology, 56*, 67–76. phttps://doi.org/10.1080/08856559.1940.9944063

Platt, J. J., & Spivack, G. (2006). Unidimensionality of the means-ends problem-solving (MEPS) procedure. *Journal of Clinical Psychology, 31*(1), 15–16. https://doi.org/10.1002/1097-4679(197501)31:1<15::AID-JCLP2270310106>3.0.CO;2-8

Prados, J. M. (2011). Do beliefs about the utility of worry facilitate worry? *Journal of Anxiety Disorders, 25*(2), 217–223. https://doi.org/10.1016/j.janxdis.2010.09.005

Qiu, L., Su, J., Ni, Y., Bai, Y., Zhang, X., Li, X., & Wan, X. (2018). The neural system of metacognition accompanying decision-making in the prefrontal cortex. *PLOS Biology, 16*(4), e2004037. https://doi.org/10.1371/journal.pbio.2004037

Quach, A. S., Epstein, N. B., Riley, P. J., Falconier, M. K., & Fang, X. (2015). Effects of parental warmth and academic pressure on anxiety and depression symptoms in Chinese adolescents. *Journal of Child and Family Studies, 24*(1), 106–116. https://doi.org/10.1007/s10826-013-9818-y

Rafetseder, E., & Perner, J. (2012). When the alternative would have been better: Counterfactual reasoning and the emergence of regret. *Cognition & Emotion, 26*(5), 800–819. https://doi.org/10.1080/02699931.2011.619744

Reale, L., Bartoli, B., Cartabia, M., Zanetti, M., Costantino, M. A., Canevini, M. P., Termine, C., Bonati, M., Conte, S., Renzetti, V., Salvoni, L., Molteni, M., Salandi, A., Trabattoni, S., Effedri, P., Filippini, E., Pedercini, E., Zanetti, E., ... Rossi, G. (2017). Comorbidity prevalence and treatment outcome in children and adolescents with ADHD. *European Child & Adolescent Psychiatry; New York, 26*(12), 1443–1457. http://dx.doi.org/10.1007/s00787-017-1005-z

Reinholdt-Dunne, M. L., Blicher, A., Nordahl, H., Normann, N., Esbjørn, B. H., & Wells, A. (2019). Modeling the relationships between metacognitive beliefs, attention control and symptoms in children with and without anxiety disorders: A test of the S-REF model. *Frontiers in Psychology, 10,* 1025. https://doi.org/10.3389/fpsyg.2019.01205

Reynolds, C. R. (1980). Concurrent validity of what I think and feel: The revised children's manifest anxiety scale. *Journal of Consulting and Clinical Psychology, 48*(6), 774–775. https://doi.org/10.1037/0022-006X.48.6.774

Reynolds, C. R., & Richmond, B. O. (1978). What I think and feel: A revised measure of children's manifest anxiety. *Journal of Abnormal Child Psychology, 6*(2), 271–280. https://doi.org/10.1007/BF00919131

Riggs, K. J., Peterson, D. M., Robinson, E. J., & Mitchell, P. (1998). Are errors in false belief tasks symptomatic of a broader difficulty with counterfactuality? *Cognitive Development, 13*(1), 73–90. https://doi.org/10.1016/S0885-2014(98)90021-1

Roberts, R. E., & Duong, H. T. (2017). Is there an association between short sleep duration and adolescent anxiety disorders? *Sleep Medicine, 30,* 82–87. https://doi.org/10.1016/j.sleep.2016.02.007

Robinson, E. J., & Beck, S. (2000). What is difficult about counterfactual reasoning? In P. Mitchell, & K. Riggs (Eds.), *Children's reasoning and the mind* (pp. 101–119). London: Psychology Press/Taylor & Francis.

Rodríguez-Biglieri, R., & Vetere, G. L. (2011). Psychometric characteristics of the Penn State Worry Questionnaire in an Argentinean sample: A cross-cultural contribution. *The Spanish Journal of Psychology, 14*(1), 452–463. https://doi.org/10.5209/rev_SJOP.2011.v14.n1.41

Roebers, C. M. (2017). Executive function and metacognition: Towards a unifying framework of cognitive self-regulation. *Developmental Review, 45,* 31–51. https://doi.org/10.1016/j.dr.2017.04.001

Roelofs, J., Meesters, C., ter Huurne, M., Bamelis, L., & Muris, P. (2006). On the links between attachment style, parental rearing behaviors, and internalizing and externalizing problems in non-clinical children. *Journal of Child and Family Studies, 15*(3), 319–332. https://doi.org/10.1007/s10826-006-9025-1

Roemer, L., & Orsillo, S. M. (2002). Expanding our conceptualization of and treatment for generalized anxiety disorder: Integrating mindfulness/acceptance-based approaches with existing cognitive-behavioral models. *Clinical Psychology: Science and Practice, 9*(1), 54–68. https://doi.org/10.1093/clipsy.9.1.54

Roemer, L., Salters, K., Raffa, S. D., & Orsillo, S. M. (2005). Fear and avoidance of internal experiences in GAD: Preliminary tests of a conceptual model. *Cognitive Therapy and Research, 29*(1), 71–88. https://doi.org/10.1007/s10608-005-1650-2

Roese, N. J., & Olson, J. M. (1997). Counterfactual thinking: The intersection of affect and function. In M. P. Zanna (Ed.), *Advances in experimental social psychology* (Vol. 29, pp. 1–59). Academic Press. https://doi.org/10.1016/S0065-2601(08)60015-5

Roisman, G. I., Padrón, E., Sroufe, L. A., & Egeland, B. (2002). Earned–secure attachment status in retrospect and prospect. *Child Development, 73*(4), 1204–1219. https://doi.org/10.1111/1467-8624.00467

Ronald, A., Sieradzka, D., Cardno, A. G., Haworth, C. M. A., McGuire, P., & Freeman, D. (2014). Characterization of psychotic experiences in adolescence using the specific psychotic experiences questionnaire: Findings from a study of 5000 16-year-old twins. *Schizophrenia Bulletin, 40*(4), 868–877. https://doi.org/10.1093/schbul/sbt106

Rovira, J., Albarracin, G., Salvador, L., Rejas, J., Sánchez-Iriso, E., & Cabasés, J. M. (2012). The cost of generalized anxiety disorder in primary care settings: Results of the ANCORA study. *Community Mental Health Journal, 48*(3), 372–383. https://doi.org/10.1007/s10597-012-9503-4

Rubin, K. H., & Rose-Krasnor, L. (1992). Interpersonal problem solving and social competence in children. In V. B. Van Hasselt & M. Hersen (Eds.), *Handbook of Social Development* (pp. 283–323). New York: Springer US. https://doi.org/10.1007/978-1-4899-0694-6_12

Rucker, L. S., West, L. M., & Roemer, L. (2010). Relationships among perceived racial stress, intolerance of uncertainty, and worry in a black sample. *Behavior Therapy, 41*(2), 245–253. https://doi.org/10.1016/j.beth.2009.04.001

Ruscio, A. M. (2002). Delimiting the boundaries of generalized anxiety disorder: Differentiating high worriers with and without GAD. *Journal of Anxiety Disorders, 16*(4), 377–400. https://doi.org/10.1016/S0887-6185(02)00130-5

Russell, E., & Sofronoff, K. (2005). Anxiety and social worries in children with Asperger syndrome. *Australian and New Zealand Journal of Psychiatry, 39*(7), 633–638. https://doi.org/10.1111/j.1440-1614.2005.01637.x

Saiphoo, A. N., & Vahedi, Z. (2019). A meta-analytic review of the relationship between social media use and body image disturbance. *Computers in Human Behavior, 101*, 259–275. https://doi.org/10.1016/j.chb.2019.07.028

Sala, M., & Levinson, C. A. (2016). The longitudinal relationship between worry and disordered eating: Is worry a precursor or consequence of disordered eating? *Eating Behaviors, 23*, 28–32. https://doi.org/10.1016/j.eatbeh.2016.07.012

Salari, E., Shahrivar, Z., Mahmoudi-Gharaei, J., Shirazi, E., & Sepasi, M. (2018). Parent-only group cognitive behavioral intervention for children with anxiety disorders: A control group study. *Journal of the Canadian Academy of Child and Adolescent Psychiatry, 27*(2), 130–136.

Salters-Pedneault, K., Roemer, L., Tull, M. T., Rucker, L., & Mennin, D. S. (2006). Evidence of broad deficits in emotion regulation associated with chronic worry and generalized anxiety disorder. *Cognitive Therapy and Research, 30*(4), 469–480. https://doi.org/10.1007/s10608-006-9055-4

Sanchez, A. L., Kendall, P. C., & Comer, J. S. (2016). Evaluating the intergenerational link between maternal and child intolerance of uncertainty: A preliminary cross-sectional examination. *Cognitive Therapy and Research, 40*(4), 532–539. https://doi.org/10.1007/s10608-016-9757-1

Sankar, R., Robinson, L., Honey, E., & Freeston, M. H. (2017). We know intolerance of uncertainty is a transdiagnostic factor but we don't know what it looks like in everyday life. *Clinical Psychology Forum, 296*, 10–15.

Sassaroli, S., Bertelli, S., Decoppi, M., Crosina, M., Milos, G., & Ruggiero, G. M. (2005). Worry and eating disorders: A psychopathological association. *Eating Behaviors, 6*(4), 301–307. https://doi.org/10.1016/j.eatbeh.2005.05.001

Sassaroli, S., & Ruggiero, G. M. (2005). The role of stress in the association between low self-esteem, perfectionism, and worry, and eating disorders. *International Journal of Eating Disorders, 37*(2), 135–141. https://doi.org/10.1002/eat.20079

Schmidt, L. A., & Fox, N. A. (1998). Fear-potentiated startle responses in temperamentally different human infants. *Developmental Psychobiology: The Journal of the International Society for Developmental Psychobiology, 32*(2), 113–120. https://doi.org/10.1002/(SICI)1098-2302(199803)32:2<113::AID-DEV4>3.0.CO;2-S

Schneider, S., Houweling, J. E. G., Gommlich-Schneider, S., Klein, C., Nündel, B., & Wolke, D. (2009). Effect of maternal panic disorder on mother–child interaction and relation to child anxiety and child self-efficacy. *Archives of Women's Mental Health, 12*(4), 251–259. https://doi.org/10.1007/s00737-009-0072-7

Segerstrom, S. C., Tsao, J. C. I., Alden, L. E., & Craske, M. G. (2000). Worry and rumination: Repetitive thought as a concomitant and predictor of negative mood. *Cognitive Therapy and Research, 24*(6), 671–688. https://doi.org/10.1023/A:1005587311498

Seligman, L. D., Hovey, J. D., Ibarra, M., Hurtado, G., Marin, C. E., & Silverman, W. K. (2019). Latino and Non-Latino parental treatment preferences for child and adolescent anxiety disorders. *Child Psychiatry & Human Development, 51*, 617–624. https://doi.org/10.1007/s10578-019-00945-x

Settipani, C. A., Puleo, C. M., Conner, B. T., & Kendall, P. C. (2012). Characteristics and anxiety symptom presentation associated with autism spectrum traits in youth with anxiety disorders. *Journal of Anxiety Disorders, 26*(3), 459–467. https://doi.org/10.1016/j.janxdis.2012.01.010

Sexton, K. A., & Dugas, M. J. (2009). An investigation of factors associated with cognitive avoidance in worry. *Cognitive Therapy and Research, 33*(2), 150–162. https://doi.org/10.1007/s10608-007-9177-3

Shanahan, L., Copeland, W. E., Angold, A., Bondy, C. L., & Costello, E. J. (2014). Sleep problems predict and are predicted by generalized anxiety/depression and oppositional defiant disorder. *Journal of the American Academy of Child & Adolescent Psychiatry, 53*(5), 550–558. https://doi.org/10.1016/j.jaac.2013.12.029

Sharpe, H., Damazer, K., Treasure, J., & Schmidt, U. (2013). What are adolescents' experiences of body dissatisfaction and dieting, and what do they recommend for prevention? A qualitative study. *Eating and Weight Disorders—Studies on Anorexia, Bulimia and Obesity, 18*(2), 133–141. https://doi.org/10.1007/s40519-013-0023-1

Shekim, W. O., Asarnow, R. F., Hess, E., Zaucha, K., & Wheeler, N. (1990). A clinical and demographic profile of a sample of adults with attention deficit hyperactivity disorder, residual state. *Comprehensive Psychiatry, 31*(5), 416–425. https://doi.org/10.1016/0010-440X(90)90026-O

Shenk, C. E., Putnam, F. W., & Noll, J. G. (2012). Experiential avoidance and the relationship between child maltreatment and PTSD symptoms: Preliminary evidence. *Child Abuse & Neglect, 36*(2), 118–126. https://doi.org/10.1016/j.chiabu.2011.09.012

Shiels, K., & Hawk, L. W. (2010). Self-regulation in ADHD: The role of error processing. *Clinical Psychology Review, 30*(8), 951–961. https://doi.org/10.1016/j.cpr.2010.06.010

Sibrava, N. J., & Borkovec, T. D. (2006). The cognitive avoidance theory of worry. In G. C. L. Davey, & A. Wells (Eds.), *Worry and its psychological disorders: Theory, assessment and treatment* (pp. 239–256). Chichester: John Wiley & Sons Ltd. https://doi.org/10.1002/9780470713143.ch14

Silverman, W. K., Greca, A. M., & Wasserstein, S. (1995). What do children worry about? Worries and their relation to anxiety. *Child Development, 66*(3), 671–686. https://doi.org/10.2307/1131942

Silverman, W. K., Marin, C. E., Rey, Y., Kurtines, W. M., Jaccard, J., & Pettit, J. W. (2019). Group-versus parent-involvement CBT for childhood anxiety disorders: Treatment specificity and long-term recovery mediation. *Clinical Psychological Science, 7*(4), 840–855. https://doi.org/10.1177/2167702619830404

Simon, A., & Ward, L. O. (1974). Variables influencing the sources, frequency and intensity of worry in secondary school pupils. *British Journal of Social & Clinical Psychology, 13*(4), 391–396. https://doi.org/10.1111/j.2044-8260.1974.tb00134.x

Simonds, J., & Rothbart, M. (2004). *The temperament in middle childhood questionnaire (TMCQ): A computerized self-report measure of temperament for ages 7–10.* Occasional Temperament Conference, Athens, Greece.

Simons, L. E., Sieberg, C. B., & Lewis Claar, R. (2012). Anxiety and functional disability in a large sample of children and adolescents with chronic pain. *Pain Research and Management, 17*(2), 93–97. https://doi.org/10.1155/2012/420676

Siqueland, L., Rynn, M., & Diamond, G. S. (2005). Cognitive behavioral and attachment based family therapy for anxious adolescents: Phase I and II studies. *Journal of Anxiety Disorders, 19*(4), 361–381. https://doi.org/10.1016/j.janxdis.2004.04.006

Smetana, J. G. (1985). Preschool children's conceptions of transgressions: Effects of varying moral and conventional domain-related attributes. *Developmental Psychology, 21*(1), 18–29. https://doi.org/10.1037/0012-1649.21.1.18

Smetana, J. G. (1993). Understanding of social rules. In M. Bennett (Ed.) *The development of social cognition: The child as psychologist* (pp. 111–141). New York: Guilford Press.

Smink, F. R. E., van Hoeken, D., & Hoek, H. W. (2012). Epidemiology of eating disorders: incidence, prevalence and mortality rates. *Current Psychiatry Reports, 14*(4), 406–414. https://doi.org/10.1007/s11920-012-0282-y

Smith, A. M., Flannery-Schroeder, E. C., Gorman, K. S., & Cook, N. (2014). Parent cognitive-behavioral intervention for the treatment of childhood anxiety disorders: A pilot study. *Behaviour Research and Therapy, 61*, 156–161. https://doi.org/10.1016/j.brat.2014.08.010

Smith, J. M., & Alloy, L. B. (2009). A roadmap to rumination: A review of the definition, assessment, and conceptualization of this multifaceted construct. *Clinical Psychology Review, 29*(2), 116–128. https://doi.org/10.1016/j.cpr.2008.10.003

Smith, J. P., Glass, D. J., & Fireman, G. (2015). The understanding and experience of mixed emotions in 3–5-year-old children. *The Journal of Genetic Psychology, 176*(2), 65–81. https://doi.org/10.1080/00221325.2014.1002750

Smith, K. E., & Hudson, J. L. (2013). Metacognitive beliefs and processes in clinical anxiety in children. *Journal of Clinical Child & Adolescent Psychology, 42*(5), 590–602. https://doi.org/10.1080/15374416.2012.755925

Songco, A., Hudson, J. L., & Fox, E. (2020). A cognitive model of pathological worry in children and adolescents: A systematic review. *Clinical Child and Family Psychology Review, 23*(2), 229–249. https://doi.org/10.1007/s10567-020-00311-7

Sørensen, L., Plessen, K. J., Nicholas, J., & Lundervold, A. J. (2011). Is behavioral regulation in children with ADHD aggravated by comorbid anxiety disorder? *Journal of Attention Disorders, 15*(1), 56–66. https://doi.org/10.1177/1087054709356931

South, M., & Rodgers, J. (2017). Sensory, emotional and cognitive contributions to anxiety in autism spectrum disorders. *Frontiers in Human Neuroscience, 11.* https://doi.org/10.3389/fnhum.2017.00020

Southam-Gerow, M. A., & Kendall, P. C. (2000). A preliminary study of the emotion understanding of youths referred for treatment of anxiety disorders. *Journal of Clinical Child Psychology, 29*(3), 319–327. https://doi.org/10.1207/S15374424JCCP2903_3

Spain, D., Sin, J., Linder, K. B., McMahon, J., & Happé, F. (2018). Social anxiety in autism spectrum disorder: A systematic review. *Research in Autism Spectrum Disorders, 52,* 51–68. https://doi.org/10.1016/j.rasd.2018.04.007

Spears, M., Montgomery, A. A., Gunnell, D., & Araya, R. (2014). Factors associated with the development of self-harm amongst a socio-economically deprived cohort of adolescents in Santiago, Chile. *Social Psychiatry and Psychiatric Epidemiology, 49*(4), 629–637. https://doi.org/10.1007/s00127-013-0767-y

Speckens, A. E. M., & Hawton, K. (2011). Social problem solving in adolescents with suicidal behavior: A systematic review. *Suicide and Life-Threatening Behavior, 35*(4), 365–387. https://doi.org/10.1521/suli.2005.35.4.365

Spence, S. H. (1995). *Social skills training, enhancing social competence with children and adolescents: Research and technical support.* Slough: NFER-Nelson.

Spence, S. H. (1998). A measure of anxiety symptoms among children. *Behaviour Research and Therapy, 36*(5), 545–566. https://doi.org/10.1016/s0005-7967(98)00034-5

Spitzer, R. (1980). *Diagnostic and statistical manual of mental disorders* (Vol. III). Arlington: American Psychiatric Association Publishing.

Stallard, P., Spears, M., Montgomery, A. A., Phillips, R., & Sayal, K. (2013). Self-harm in young adolescents (12–16 years): Onset and short-term continuation in a community sample. *BMC Psychiatry, 13*(1), 328. https://doi.org/10.1186/1471-244X-13-328

Stanford, E. A., Chambers, C. T., Biesanz, J. C., & Chen, E. (2008). The frequency, trajectories and predictors of adolescent recurrent pain: A population-based approach. *PAIN, 138*(1), 11. https://doi.org/10.1016/j.pain.2007.10.032

Startup, H., Freeman, D., & Garety, P. A. (2007). Persecutory delusions and catastrophic worry in psychosis: Developing the understanding of delusion distress and persistence. *Behaviour Research and Therapy, 45*(3), 523–537. https://doi.org/10.1016/j.brat.2006.04.006

Startup, H., Lavender, A., Oldershaw, A., Stott, R., Tchanturia, K., Treasure, J., & Schmidt, U. (2013). Worry and rumination in anorexia nervosa. *Behavioural and Cognitive Psychotherapy, 41*(3), 301–316. https://doi.org/10.1017/S1352465812000847

Stein, A., Craske, M. G., Lehtonen, A., Harvey, A., Savage-McGlynn, E., Davies, B., Goodwin, J., Murray, L., Cortina-Borja, M., & Counsell, N. (2012). Maternal cognitions and mother–infant interaction in postnatal depression and generalized anxiety disorder. *Journal of Abnormal Psychology, 121*(4), 795. https://doi.org/10.1037/a0026847

Steinberg, L. (2005). Cognitive and affective development in adolescence. *Trends in Cognitive Sciences, 9*(2), 69–74. https://doi.org/10.1016/j.tics.2004.12.005

Steinsbekk, S., Berg-Nielsen, T. S., & Wichstrøm, L. (2013). Sleep disorders in preschoolers: Prevalence and comorbidity with psychiatric symptoms. *Journal of Developmental and Behavioral Pediatrics, 34*(9), 633–641. https://doi.org/10.1097/01.DBP.0000437636.33306.49

Sternheim, L., Startup, H., Saeidi, S., Morgan, J., Hugo, P., Russell, A., & Schmidt, U. (2012). Understanding catastrophic worry in eating disorders: Process and content characteristics. *Journal of Behavior Therapy and Experimental Psychiatry, 43*(4), 1095–1103. https://doi.org/10.1016/j.jbtep.2012.05.006

Stevenson-Hinde, J., & Shouldice, A. (1995). 4.5 to 7 years: Fearful behaviour, fears and worries. *Journal of Child Psychology and Psychiatry, 36*(6), 1027–1038. https://doi.org/10.1111/j.1469-7610.1995.tb01348.x

Stokes, C., & Hirsch, C. R. (2010). Engaging in imagery versus verbal processing of worry: Impact on negative intrusions in high worriers. *Behaviour Research and Therapy, 48*(5), 418–423. https://doi.org/10.1016/j.brat.2009.12.011

Stuijfzand, S., Creswell, C., Field, A. P., Pearcey, S., & Dodd, H. (2018). Research review: Is anxiety associated with negative interpretations of ambiguity in children and adolescents? A systematic review and meta-analysis. *Journal of Child Psychology and Psychiatry, 59*(11), 1127–1142. https://doi.org/10.1111/jcpp.12822

Stuijfzand, S., & Dodd, H. F. (2017). Young children have social worries too: Validation of a brief parent report measure of social worries in children aged 4–8 years. *Journal of Anxiety Disorders, 50*, 87–93. https://doi.org/10.1016/j.janxdis.2017.05.008

Suddendorf, T. (2010). Linking yesterday and tomorrow: Preschoolers ability to report temporally displaced events. *British Journal of Developmental Psychology, 258*(2), 491–498. https://doi.org/10.1016/j.cub.2014.10.058

Suddendorf, T., Nielsen, M., & von Gehlen, R. (2011). Children's capacity to remember a novel problem and to secure its future solution: Future solutions of novel problems. *Developmental Science, 14*(1), 26–33. https://doi.org/10.1111/j.1467-7687.2010.00950.x

Suh, E. M., Schwartz, S. H., & Melech, G. (2000). National differences in micro and macro worry: Social, economic, and cultural explanations. In E. Diener & E. M. Suh (Eds.), *Culture and subjective well-being*. Cambridge, MA: The MIT Press.

Suveg, C., Morelen, D., Brewer, G. A., & Thomassin, K. (2010). The emotion dysregulation model of anxiety: A preliminary path analytic examination. *Journal of Anxiety Disorders, 24*(8), 924–930. https://doi.org/10.1016/j.janxdis.2010.06.018

Suveg, C., Sood, E., Comer, J. S., & Kendall, P. C. (2009). Changes in emotion regulation following cognitive-behavioral therapy for anxious youth. *Journal of Clinical Child & Adolescent Psychology, 38*(3), 390–401. https://doi.org/10.1080/15374410902851721

Suveg, C., & Zeman, J. (2004). Emotion regulation in children with anxiety disorders. *Journal of Clinical Child and Adolescent Psychology, 33*(4), 750–759. https://doi.org/10.1207/s15374424jccp3304_10

Suveg, C., Zeman, J., Flannery-Schroeder, E., & Cassano, M. (2005). Emotion socialization in families of children with an anxiety disorder. *Journal of Abnormal Child Psychology, 33*(2), 145–155. https://doi.org/10.1007/s10802-005-1823-1

Szabó, M. (2007). Do children differentiate worry from fear? *Behaviour Change, 24*(4), 195–204.

Takahashi, F., Koseki, S., & Shimada, H. (2009). Developmental trends in children's aggression and social problem-solving. *Journal of Applied Developmental Psychology, 30*(3), 265–272. https://doi.org/10.1016/j.appdev.2008.12.007

Tallis, F., Davey, G. C. L., & Capuzzo, N. (1994). The phenomenology of non-pathological worry: A preliminary investigation. In G. C. L. Davey, & F. Tallis (Eds.), *Worrying: Perspectives on theory, assessment and treatment* (pp. 61–89). Chichester: John Wiley & Sons.

Thayer, J. F., Friedman, B. H., & Borkovec, T. D. (1996). Autonomic characteristics of generalized anxiety disorder and worry. *Biological Psychiatry, 39*(4), 255–266. https://doi.org/10.1016/0006-3223(95)00136-0

Thielsch, C., Ehring, T., Nestler, S., Wolters, J., Kopei, I., Rist, F., Gerlach, A. L., & Andor, T. (2015). Metacognitions, worry and sleep in everyday life: Studying bidirectional pathways using ecological momentary assessment in GAD patients. *Journal of Anxiety Disorders, 33*, 53–61. https://doi.org/10.1016/j.janxdis.2015.04.007

Thienemann, M., Moore, P., & Tompkins, K. (2006). A parent-only group intervention for children with anxiety disorders: Pilot study. *Journal of the American Academy of Child & Adolescent Psychiatry, 45*(1), 37–46. https://doi.org/10.1097/01.chi.0000186404.90217.02

Thirlwall, K., Cooper, P. J., Karalus, J., Voysey, M., Willetts, L., & Creswell, C. (2013). Treatment of child anxiety disorders via guided parent-delivered cognitive–behavioural therapy: Randomised controlled trial. *British Journal of Psychiatry, 203*(6), 436–444. https://doi.org/10.1192/bjp.bp.113.126698

Thomas, K. M., Drevets, W. C., Dahl, R. E., Ryan, N. D., Birmaher, B., Eccard, C. H., Axelson, D., Whalen, P. J., & Casey, B. J. (2001). Amygdala response to fearful faces in anxious and depressed children. *Archives of General Psychiatry, 58*(11), 1057–1063. https://doi.org/10.1001/archpsyc.58.11.1057

Topper, M., Emmelkamp, P. M. G., Watkins, E., & Ehring, T. (2017a). Prevention of anxiety disorders and depression by targeting excessive worry and rumination in adolescents and young adults: A randomized controlled trial. *Behaviour Research and Therapy, 90*, 123–136. https://doi.org/10.1016/j.brat.2016.12.015

Topper, M., Emmelkamp, P. M. G., Watkins, E., & Ehring, T. (2017b). Prevention of anxiety disorders and depression by targeting excessive worry and rumination in adolescents and young adults: A randomized controlled trial. *Behaviour Research and Therapy, 90*, 123–136. https://doi.org/10.1016/j.brat.2016.12.015

Tracey, S. A., Chorpita, B. F., Douban, J., & Barlow, D. H. (1997). Empirical evaluation of DSM-IV generalized anxiety disorder criteria in children and adolescents. *Journal of Clinical Child Psychology, 26*(4), 404–414. https://doi.org/10.1207/s15374424jccp2604_9

Treanor, M., Erisman, S. M., Salters-Pedneault, K., Roemer, L., & Orsillo, S. M. (2011). Acceptance-based behavioral therapy for GAD: Effects on outcomes from three theoretical models. *Depression and Anxiety, 28*(2), 127–136. https://doi.org/10.1002/da.20766

Triantafyllou, K., Cartwright-Hatton, S., Korpa, T., Kolaitis, G., & Barrowclough, C. (2012). Catastrophic worries in mothers of adolescents with internalizing disorders: Maternal catastrophic worries and adolescents' internalizing disorders.

British Journal of Clinical Psychology, 51(3), 307–322. https://doi.org/10.1111/j.2044-8260.2011.02029.x

Tsujimoto, S. (2008). The prefrontal cortex: Functional neural development during early childhood. *The Neuroscientist, 14*(4), 345–358. https://doi.org/10.1177/1073858408316002

Turk, C. L., Heimberg, R. G., Luterek, J. A., Mennin, D. S., & Fresco, D. M. (2005). Emotion dysregulation in generalized anxiety disorder: A comparison with social anxiety disorder. *Cognitive Therapy and Research, 29*(1), 89–106. https://doi.org/10.1007/s10608-005-1651-1

Turner, L., & Wilson, C. (2010). Worry, Mood and Stop Rules in Young Adolescents: Does the Mood-as-Input Theory Apply? *Journal of Experimental Psychopathology, 1*(1), 34–51. https://doi.org/10.5127/jep.007810

Turner, S. M., & Beidel, D. C. (1996). Is behavioral inhibition related to the anxiety disorders. *Clinical Psychology Review, 16*(2), 157–172. https://doi.org/10.1016/0272-7358(96)00010-4

Turner, S. M., Beidel, D. C., Roberson-Nay, R., & Tervo, K. (2003). Parenting behaviors in parents with anxiety disorders. *Behaviour Research and Therapy, 41*(5), 541–554. https://doi.org/10.1016/S0005-7967(02)00028-1

Ursache, A., & Raver, C. C. (2014). Trait and state anxiety: Relations to executive functioning in an at-risk sample. *Cognition and Emotion, 28*(5), 845–855. https://doi.org/10.1080/02699931.2013.855173

Vaclavik, D., Buitron, V., Rey, Y., Marin, C. E., Silverman, W. K., & Pettit, J. W. (2017). Parental acculturation level moderates outcome in peer-involved and parent-involved CBT for anxiety disorders in Latino youth. *Journal of Latina/o Psychology, 5*(4), 261–274. https://doi.org/10.1037/lat0000095

Vahedi, A., Krug, I., Fuller-Tyszkiewicz, M., & Westrupp, E. M. (2018). Longitudinal associations between work-family conflict and enrichment, inter-parental conflict, and child internalizing and externalizing problems. *Social Science & Medicine, 211*, 251–260. https://doi.org/10.1016/j.socscimed.2018.06.031

Van Ameringen, M., Mancini, C., Simpson, W., & Patterson, B. (2011). Adult attention deficit hyperactivity disorder in an anxiety disorders population. *CNS Neuroscience & Therapeutics, 17*(4), 221–226. https://doi.org/10.1111/j.1755-5949.2010.00148.x

van Eijck, F. E. A. M., Branje, S. J. T., Hale, W. W., & Meeus, W. H. J. (2012). Longitudinal associations between perceived parent-adolescent attachment relationship quality and generalized anxiety disorder symptoms in adolescence. *Journal of Abnormal Child Psychology, 40*(6), 871–883. https://doi.org/10.1007/s10802-012-9613-z

van Steensel, F. J. A., Bögels, S. M., & Perrin, S. (2011). Anxiety disorders in children and adolescents with autistic spectrum disorders: A meta-analysis. *Clinical Child and Family Psychology Review, 14*(3), 302. https://doi.org/10.1007/s10567-011-0097-0

van Straten, A., van der Zweerde, T., Kleiboer, A., Cuijpers, P., Morin, C. M., & Lancee, J. (2018). Cognitive and behavioral therapies in the treatment of insomnia: A meta-analysis. *Sleep Medicine Reviews, 38*, 3–16. https://doi.org/10.1016/j.smrv.2017.02.001

Varela, R. E., & Hensley-Maloney, L. (2009). The influence of culture on anxiety in Latino youth: A review. *Clinical Child and Family Psychology Review, 12*(3), 217–233. https://doi.org/10.1007/s10567-009-0044-5

Varela, R. E., Sanchez-Sosa, J. J., Biggs, B. K., & Luis, T. M. (2008). Anxiety symptoms and fears in Hispanic and European American Children: Cross-cultural measurement equivalence. *Journal of Psychopathology and Behavioral Assessment, 30*(2), 132–145. https://doi.org/10.1007/s10862-007-9056-y

Varela, R. E., Sanchez-Sosa, J. J., Biggs, B. K., & Luis, T. M. (2009). Parenting strategies and socio-cultural influences in childhood anxiety: Mexican, Latin American descent, and European American families. *Journal of Anxiety Disorders, 23*(5), 609–616. https://doi.org/10.1016/j.janxdis.2009.01.012

Vasey, M. W., & Borkovec, T. D. (1992). A catastrophizing assessment of worrisome thoughts. *Cognitive Therapy and Research, 16*(5), 505–520. https://doi.org/10.1007/BF01175138

Vasey, M. W., Crnic, K. A., & Carter, W. G. (1994). Worry in childhood: A developmental perspective. *Cognitive Therapy and Research, 18*(6), 529–549.

Vasey, M. W., & Daleiden, E. L. (1994). Worry in Children. In G. C. L. Davey & F. Tallis (Eds.), *Worrying: Perspectives on theory, assessment and treatment* (pp. 185–208). Chichester: John Wiley & Sons Ltd.

Verkuil, B., Brosschot, J., Borkovec, T. D., & Thayer, J. F. (2009). Acute autonomic effects of experimental worry and cognitive problem solving: Why worry about worry? *International Journal of Clinical and Health Psychology, 9*(3), 439–453.

Verstraeten, K., Bijttebier, P., Vasey, M. W., & Raes, F. (2011). Specificity of worry and rumination in the development of anxiety and depressive symptoms in children. *British Journal of Clinical Psychology, 50*(4), 364–378. https:/doi.org/10.1348/014466510X532715

Vervoort, T., Goubert, L., Eccleston, C., Bijttebier, P., & Crombez, G. (2006). Catastrophic thinking about pain is independently associated with pain severity, disability, and somatic complaints in school children and children with chronic pain. *Journal of Pediatric Psychology, 31*(7), 674–683. https://doi.org/10.1093/jpepsy/jsj059

Viana, A. G., & Rabian, B. (2008). Perceived attachment: Relations to anxiety sensitivity, worry, and GAD symptoms. *Behaviour Research and Therapy, 46*(6), 737–747. https://doi.org/10.1016/j.brat.2008.03.002

Visu-Petra, L., Miclea, M., & Visu-Petra, G. (2013). Individual differences in anxiety and executive functioning: A multidimensional view. *International Journal of Psychology, 48*(4), 649–659. https://doi.org/10.1080/00207594.2012.656132

Voon, D., & Phillips, L. J. (2015). An investigation of relationships between cognitive factors associated with worry. *Journal of Experimental Psychopathology, 6*(4), 330–342. https://doi.org/10.5127/jep.037013

Wåhlstedt, C., Thorell, L. B., & Bohlin, G. (2008). ADHD symptoms and executive function impairment: Early predictors of later behavioral problems. *Developmental Neuropsychology, 33*(2), 160–178. https://doi.org/10.1080/87565640701884253

Wahlund, T., Andersson, E., Jolstedt, M., Perrin, S., Vigerland, S., & Serlachius, E. (2019). Intolerance of uncertainty-focused treatment for adolescents with excessive worry: A pilot feasibility study. *Cognitive and Behavioral Practice, 27*, 215–230. https://doi.org/10.1016/j.cbpra.2019.06.002

Walczak, M., Breinholst, S., Ollendick, T., & Esbjørn, B. H. (2019). Cognitive behavior therapy and metacognitive therapy: Moderators of treatment outcomes for children with generalized anxiety disorder. *Child Psychiatry & Human Development, 50*(3), 449–458. https://doi.org/10.1007/s10578-018-0853-1

Warden, D., & MacKinnon, S. (2003). Prosocial children, bullies and victims: An investigation of their sociometric status, empathy and social problem-solving strategies. *British Journal of Developmental Psychology, 21*(3), 367–385. https://doi.org/10.1348/026151003322277757

Warwick, H., Reardon, T., Cooper, P., Murayama, K., Reynolds, S., Wilson, C., & Creswell, C. (2017). Complete recovery from anxiety disorders following cognitive behavior therapy in children and adolescents: A meta-analysis. *Clinical Psychology Review, 52*, 77–91. https://doi.org/10.1016/j.cpr.2016.12.002

Waters, A. M., Bradley, B. P., & Mogg, K. (2014). Biased attention to threat in paediatric anxiety disorders (generalized anxiety disorder, social phobia, specific phobia, separation anxiety disorder) as a function of "distress" versus "fear" diagnostic categorization. *Psychological Medicine, 44*(3), 607–616. https://doi.org/10.1017/S0033291713000779

Waters, A. M., Donaldson, J., & Zimmer-Gembeck, M. J. (2008). Cognitive-behavioural therapy combined with an interpersonal skills component in the treatment of generalised anxiety disorder in adolescent females: A case series. *Behaviour Change, 25*(1), 35–43. https://doi.org/10.1375/bech.25.1.35

Waters, A. M., Groth, T. A., Purkis, H., & Alston-knox, C. (2017). Predicting outcomes for anxious children receiving group cognitive-behavioural therapy: Does the type of anxiety diagnosis make a difference?: Type of diagnosis and treatment outcomes in anxious children. *Clinical Psychologist, 22,* 344–354. https://doi.org/10.1111/cp.12128

Waters, E., Hamilton, C. E., & Weinfield, N. S. (2000). The stability of attachment security from infancy to adolescence and early adulthood: General introduction. *Child Development, 71*(3), 678–683. https://doi.org/10.1111/1467-8624.00175

Watson, D. (2005). Rethinking the mood and anxiety disorders: A quantitative hierarchical model for DSM-V. *Journal of Abnormal Psychology, 114*(4), 522–536. https://doi.org/10.1037/0021-843X.114.4.522

Watson, D., & Pennebaker, J. W. (1989). Health complaints, stress, and distress: Exploring the central role of negative affectivity. *Psychological Review, 96*(2), 234–254. https://doi.org/10.1037//0033-295X.96.2.234

Webster-Stratton, C. (1990). *Wally game: A problem-solving test.* Seattle: Unpublished manuscript, University of Washington.

Webster-Stratton, C., & Reid, M. J. (2003). Treating conduct problems and strengthening social and emotional competence in young children: The Dina Dinosaur treatment program. *Journal of Emotional and Behavioral Disorders, 11*(3), 130–143. https://doi.org/10.1177/10634266030110030101

Weems, C. F. (2008). Developmental trajectories of childhood anxiety: Identifying continuity and change in anxious emotion. *Developmental Review, 28*(4), 488–502. https://doi.org/10.1016/j.dr.2008.01.001

Weems, C. F., Silverman, W. K., & La Greca, A. M. (2000). What do youth referred for anxiety problems worry about? Worry and its relation to anxiety and anxiety disorders in children and adolescents. *Journal of Abnormal Child Psychology, 28*(1), 63–72. https://doi.org/10.1023/A:1005122101885

Weems, C. F., & Stickle, T. R. (2005). Anxiety disorders in childhood: Casting a nomological net. *Clinical Child and Family Psychology Review, 8*(2), 107–134. https://doi.org/10.1007/s10567-005-4751-2

Weems, C. F., Zakem, A. H., Costa, N. M., Cannon, M. F., & Watts, S. E. (2005). Physiological response and childhood anxiety: Association with symptoms of anxiety disorders and cognitive bias. *Journal of Clinical Child and Adolescent Psychology, 34*(4), 712–723. https://doi.org/10.1207/s15374424jccp3404_13

Weil, L. G., Fleming, S. M., Dumontheil, I., Kilford, E. J., Weil, R. S., Rees, G., Dolan, R. J., & Blakemore, S.-J. (2013). The development of metacognitive ability in adolescence. *Consciousness and Cognition, 22*(1), 264–271 https://doi.org/10.1016/j.concog.2013.01.004

Weise, S., Ong, J., Tesler, N. A., Kim, S., & Roth, W. T. (2013). Worried sleep: 24-h monitoring in high and low worriers. *Biological Psychology, 94*(1), 61–70. https://doi.org/10.1016/j.biopsycho.2013.04.009

Wells, A. (1995). Meta-cognition and worry: A cognitive model of generalized anxiety disorder. *Behavioural and Cognitive Psychotherapy, 23*(3), 301–320. https://doi.org/10.1017/S1352465800015897

Wells, A. (2011). *Metacognitive therapy for anxiety and depression.* New York: Guilford Press.

Wells, A., & Carter, K. E. P. (2009). Maladaptive thought control strategies in generalized anxiety disorder, major depressive disorder, and nonpatient groups and relationships with trait anxiety. *International Journal of Cognitive Therapy, 2*(3), 224–234. https://doi.org/10.1521/ijct.2009.2.3.224

Wells, A., & Cartwright-Hatton, S. (2004). A short form of the metacognitions questionnaire: Properties of the MCQ-30. *Behaviour Research and Therapy, 42*(4), 385–396. https://doi.org/10.1016/S0005-7967(03)00147-5

Wells, A., & Davies, M. I. (1994). The thought control questionnaire: A measure of individual differences in the control of unwanted thoughts. *Behaviour Research and Therapy, 32*(8), 871–878. https://doi.org/10.1016/0005-7967(94)90168-6

Werner, N. E., & Crick, N. R. (2004). Maladaptive peer relationships and the development of relational and physical aggression during middle childhood. *Social Development, 13*(4), 495–514. https://doi.org/10.1111/j.1467-9507.2004.00280.x

Whaley, S., Pinto, A., & Sigman, M. (1999). Characterizing interactions between anxious mothers and their children. *Journal of Consulting and Clinical Psychology, 67*(6), 826–836. https://doi.org/10.1037/0022-006X.67.6.826

White, J. A., & Hudson, J. L. (2016). The metacognitive model of anxiety in children: Towards a reliable and valid measure. *Cognitive Therapy and Research, 40*(1), 92–106. https://doi.org/10.1007/s10608-015-9725-1

Whiting, S. E., May, A. C., Rudy, B. M., & Davis, T. E. (2014). Strategies for the control of unwanted thoughts in adolescents: The adolescent thought control questionnaire (TCQ-A). *Journal of Psychopathology and Behavioral Assessment, 36*(2), 276–287. https://doi.org/10.1007/s10862-013-9369-y

Whitton, S. W., Luiselli, J. K., & Donaldson, D. L. (2006). Cognitive-behavioral treatment of generalized anxiety: Disorder and vomiting phobia in an elementary-age child. *Clinical Case Studies, 5*(6), 477–487. https://doi.org/10.1177/1534650105284476

Wijsbroek, S. A. M., Hale III, W. W., Raaijmakers, Q. A. W., & Meeus, W. H. J. (2011). The direction of effects between perceived parental behavioral control and psychological control and adolescents' self-reported GAD and SAD symptoms. *European Child & Adolescent Psychiatry, 20*(7), 361–371. https://doi.org/10.1007/s00787-011-0183-3

Williams, S. R., Kertz, S. J., Schrock, M. D., & Woodruff-Borden, J. (2012). A sequential analysis of parent–child interactions in anxious and nonanxious families. *Journal of Clinical Child & Adolescent Psychology, 41*(1), 64–74. https://doi.org/10.1080/15374416.2012.632347

Wilson, C. (2008, July). *Worry and meta-cognition in children: Developmental patterns.* BABCP Annual Conference, Edinburgh.

Wilson, C. (2010). Pathological worry in children: What is currently known? *Journal of Experimental Psychopathology, 1*(1), 6–33. https://doi.org/10.5127/jep.008110

Wilson, C., Bourne, S., & Cuddy, S. (in preparation). *Catastrophising in children: Relationships with verbal ability, verbal fluency, worry and anxiety.*

Wilson, C., Budd, B., Chernin, R., King, H., Leddy, A., Maclennan, F., & Mallandain, I. (2011). The role of meta-cognition and parenting in adolescent worry. *Journal of Anxiety Disorders, 25*(1), 71–79. https://doi.org/10.1016/j.janxdis.2010.08.005

Wilson, C., Curtin, R., O'Brien, D., Skelton, S., & Easton, A. (in preparation). *Impact of mood on future thinking: A developmental investigation.*

Wilson, C., & Hall, M. (2012). Thought control strategies in adolescents: Links with OCD symptoms and meta-cognitive beliefs. *Behavioural and Cognitive Psychotherapy, 40*(4), 438–451. https://doi.org/10.1017/S135246581200001X

Wilson, C., & Hughes, C. (2011). Worry, beliefs about worry and problem solving in young children. *Behavioural and Cognitive Psychotherapy, 39*(5), 507–521. https://doi.org/10.1017/S1352465811000269

Wilson, C., McEnaney, E., & Felekki, A. (in preparation). *Can and do children differentiate between fear and worry?*

Wilson, C., McKinney, R., Mullen, J., & Ryan, H. (2019, October). *Thought control strategies in children.* European Association of Clinical Psychology, Dresden, Germany.

Wilson, C., Mullen, J., McKinney, R., & Ryan, H. (in preparation). *The control of unwanted thoughts: A developmental perspective.*

Wilson, T. D., & Gilbert, D. T. (2005). Affective forecasting: Knowing what to want. *Current Directions in Psychological Science, 14*(3), 131–134. https://doi.org/10.1111/j.0963-7214.2005.00355.x

Wolters, L. H., Hogendoorn, S. M., Oudega, M., Vervoort, L., de Haan, E., Prins, P. J. M., & Boer, F. (2012). Psychometric properties of the Dutch version of the meta-cognitions questionnaire-adolescent version (MCQ-A) in non-clinical adolescents and adolescents with obsessive-compulsive disorder. *Journal of Anxiety Disorders, 26*(2), 343–351. https://doi.org/10.1016/j.janxdis.2011.11.013

Wong, K. K., Freeman, D., & Hughes, C. (2014). Suspicious young minds: Paranoia and mistrust in 8- to 14-year-olds in the UK and Hong Kong. *The British Journal of Psychiatry, 205*(3), 221–229. https://doi.org/10.1192/bjp.bp.113.135467

Wood, J. J., Piacentini, J. C., Southam-Gerow, M., Chu, B. C., & Sigman, M. (2006). Family cognitive behavioral therapy for child anxiety disorders. *Journal of the American Academy of Child & Adolescent Psychiatry, 45*(3), 314–321. https://doi.org/10.1097/01.chi.0000196425.88341.b0

Wright, M., Banerjee, R., Hoek, W., Rieffe, C., & Novin, S. (2010). Depression and social anxiety in children: Differential links with coping strategies. *Journal of Abnormal Child Psychology, 38*(3), 405–419. https://doi.org/10.1007/s10802-009-9375-4

Wurm, M., Anniko, M., Tillfors, M., Flink, I., & Boersma, K. (2018). Musculoskeletal pain in early adolescence: A longitudinal examination of pain prevalence and the role of peer-related stress, worry, and gender. *Journal of Psychosomatic Research, 111*, 76–82. https://doi.org/10.1016/j.jpsychores.2018.05.016

Xing, X., & Wang, M. (2017). Gender differences in the moderating effects of parental warmth and hostility on the association between corporal punishment and child externalizing behaviors in China. *Journal of Child and Family Studies, 26*(3), 928–938. https://doi.org/10.1007/s10826-016-0610-7

Xu, J., Ni, S., Ran, M., & Zhang, C. (2017). The relationship between parenting styles and adolescents' social anxiety in migrant families: A study in Guangdong, China. *Frontiers in Psychology, 8*, 626. https://doi.org/10.3389/fpsyg.2017.00626

Yalom, I. D. (1985). *The theory and practice of group psychotherapy*. New York: Basic Books.

Yap, M. B. H., & Jorm, A. F. (2015). Parental factors associated with childhood anxiety, depression, and internalizing problems: A systematic review and meta-analysis. *Journal of Affective Disorders, 175*, 424–440. https://doi.org/10.1016/j.jad.2015.01.050

Yap, M. B. H., Pilkington, P. D., Ryan, S. M., & Jorm, A. F. (2014). Parental factors associated with depression and anxiety in young people: A systematic review and meta-analysis. *Journal of Affective Disorders, 156*, 8–23. https://doi.org/10.1016/j.jad.2013.11.007

Yılmaz, A. E., Gençöz, T., & Wells, A. (2008). Psychometric characteristics of the Penn State Worry Questionnaire and Metacognitions Questionnaire-30 and metacognitive predictors of worry and obsessive–compulsive symptoms in a Turkish sample. *Clinical Psychology & Psychotherapy, 15*(6), 424–439. https://doi.org/10.1002/cpp.589

Young, C. C., & Dietrich, M. S. (2015). Stressful life events, worry, and rumination predict depressive and anxiety symptoms in young adolescents. *Journal of Child and Adolescent Psychiatric Nursing, 28*(1), 35–42. https://doi.org/10.1111/jcap.12102

Zainal, N. H., Newman, M. G., & Hong, R. Y. (2019). Cross-cultural and gender invariance of transdiagnostic processes in the United States and Singapore. *Assessment,* 1073191119869832. https://doi.org/10.1177/1073191119869832

Zeligs, R. (1939). Children's worries. *Sociology & Social Research, 24,* 22–32.

INDEX

Note: **Bold** page numbers refer to tables and *italic* page numbers refer to figures.

acceptance model of GAD 79, 88, 93–96, 126
ADHD *see* attention deficit hyperactivity disorder (ADHD)
adolescent: anxiety and depression 58–59, *58*, 110; eating disorders 112–113; experience of worry 9, 11; meta-cognition 15, 68–69, 82–84, 86–87, *86*; pain 116–118; parenting and worry 60–61; psychosis 111–112; worry 17–18, 73
Alfano, C. A. 126
Alternative Solutions Test 6
AMAS 54, 55
Angelino, H. 28, 29
Angold, A. 54, 105, 107, 115, 142
anxiety disorder 20, 30, 53, 54, 60, 62–64, 65, 104–109, 142, 148; treatment of 71–74, 123–126
Atance, C. M. 31–32, 34–36
attachment 65–67, **79**, 101, *101*
attentional control 44
attentional biases 45–47, 65
attentional processes 140, 145
attention deficit hyperactivity disorder (ADHD) 121–123
autistic spectrum conditions (ASC) 119–121
avoidance model of GAD 8, 78, **79**, 80, 87–89, 100

Bacow, T. L. 83, 85
Bandura, A. 41
Barahmand, U. 15, 28, 90
Barrett, P. M. 6, 71
Beck, A. T. 54, 110
Beck, S. 33, 34
Beck Anxiety Inventory for adults (BAI) 54
Behar, E. 8, **79**, 115
behavioural inhibition (BI) 96–97
Beidel, D. C. 53, 97
beliefs about worry 13–15, 109, 136, 140; in adults 78, **79**, 80–82; in children 82–87, *86*; parent-child concordance in 68–69
BI *see* behavioural inhibition (BI)
Blake, M. J. 115, 116
Blakemore, S. J. 41
Bögels, S. M. 55, 61, 62, 119, 123
Bolton, D. 15, 74, 86, 88, 99, 124, 125
Borkovec, T. D. 3, 10, 13, 22, 78, 80, 87, 90
Breinholst, S. 66, 68, 71, 74
Brown, A. M. 60, 66

Calamari, J. E. 68, 69
Campbell, M. A. 11, 12, 13
Carney, C. E. 114
Carter, W. G. 48–49, 53
Cartwright-Hatton, S. 14, 15, 29, 67, 73, 74, 82, 105
Cassidy, J. 65, 100

INDEX

catastrophisation 47–50, 56, 115, 117–118, 128, 140
catastrophising interview 23–25, *24*, 47–49
Chessor, D. 74, 126
Clementi, M. A. 115, 126
cognitive ability 29, 39, 42–44
cognitive avoidance **79**, 87–89, 109, 145
Cognitive Behaviour Therapy (CBT) 71–74, 122–126, 143–145; CBT-I 114–115
Comer, J. S. 69
co-morbidity 106, 108, 117, 121, 122, 125
control: attentional 44, 132; thought control strategies 90–91, *91*; uncontrollability 17, 19, 69, 77, 128, 135, 138–140, 148
Costello, E. J. 105, 107, 142
counterfactual thinking 33, 34
Creswell, C. 6, 45, 62, 63, 67, 73, 74, 90, 99, 124
Crick, N. 5, 43
Crnic, K. A. 48–49

Daleiden, E. L. 5, 27
Davey, G. C. L. 3–6, 23, 47, 90
delusions 111–113, 143
depression 57–58, *58*, 64, 94, 106, 110–111, 143
Depression Anxiety Stress Scale 8–9
Derakshan, N. 6
distraction 87, 90–91, 94
Dodge, K. A. 5
Donovan, C. L. 15, 56, 74, 88, 90, 109, 125
Dugas, M. J. 13–15, 69, 78, 80, 87–90, 98–99, 124–125
Dunn, J. 40
D'Zurilla, T. J. 5

eating disorders 112–114
Eccleston, C. 116–117
Egger, H. L. 105, 107, 142
Ehrenreich-May, J. 94
Eijck, F. E. A. M. van 100–101, *101*
Ellis, D. M. 85
emotional avoidance 93, 94
Emotional Avoidance Strategy Inventory for Adolescents 94
emotional dysregulation model of GAD **79**, 93, 95

emotional experience 8, 80, 95, 131, 136, 146
emotional over-reactivity 93
emotions: management/regulation of 66–67, 93; strategies for managing 89–92, *91*
Engels, R. 60
Esbjørn, B. H. 66, 68, 72, 74, 83, 86, 91, 125, 126
executive functions (EF) 38, 39, 42, 43–47, 121–123
experiential avoidance **79**, 87–89, 145
Eysenck, M. W. 6, 44

family CBT (fCBT) 71–74
Farrell, L. J. 56
fear 2–3, 9, 30; -based disorders 107, 142, 143–144; questionnaire measure of 11; *vs.* worry 11–13, *12*, 131, 134
Fialko, L. 15, 86, 88
Fisak, B. 56, 86
Fisher, E. 117
Flavell, J. H. 82
Fogliati, V. J. 126
Fowler, S. 8–9
Fox, E. 45
Fox, N. A. 54, 96, 97, 100
Francis, K. 13
Freeman, D. 111–112
future emotion 38, 46
future thinking 31–39, *32*

GAD *see* generalised anxiety disorder (GAD)
Gallagher, M. 66, 100
Garety, P. A. 111–112
gender differences 17, 19, 38, 55, 61, 65, 100
generalised anxiety disorder (GAD) 15, 16, 20, 42, 45, 73, 74, 104, 133; adults with 13, 22; attachment behaviours 65–67; diagnosis of 109; diagnostic criteria for 77; in children 104–107; models of 101–102; in parenting behaviours 60–64, *61*, *62*; pathological/problem worry and (*see* problematic worry); shared and unique components of models 78, **79**; standard interventions for 145; treatment of children with 123–126

generic CBT 74, 124–126, 143
Geronimi, E. M. C. 45
Gill, A. H. 90
Goldfried, M. R. 5
Gracey, C. 120
Gramszlo, C. 8, 45–46
Greca, A. M. 18, 28, 30, 72, 108
group-based CBT 72, 124
Grüner, K. 61, *62*
Guerreiro, D. F. 43

Hale, W. W. 60
Hare, D. J. 120
Harvey, A. G. 114
Hearn, C. S. 109
Heffernan, M. 118
heightened internal experiences 94–98, *97*
Hirsch, C. R. 10, 44–46, 122
Holmes, M. C. 56
Hudson, J. L. 15, 45, 73, 74, 83, 85, 86, 124
Hughes, C. 6, 14, 42, 83, 90

implicit association test (IAT) 25
insomnia 114–116
internal experiences, problematic relationships with **79**, 88, 92–94, 145
inter-parental conflict 57, *58*, 59
interpersonal problem-solving deficits 4–7, 90
interviews 16–20; catastrophising 23–25, *24*, 47–49; semi-structured 28
intolerance of uncertainty (IU) **79**, 108, 109, 118–120, 134; in children 99–100; definition 98; parent-child concordance 69; problem worry 98–100; treatment based on 124
Intolerance of Uncertainty Scale 69

Jorm, A. F. 57, *58*

Kendall, P. C. 69, 93, 123
Kennedy, S. M. 94
Klemanski, D. H. 111
Knott, F. 120

Lagattuta, K. H. 38, 46
La Greca, A. M. 108

language: development of 29, 31, 136; reliance on 25, 33; uncertainty ratings and 38
language processes 132
Levinson, C. A. 113
Lewis Claar, R. 117
Liew, S. M. 120
Luhmann, M. 115

Magiati, I. 120
Majdandžić, M. 61, 62
maternal anxious parenting 61–62, *62*
maternal social anxiety 63
maternal worry 56
Mathews, A. 44, 45, 122
McEvoy, P. M. 81
McGowan, S. K. 114, 115
McKinney, R. 91
McKinnon, A. 74, 124
McLeod, B. D. 57–59
McMahon, A. 94
Meagher, R. 126
Meeus, W. H. J. 60
Meltzoff, A. N. 32, 34, 35–36
Merckelbach, H. 2, 16, 28, 29, 54, 61, *62*
meta-cognition 92, 108; in adolescents 85–87; in children 85–87; cross-culturally 81; in parents and children 68–69
Meta-Cognitions Questionnaire (MCQ) 14, 81–83, 85, 86; positive beliefs sub-scale of 15
metacognitive ability 41
meta-cognitive beliefs, developmental progression of 87
meta-cognitive development 92
meta-cognitive model of GAD **79**, 90; positive beliefs 80
meta-cognitive therapy 125
Miranda, R. 66, 93, 100
Mogg, K. 45
Möller, E. L. 61
mood disorders, in children and adolescents 110–111
mood induction 36
mood manipulation 36
Multi-dimensional Anxiety Scale for Children (MASC) 20, 54

Muris, P. 2, 16, 22, 54, 59, 61, *62*, 66, 111
Murray, L. 63, 64

negative affect 7–9, 96, 117
negative beliefs **79**, 80, 81, 84–87, *86*, 109, 148
negative emotions 38, 67, 138
negative mood induction condition 36
negative problem orientation (NPO) 7, **79**, 89–90, 109
negative thinking 110, 114
Nelemans, S. A. 61
new developmental understanding of worry 139–141; clinical implications 142–145; developmental implications 141; systemic and wider system implications 146
NPO *see* negative problem orientation (NPO)

OCD 69, 83
O'Neill, D. K. 31–32
Osleger, C. *24*, 48
Osmanağaoğlu, N. 99
over-anxious disorder (OAD) 104–107, 123
Ozsivadjian, A. 120

pain 116–119
pain catastrophisation 117
pain-related disability 117–118
panic attacks disorder 63, 96, 104, 106
parental anxiety *vs.* child anxiety 53–56
parent-child relationships 58, 71–72, 101, *101*
parenting behaviours 56–57, 75, 132; GAD symptoms 60–64, *61*, *62*; predict child and adolescent anxiety and depression 57–59, *58*; role in childhood worry and generalised anxiety disorder 64–65
parent-involved CBT 72
parents: involvement in worried children treatment 70–74; meta-cognitions in 68–69; role in development of children's worry 132; uncertainty intolerance in 69
Parkinson, M. 6, 90
paternal anxiety 62

paternal behaviours 61–62, *62*
Payne, S. 99, 124
peers: relationships with 42–43; worries about 15, 117, 122
Penney, A. M. 81
Penn State Worry Questionnaire (PSWQ) 22, 23, 55, 112
Penn State Worry Questionnaire for Children (PSWQ-C) 8, 9, 22, 55
Perrin, S. 86, 88, 99, 119, 122, 124, 125
persecutory delusions 111–112
Pinquart, M. 59
poor sleep 53, 114–116, 143
positive beliefs about worry 13–15, 68, 80, 81, 84–87, *86*, 109, 128, 148
Prados, J. M. 81
problematic relationships with internal experiences **79**, 88, 92–94, 145
problematic worry 47, 133, 138, 140, 143, 145, 148; attachment and previous trauma 100–101, *101*; beliefs about worry 78, 80–87; cognitive/experiential avoidance 87–89; development of 146; heightened internal experiences 94–98, *97*; intolerance of uncertainty 98–100; problematic relationships with internal experiences 92–94; processes involved in 77–78, **79**; strategies for managing problems/emotions 89–92, *91*
problem solving 3–7, 30, 39–43, *40*, 134; confidence 5, 90, ineffective **79**; interpersonal 90; positive beliefs about 14; social 40–43, *40*; and worry 4, 4–7
problem-solving deficits 43, 89; and negative outcomes 42
PSWQ *see* Penn State Worry Questionnaire (PSWQ)
PSWQ-C *see* Penn State Worry Questionnaire for Children (PSWQ-C)
psychosis 111–112

quality of life 77, 125
questionnaire 16–18, 21–22; formal 28; MCQ 81–83, 85, 86; measure of fear 11; measure of worry 11; PSWQ 22, 23, 55, 112; PSWQ-C 8, 9, 22, 55;

Social Worries Questionnaire for parents 21; TCQ 90, 91; Temperament in Middle Childhood Questionnaire 8

Rapee, R. M. 11, 13
rejection 24, 57, 60, 61, 64; parental 57, 60, 61
repetitive negative thinking (RNT) 110, 127
Revised Children's Manifest Anxiety Scale (RCMAS) 20, 54, 55, 117
Roemer, L. 13, 78, 80, 87, 88, 93, 95, 98
rumination 36, 43, 104, 110–111, 114, 143; overlap with worry 31, 104, 110–111

Sala, M. 113
Sanchez, A. L. 69
Schmidt, L. A. 96
Screen for Child Anxiety Related Disorders (SCARED) 20, 54
self-report 62, 93; of anxiety 34; measures of child and parent anxiety 54; of repetitive negative thinking, anxiety, and depression 127
separation anxiety disorder 104, 123
Settipani, C. A. 120
Shedd, C. L. 28, 29
Sieberg, C. B. 117
Silverman, W. K. 18, 28, 72, 108, 124
Simon, A. 16, 17
Simons, L. E. 117
sleep disturbance 115–116
sleep problems 126
sleep quality 114–115
Smetana, J. G. 40
social anxiety disorder 20, 63, 64, 73, 74, 109, 124, 125; mothers with 63
social desirability 30
social problem solving 5–6, 30, 40–42, *40*
Social Worries Anxiety Index for Young Children 21
Social Worries Questionnaire for parents 21
Spence Anxiety Scale 54
Spence Children's Anxiety Scale (SCAS) 20, 54
Spence, S. H. 11, 13, 20, 54, 71

spontaneous counterfactual thinking 34
Stein, A. 64
Steinberg, L. 41
Suddendorf, T. 31, 33
Suveg, C. 95
Szabó, M. 8, 9, 11, 12, 13

Tallis, F. 4
TCQ *see* Thought Control Questionnaire (TCQ)
temperament 8, 46, 54, 61, 89, 96, 102, 127, 133, 140
temperamental negative affectivity 8
Temperament in Middle Childhood Questionnaire 8
theory of mind 38; development of 42
Thielsch, C. 86, 115
Thought Control Questionnaire (TCQ) 90, 91
thought control strategies 90–91, *91*
Topper, M. 127
Triantafyllou, K. 56
Turner, L. 23, 25, 48, 49
Turner, S. M. 53, 97

uncertainty 2, 14, 17, 40, 63; in verbal justifications 36, 38
unconscious processing 135, 139, 140, 146, 148
uncontrollability 16, 17, 19, 77, 128, 135, 138, 148
unexplained pain 143
unwanted thoughts 90, 91, 102

Varela, R. E. 30, 59
Vasey, M. W. 5, 23, 27, 37, 48–49
verbal ability 36, 48, 49
verbal-linguistic nature, of worry 9–13, *12*, 131–132, 134

Wahlund, T. 125
Wally Problem Solving task 6
Ward, L. O. 16–17
warmth *58*, 59, 61–62
WASI *see* Weschler Abbreviated Scale of Intelligence (WASI)
Wasserstein, S. 18, 28, 30, 72

Waters, A. M. 45, 124
Weems, C. F. 54, 95, 96, 100, 108, 142
Weisz, J. R. 57
Wells, A. 78, 80, 90, 125
Weschler Abbreviated Scale of Intelligence (WASI) 48
Whiteside, S. P. 60, 66
Why Worry II 15
Wilson, C. 6, 23, 48, 49, 55, 60, 68, 83, *86*, 94, 109
Woodard, J. L. 68–69
Wood, C. 120
Wood, J. J. 57, 71
Woodruff-Borden, J. 8, 46
Worries Inventory 17
worry: across different psychological disorders 127–128, *129*; in anxiety disorders in childhood 107–109; assessing content of 16–18; assessment of children's 15–16; attachment and 65–67; in attention deficit hyperactivity disorder 121–123; in autistic spectrum conditions 119–121; beliefs about 78, 80–87 (*see also* beliefs about worry); catastrophisation 47–50; categories of 13; child *vs.* parent anxiety 53–56; components of 30–31; definitions of 2–3, 29; in depression and mood disorders 110–111; development across childhood 27–30; developmental progression from infancy to adolescence 133–137; development of 81; in eating disorders 112–114; executive functions 43–47; fear *vs.* 11–13, *12*; function of 13–15, 135; future thinking 31–39, *32*; in insomnia 114–116; measurement of children 15–25; negative affect and 7–9; in pain 116–119; parenting behaviours and 56–65, *58*, *61*, *62*; in parents and children 67–69; positive beliefs about 13–14; presentation and experience of 51; private nature of 53; problematic features development 138–139; problem solving and 4, 4–7, 39–43, *40*; in psychosis 111–112; questionnaire measure of 11; research agenda for 147–148; symptom-based measures of 20; treatment in children 143–145; treatment of 123–127; verbal-linguistic nature of 9–13, *12*
worry-based disorders 16, 73, 107, 135, 141, 143–144
Worry List Questionnaires 17
Worry Tendency Questionnaire for Chinese Adolescents 17
Wurm, M. 117

Yap, M. B. H. 57, 58–59, *58*